SAVE "NATIVE AND UNSPOILED FOR FUTURE GENERATIONS"

SAVE "NATIVE AND UNSPOILED FOR FUTURE GENERATIONS"

TWO HUGE NATIONAL PARK SITES IN AFRICA ONE IN ALASKA

John Perrott

.

SAVE "NATIVE AND UNSPOILED FOR FUTURE GENERATIONS"
TWO HUGE NATIONAL PARK SITES IN AFRICA AND ONE IN ALASKA

Copyright © (2016) by John Richard Perrott

ISBN-13: 978-1533270764

ISBN-10: 1533270767

ACKNOWLEDGEMENTS AND DEDICATIONS

Many authors dedicate their work to a person or two as close family. I herewith do a bit more or less. I acknowledge a few who especially helped with this specific focus on the (a) next stage of three `green causes (1) an enlarged NP in Botswana, increasing the 38% of Botswana's Kalahari semi-desert `sands' already NPs to near 70% of Botswana for a consolidated one huge NP essentially of all western Botswana's Kalahari Desert to be restocked with endangered African wildlife, then developed as an International African wildlife National Park (NP) sanctuary-cum-Kalahari Bushman homeland reserve. I herewith dedicate this book to the Huguenot (French name for Protestants) Humboldt Perrott family and take off my hat especially to the 1st three generations of William Perrott and his West via covered-wagon-in 1848 (at age of three) California pioneer wife Sarah Jane Van Duzer Perrott and their spunky artist daughter Laura Perrott Mahan as key contributors in the Humboldt Save The Redwoods movement and its success in saving some of the world's tallest trees in CA State Parks. Then to third generation Vera Perrott Vietor for creating the Lynn Vietor Nature Preserve (LVNP) and founding Humboldt Area Foundation (HAF) charity. Then I make dedications to several individuals who contributed materially to my sturdy bringing up for a strong foundation for a then International career-cum-odyssey as recorded in my previous 2015 book via 3rd generation Humboldt Table Bluff Ranch father Henry William Perrott, our mother eastern OR `wheat Finn' Blanche Marie Hendrickson Perrott, plus our Humboldt aunt Vera Perrott Vietor.

ACKNOWLEDGEMENTS: To Brother Bill and Sister Sally for moral support in taking off my construction `hard hat' to be a shiny-back sided `author in retirement' from an International hard-nosed construction stiff career. Here's to my TX Internet guru Jessica Davis for critical help in word processing know-how, navigating between net programs, photographic presentations, tricks of the trade for electronic publishing in this and my previous `book 3'now this book 4's unusual, colorful covers, ny baxic design approach, her detailing. .

DEDICATIONS: I Thank God our Creator for what I suspect were several 'divine interventions' not least of which was Dr. Jack Wheeler's introduction to `adventure travel' which led to visiting the Kalahari Bushman, thus indirectly to my Botswana NP and Mozambique Elephant Coast CPD-NP two African sagas the major subjects of this my 4th book. Then God and `Life' for delivering me to my father Henry William and mother Blanche Marie for a now much appreciated tough-love-work-ethic Northern CA Redwood Empire bringing up, assisted in that effort by our childless aunt Vera Perrott Vietor's "You're still going up jackass hill" admonishments, other common sense conservative philosophies, providing oral roots history back to our being French Huguenots and 4th generation Humboldt Perrotts plus introduction to green causes like those visited in this book, then her husband uncle Lynn Vietor's insights into life philosophies, career encouragement. Thanks to my four-grew-up-with-me siblings as elder brother Bill, younger sister Sally, younger brother Henry Albert, youngest sister Carol Ann.

To Bechtel's Project Manager Jim Leaver for hiring me sight unseen to an entry level 1958 Bechtel engineering-construction job in Paris, France on a major-trans-Saharan-Desert oil pipeline leading to a then 30 year plus international Bechtel mega-project career. Then to Jack Burkhalter my pipeline 'spread man' (boss) in Libya who got me out of our desert field office (desk job) onto the jobsite ROW (off the bench onto the playing field) where I was given chances thereafter to have a meaningful Bechtel career. To Bechtel's Tom Oxman (plus Jim Leaver) who together gave me a shot at the HNICC position (2015's book 3's Chapter 21) on the $8-billion-trans-Alaska-1970s-oil pipeline. That's which gave me the `been there' experiences to stick my nose into the ANWR conundrum to try to get that Mother Nature's annual summer `green' wildlife migration extravaganza available as a developed International nature lover's wildlife watching destination via frozen winter built roads for BLM allowed thawed tundra summer access. That's me as a UC Berkeley engineer, Bechtel construction stiff `key man', now proponent of creating International class National Parks to save more ecosystems and wildlife (plus Kalahari Bushman) as "native and unspoiled for future generations" International green wildlife (Bushman) wildlife-watching NP destinations in Botswana's Kalahari Desert, even resurrecting our CPD-NP (1996) in Mozambique.

Here's to a list far too long to relate to of friends, other associates in my career, grammar school, high school, colleges, fraternity and military then with Bechtel worldwide. Or in life in general like Dr Jack Wheeler's adventure trips I give my appreciation, thanks. I've enjoyed what I call a `good life' which I have appreciated and enjoyed as see my 3rd bOok HUGUENOT ROOTS-cum-SIX CONTINENT ODYSSEY (2015).

ACRONYMS Used In SAVE "NATIVE AND UNSPOILED FOR FUTURE GENERATIONS"

In this day and age acronyms are all the rage. But they are not well dealt with from the dictionary prospective (some now via net search). We all know acronyms such as USA or IRS. Many of today's now profusion of acronyms are not so familiar. When new (mostly this book only) acronyms are introduced as a reader forgets and must then go mad going back thru pages to see where an acronym was first introduced. It can be like searching for a needle in a haystack. Thus herein is a list of this book's mostly private acronyms to aid readers and avoid confusion, frustration, mental stress and irritation.

ANWR (Arctic National Wildlife Reserve) Alaska a herein win-win plan how to get oil out, world tourists in
ASAP (As soon as possible) a more known old time acronym
ATV (All-terrain Vehicle) or 4x4 vehicles, skidoo, Rolligon (on Arctic tundra) as in ANWR with no road access
BFTB (BUSH FOR THE BUSHMAN (92) book re The Gods Must Be Crazy (86) Kalahari movie's people
BKBE (Botswana Kalahari Bushman Encampment) where we visited nomadic Bushman in 1988
BLM (US Bureau of Land Management) Alaska pipeline guardians of permafrost tundra, as ANWR
BME (Blanchard Mozambique Enterprises) back of T-shirt Bk 4 Cpt 2, later outdated by bigger 914 Sq Mi NP
CAP (Carol Ann Perrott) of our 4th generation of Humboldt Table Bluff ranch reared sibling Perrott's
CAPA (Carol Ann Perrott Armstrong) of Perrott 4th generation married name
CCR (Cape to Cairo Road) Africa's Cape to Cairo Road 'concept' never built (or completed) per se
CKGR (Central Kalahari Game Reserve) UK created for Bushman by Brits, independent GoB later ejected them
CPD (Center of Plant Diversity) established via UN International Biodiversity Accord, Rio 92 Earth Summit
CPD-NP (as the 1996 combined NP and CPD of 914 Sq Mi created (concept) in MZB in 1996
CYA (cover your ass) a self-serving cop out excuse, bureaucratic cover up, dogma, human failing
DNA (Deoxyribonucleic acid) containing genetic instructions (genes) in living things Bushman our world's oldest
Dar or DSM (Dar es Salaam) TNZ Indian Ocean harbor, capital of independent Tanzania (TNZ)
DPI (Dots per inch) the density of print in photographs, as 300 DPI or greater to publish a good book photo
Dr JW (Dr Jack Wheeler) of TTPN Internet blog, leader of adventure travel' like 1988 Kalahari Bushman visit
E (east) abbreviation to save space especially in image captions, N, S, W, E or further NE or SW used throughout
EC (European Community) wrongly encouraging cattle into Botswanan's fragile 'thorn-thirst' Kalahari in 1980s
EC (Elephant Coast in Mozambique0 s8te 9four 1995-6 development
ECNP (Elephant Coast NP) 1996 GoM adopted 914 Sq Mi development as CPD-NP development plan in S MZB
ECONOMIST (The UK Economist mag who did a positive article on our create MZBECNP project in 1995)
EPA (Environmental Protection Agency) USA Government environmentalist protection bureaucracy
EPC (engineer-procure-construct) construction lingo, a grass-roots-turn-key construction project
EPCM (engineer, procure, construction manage) often to manage selection of the contractor by competitive bid
FOR (Fair Oaks Ranch, TX) my first "roof" (vs overseas camp) in USA post-1988 off IH 10 N of San Antonio, TX
GDP (Gross Domestic Product) broken down in segments as gold mining vs. tourism for South Africa
GLTP (Grand Limpopo TransFrontier Park) 38,500 Sq Mi in three nation South Africa, Zimbabwe, MZB
GoB (Government of Botswana) who unfortunately often look down on Bushman as "Stone Age embarrassments"
GoM (Government of Mozambique) hoped for partners in the Elephant Coast Wildlife National Park effort
GP (Game Park) as Makgadikgadi Pan Game Park (GP) in Botswana to be upgraded to full NP status
GR (Game Reserve) as Gonareshou GR in Zimbabwe (to full wildlife-NP status)
HAP (Henry Albert Perrott) of our fourth generation Humboldt Table Bluff Perrott's, my younger brother
HCFWC (Humboldt County Federation of Women's Clubs) active in Save the Redwoods cause early 1900s
HNICC (Head N In Complete Charge) acting front end PM on 1970s $8 billion Bechtel managed Alaska Oil Pipeline
HWP (Henry William Perrott) our father 3rd Perrott generation owner-operator of Perrott Table Bluff ranch
HWSTRL (Humboldt Women's Save the Redwoods League) cofounded 1919 by Laura Perrott Mahan
HQ (Headquarters) of ranch, Bechtel, whatever organization or entity being discussed
IUCN-(The World Conservation Union) co-publishers of CPD 1994 three book volumes (Vol 1 Africa et al)
IT (International Tourist) who can't access ANWR lacking frozen winter built `summer access" roads
IWP (International World Park) for three country collective TransFrontier Park in S Africa, Zimbabwe, MZB
JRP (John Richard Perrott) fourth generation of 1865 established Table Bluff Ranch (author herein)
JHP (John Henry Perrott) 5th generation son of HAP and Jan Perrott now CA lawyer, author's nephew
JNB (Johannesburg South Africa) airport international entry site for southernAfican wildlife-watching of
JW (Dr Jack Wheeler) leader of several 'adventure' travels trips reported as our 1988 Kalahari Bushman visit
KZN (KwaZulu-Natal) the Natal Province in NE (Indian Ocean coast) of South Africa where Zulu tribe originated

LA (Los Angeles) the southern CA metropolis
LM (Lorenzo Marques) was capital of MZB pre-1975 now Maputo in post-independence from Portugal
LR (Land Rover) a main 4x4 Brit hunting vehicle in Africa along with Japanese 4x4 Toyotas
LTCG (IRS Long Term Capital Gain) income tax paid on long held property's appreciation (or inflation loss)
LV (Lynn Vietor, Vera Perrott Vietor's husband, our Humboldt Perrott 4th generation's uncle
LVNP (Lynn Vietor Nature Preserve) 14.3 acres created by Vera Perrott Vietor's 1972 will of her home site
MER (Mapupt Elephant Reserve) shot out by Cuban Military postb1975 in MZB
MGR (Makgadikgadi Game Reserve) in Botswana created by Brits pre 1966.
ML (Merrill Lynch) brokers aided in sorting our Perrott Ed Fund taken over from Vera's rip off SF bank
MZB (Mozambique) Africa's S Indian Ocean Coast nation (in Elephant Coast CPD-NP 914 Sq Mi saga)
MZBECNP (MZB Elephant Coast NP) development effort to resurrect 914 Sq Mi to 4000 Sq Mi version
NGO (Non-Governmental Organization) here usually pro conservationist not for profits
N (north) an abbreviation vs. acronym to save space especially in short electronic book image captions
NAUFFG ("Native and Unspoiled for Future Generations") in a Nature Preserve or National Park
NNFN (Nick Nobody From Nowhere) JRP in CPD-NP effort in MZB in 1995 and thereafter
NO (New Orleans USA) NOJim's home and office location in the MZB Elephant Coast 1990s saga
NOJim (Jim Blanchard III of New Orleans) entrepreneur in the MZB CPD-NP development project 1995-6
NOL (New Orleans Lawyer) Jim Blanchard III's lawyer who sabotaged and killed his MZB Elephant Coast Project
NOO (in the ANWR saga proponents of No Oil Out) or against extracting crude oil, other opposite goals
NOY (North of the Yukon River) midway on the Alaska 1970's 800 Mi crude oil pipeline
NP (National Park) often mentioned in African chapters et al in efforts to create more or larger protective NPs
NP (Nature Preserve) like Aunt Vera's LVNP (Lynn Vietor Nature Preserve) in northern CA.
NYMMA (New York Museum of Modern Art) displayed Yeon's Vietor residence photographically early 1940s
NYT (New York Times) did a 1995 article on our MZB Elephant Coast CPD-NP Development Project
OOA (Out of Africa) the second wave to walk out of Africa 60,000 years ago to now inhabit the globe.
OO (Oil Out in the ANWR saga) Oil Cos to build roads for its quid pro quo to be allowed to extract oil
OPCM (Other People's Charitable Money) As Vera's charity's destroying LVNP pretending charity
OSAC (Oregon State Agricultural College) pre-1927 College since 1856 in Corvallis Oregon
OSC (Oregon State College) later upgraded university title
OSU (Oregon State University) current `upgraded' university title
PM (Project Manager, Program Manager) of a construction project or site (the buck-stops-here guy)
PP (Peace Parks) South African not for profit creates wildlife (TFPs) parks Nelson Mandela of 3 cofounders
PR (public relations) efforts to sell a product, idea, political or environmental wildlife NP concept
RWP (Robert William Perrott) patriarch of Table Bluff Perrott's fourth generation author's Brother Bill herein
RWR (Rowland Ward Record) as per Rowland Ward's Records of African Big Game (UK) hunting trophy book
S (South) used as an abbreviation vs. acronym to save space especially in image captions
SA (San Antonio TX, South Africa, or Saudi Arabia) according to context of story or statement where used
SAPPI (South African Paper and Pulp Inc.) who would have destroyed MZB's southern CPD as our CPD-NP
SF (San Francisco) historic major city south in relation to Humboldt County Perrott clan's family ranch
SJP (Sarah Jane Perrott) Perrott's first Humboldt tribal clan matriarch (1845-1937) outlived her 3 children
SJVDP (Sarah Jane Van Duzer Perrott) as above with 'maiden' middl7e name as Humboldt pioneer lady
SMEC (SAVE MOZAMBIQUE'S ELEPHANT COAST (2007) 501 (c) (3) book) see at www.savemec.org
SMPH (Sally Mae Perrott Hammack) married to Lou Hammack in Germany in 1961 lived in TX author's sister
SMP (Sally Mae Perrott) fourth generation Humboldt Perrott born 1935 grad of U of Arizona
STOL (Short Take Off Landing) class of aircraft used in bush and river bar landings in Alaska
TFP (TransFrontier Park) multi country NPs like the Kalagadi between South Africa and Botswana or GLTP
TNZ (Tanzania) country (Tanganyika Zanzibar) an East Africa country abbreviation thereof
TTPN (To The Point News) Dr Jack Wheeler's news update blog plus for Dr Jack's adventure travel news
UAE (United Arab Emirates) on Arabian Sea (or Persian Gulf to Iranians) where Dubai tourist destination is
VPV (Vera Perrott Vietor) 3rd gen Table Bluff Perrott who created HAF Charity plus LVNP in her 1972 will
VR (Vietor's John Yeon designed residence) as was shown at NYMMA in early 1940s
W (west) an abbreviation vs. acronym used to save space especially in book image captions
WP (William Perrott) first Humboldt generation to establish CA Perrott Table Bluff Ranch in 1865
WSJ (the Wall Street Journal) did a 1995 article of the MZB Elephant Coast Development Project
WWF (World Wildlife Fund for Nature) co-publishers of CPD book 3 volumes (Vol 1 Africa et al)

BOOK COVER COLOR IMAGE CAPTIONS

Books FRONT COVER (L to R top down)

01 1968 Serengeti NP TNZ night shift leopard naps in daytime roost tree on Seronara River
02 1988 three Kalahari Bushman gals perform their `tasama melon dance' for we visiting white Amero Africans
03 1967 Serengeti NP in TNZ male topi antelope atop termite mound on lookout for prowling lions
04 1971 Masai Steppe TNZ barefoot Masai mother with baby on back harvests milk and blood in gourd their diet
05 1971 Masai Steppe TNZ gal wades in water hole elephants bath and drink from at night, baobab tree in back
06 1965 Serengeti NP flat top acacia thorn tree as sun goes down at 6 PM
07-1971 Singida TNZ `poacher's tree', baobab with ladder to hut in the tree
08 1973 Wimbe camp out TNZ, double exposure, beard, ostrich egg TNZ, later 2nd exposure Linda in Oakland CA
09 1973, Marsabit NP, Kenya, home of elephant Ahmed, died in 1974, now full body mount in Nairobi, Kenya

Books BACK COVER (L to R top down)

10-Australia 1989 visit Kakadu NP colorful Aborigine rock paintings many centuries old
11-Kenya 1965 police measure Man-eater of Darajani victim's corpse, cover story OUTDOOR LIFE mag Dec 1965
12-1968 Masai Steppe TNZ Wandorobo tribe elephant tracker Swahili speaking pal Ngwira
13-1993 FL book fest give Margaret Thatcher a BFTB book, discuss Bushman `death by dispossession' in Kalahari
14-CPD book Volume 1 from 1992 Rio Earth Summit Int Biodiversity Accord, creates 250 CPDs internationally
15-1988 Zambia-Zimbabwe, Victoria Falls on Zambesi River gorge, with rainbow world's greatest waterfall
xx Author's picture with decorated in Sumatra hard hat which he never wore on job (too heavy)

CONTENTS

1

Prologue

Any curious reader might ask why this my 4th book was written. It is a focus on three green causes to create or enlarged National Parks (NPs) having 3rd book chapters but WHERE they might be lost in that 2015 book's some 44 chapters of a larger career `TELL ALL' odyssey. This is a much shorter book focusing on, or zeroing in on only those three 2015 third book chapters as to recruit billionaire developers or investors et al (all interested) to create these green cause NPs. That's wherein I would volunteer as a Program Manager or site key man or advisor as I did for the MZB Elephant Coast botanical-wildlife CPD-NP (1995). That's from a 63 Sq MI offered Indian Coast Peninsula site to a 914 Sq MI GoM awarded 99 year lease develop and operate Elephant Coast NP in 10 months in 1995-6. Where does this book's title come from. Aunt Vera for her Lynn Vietor Nature Preserve (LVNP in her 1972 will) used that phrase for the Nature Preserve her will created. That's it was to guard her gift to Public "Native and Unspoiled for future generations." Then in 1992 at the Rio Earth Summit the new paradigm of CENTERS OF PLANT DIVERSITY (CPDs) was created which the UN mandated any nation lucky enough to have such a CPD created (250 worldwide) would then be obliged to guard it "native and unspoiled for future generations" which our GoM's 1995 NP was designed to do. It's later concept was to resurrect at a full 4000 Sq MI to connect up N with the three nation GLTP. Below are the three chapters in my third book of 2015 which are repeated but expanded herein, with a higher level of focus toward their fitting this book's title of being somehow guarded "Native and unspoiled for future generations" as a CPD-NP or other wildlife sanctuary. Below is where those three chapters appear in my previous third (2015) `tell all' book proposing some version of the MZB Elephant Coast CPD-NP needs still happen.

2015 book CHAPTER 32 KALAHARI BUSHMAN'S ENDANGERED HUMAN SPECIES SURVIVAL SAGA
2015 book CHAPTER 37 MOZAMBIQUE'S ELEPHANT COAST 4000 SQ MI NATIONAL PARK SAGA
2015 book CHAPTER 39 ARCTIC NATIONAL WILDLIFE RESERVE (ANWR) TOURIST IN OIL OUT WIN WIN PLAN

Why the NOW repeated attention to those chapters? In those Cpts in my 2015 book the focus is history. In this book those NP creating or enlarging developments are featured as YET to do GREEN CAUSES in a call for action to save them "native and unspoiled for future generations." That's NOW or NEVER before it's too late. To pursue getting one or more billionaires as financers, developers et al interested in creating lasting charitable target NPs to leave some of their charitable estate money as an enduring `created international sites' protecting them "NATIVE and UNSPOILED for future generations." That is to leave their `living legacy' for long after they were gone rather than a more normal charity (beauracracy) that could go off track like we Perrott's Aunt Vera's experience as reported in my 2015's book three's Cpt 37 PUBLIC NATURE PRESERVE CREATOR VERA'S RIPPED OFF LAMENT.

At this 2016 writing a huge international current concern is the African poaching of especially elephant ivory and rhino horn that threatens the extinction of these endangered African wildlife. That's plus lions et al vs. hungry native killers of herbivores in National Parks or wherever for African meals and body parts. A big part of a solution is MORE and LARGER NPs thus with more warranting of budgets for observation helicopters, armed staff to shoot poachers as a large part of the get tough answer. This book deals with two target sites in Africa, in Botswana and Mozambique `creating National Parks' which got chapters in the late 2015 published book, plus with thoughts (actions) on how to get international wildlife watching tourists into Alaska's ANWR for its thawed tundra summer `wetlands' coastal caribou migration (via frozen-tundra's-winter-built roads) as a well-established international 'wildlife watching' destination as now booming African tourist industry (why not now Alaska too) if tourist had summer access roads. Like problems we deal with in this book's three major green cause' chapters herein.

First is in Botswana enlarging the several unconnected British created smaller NPs back before Britain's Bechuana Protectorate became Independent Botswana in 1966. That's consolidating, enlarging them into one vast all the W Kalahari Desert NP for endangered African-wildlife-Kalahari-Bushman fits protecting wildlife, endangered Kalahari Bushman their combined fragile ecosystem bill. As does resurrecting a squandered 1996 plan for a now four times as enlarged (4000 Sq Mi) MZB Elephant Coast NP in MZB to link up with the now Grand Limpopo TransFrontier Park N in protecting the UN Center of Plant Diversity territory UN mandated to be protected "native and unspoiled for future generations." An answer to stop poaching plus encroaching human developments is creating larger NPs to give wildlife room for seasonal migrations, big enough to have sufficient internally generated budget money to protect them with staff with `shoot poachers edicts' equipped with armed helicopters plus other means of protecting NATURE. In this modern epoch with a new industry, not trophy hunting endangered African wildlife, but developing NPs for `international wildlife watching" (SHOOTING WITH CAMERAS NOT GUNS) except guns in the hands of those protecting endangered African wildlife from HUMAN poachers, encroaching civilization et al. Properly designed large NPs as Africa's wildlife watching craze are cash cows that will pay for their own budgets plus give GoB and GoM cash cow GDP funding in Botswana and Mozambique NP sites.

This enlarged NP size development process entails initially doing international feasibility studies to enlighten the host black governments that this is their by far best competitive alternate land use as cash cows provided by the now booming international `wildlife watching' destinations paradigm as TNZ's Serengeti, South Africa's Kruger National Park as international-wildlife-watching destinations. But demand for many more Sq Mi to accommodate this new, now booming `wildlife watching' tourism phase to replace the days of Teddy Roosevelt and Ernest Hemingway trophy hunting thanks to the advent of still and movie camera developments. That's plus frequent immensely popular TV programs of African wildlife. Then giving affluent international inhabitants more than `native' Africans desires and opportunities to `watch wildlife' with cameras in hand. That's one of the most booming of African vacation tourist opportunities or destinations. In the case of Alaska's ANWR, oil and anti-oil elements are squabbling while international tourism can't access ANWR's caribou and waterfowl nesting thawed tundra surface wetlands fairly short summer migrations. That's the summer thaw for lack of access roads that have to be built in the frozen, dark winters when the surface tundra is frozen, not summer thawed. BLM won't allow anything but NATURE on the summer thawed tundra only reached via frozen winter built access roads.

This author was a key man on the Alaska pipeline where such pipeline access was built Yukon River to the Arctic Ocean's Prudhoe Bay primarily in the frozen darkness of winter. More of the same is needed to open up tourist access to ANWR while the `oil out' vs. `no oil out' bureaucratic factions fight endlessly leaving nature lovers no access E to Mother Nature's annual summer thawed tundra ANWR wetland extravaganza. That's while now near no one sees that annual ANWR summer migration which challenges Serengeti's annual Tanzania-Kenya one as one of the best international huge green (nature) wildlife migration tourist destinations. But now ANWR is not available due to no road access in summer (built in frozen dark winter). So this book is produced as an initial tool to target improving these green cause possibilities. That's urgent needs to save these unique special regions 'NATIVE AND UNSPOILED FOR FUTURE GENERATIONS'. This world's 1st ever NP created was in 1872 in USA.

That's Yellowstone NP as a then entirely new NP concept. 2nd was Kruger NP in SA in 1898. This book is for creating more of a dwindling few such qualified opportune sites mainly in Africa. That's in which this author has firsthand experience living, working 17 years in Africa and as key man on MZB's Elephant Coast NP 1995-6 effort. That's which fell in a crack due to our USA `developer' throwing craps, failing to perform. But that 1996 914 Sq Mi GoM awarded NP development should NOW be enlarged to 4000 Sq Mi to connect up with the since 38,500 Sq Mi (current largest in our world) three nation Grand Limpopo TransFrontier Park (GLTP). The 4000 Sq Mi NP would guard more of S MZB's Maputaland CPD resulting from Rio's Earth Summit in 1992 thus such CPD is UN mandated guarded "native and unspoiled for future generations". This book says let's help do it Now or Never! That's via an international feasibility study alerting for instance Botswana to enlarge their Kalahari NP as a best land use.

2013 New Braunfels TX author holds his first two African `green cause' books.  That's his book **BUSH FOR THE BUSHMAN**, Need "The Gods Must Be Crazy" Kalahari People Die (1992).  His 2nd book's title is **SAVE MOZAMBIQUE'S ELEPHANT COAST, Recreating Mother Nature's Wildlife Wonderland Africa (2007).**  These two earlier `green' causes books are taken up in this current 4th in Cpt 2 (Enlarged Kalahari sands wildlife-Bushman NP-Botswana) and Cpt 3 (a resurrected 4000 Sq Mi Elephant Coast wildlife-botanical MZB CPD-NP. With changing times this author points out improved reasons for these big NP development causes (1) to make all of the W Kalahari `thirst and thorn' into one enlarge consolidated wildlife-Bushman NP of an unconnected already string of British created NPs or sanctuaries preindependence. While (2) resurrecting the 914 Sq Mi Elephant Coast CPD-NP he was a key man on as GoM awarded in 1996 to a now 4000 Sq Mi CPD-NP to connect up N to now GLTP 38,500 Sq Mi of wildlife NPs created in 2002-3. His pitch, get initial dollar help to do a feasibility studies in each case to enlighten GoM and GoB this is their very best competitive land use choices in light of Africa's now wildlife-watching-destination craze to save these unique regions "native and unspoiled for future destinations" as NPs to the glee of the entire world at large, while enormous GDP `cash cows' enhancers for GoB and GoM.

Before mankind created the paradigm of protecting such region's (NPs) as new living wildlife museums or far beyond city zoo sites, especially in this book's case two such proposed new or enlarged NPs should be created, protection as NPs in Botswana and Mozambique before they are no longer available as large vs. only a few small mom-and-pop "native and unspoiled destinations protected for future generations." That's for our world's populations craving such access to Mother Nature vs. more 'asphalt jungles' as our human race `multiply like hamsters' and more native wildlife species become extinct.  Bah Humbug!  So there's no secret.  This book is written as a serious `green cause' effort to protect more of Mother Nature's gifts "native and unspoiled for future generations" as a boon for the often starving native peoples therein and their Governments to create `best land use' cash cow NPs for the good of all mankind a la SERENGETI SHALL NOT DIE 1959 documentary film-cum-follow on book that saved that world's exquisite Serengeti NP and its later added SE flank Ngorongoro Crater and Lake Manyara NP to protect the annual millions of wildebeest-zebra migration ecosystem N into Kenya's Masai Mara NP back to TNZ's Serengeti a then existing NP but which was about to be abandoned as such but for the international `Serengeti shall not die' effort. What an exciting story. Here's to a repeat story in MZB and Botswana.

In Africa this means developing such world class international tourist destinations that more affluent mostly non-Africans natives will come to from around the world to visit to add to African economies, particularly the starving Africans within the new NPs gaining employment, housing, food, schools, medical facilities now lacking. Africa has but a few such potential sites or such opportunities left. African nations don't have to create tourist destination out of camel pasture desert like in Dubai UAE with no help from Mother Nature. But too many such Mother Nature's `gifted' sites in Africa are not being protected.  It's a shame vs. saving them "native and unspoiled for future generations."  The `create a NP' path starts via a bankable international feasibility study. That's which alerts and convinces the host government of the financial and other extraordinary merits of creating or expanding their NP as a very best competitive land use. So as I embark on this my fourth book where admittedly I am not a skilled literary type despite having struggled, managed to write and get published three previous environmental *green cause* books.   That's a recent third where important chapters were devoted to these `create wildlife sanctuary NP international wildlife watching destinations   in Botswana, in MZB and in Alaska.

This 4th book revisits those earlier NP chapters as more frosting via books about them cake. That's revisited herein more in HOW TO ACHIEVE detail. So this fourth book is a more `how to' and why `we mankind need to do' these Mother Nature ecosystem protecting efforts while economically positive best land use development paradigms especially now as Africa's wildlife watching craze unfolds with cameras vs. guns. This book is written to among other things find billionaires (?) or whoever as charitable investors, to attract the support of the many `save wildlife' and `native protection' charities and enterprises. Looking for a better place for a forever charity than most charitable 501 (c) (3) charities which there is a plethora of—good on them—but to offer a billionaire or two a better choice long term `their named' legacy investment (if only `kickoff' money) in a charitable, ecologically strong activity or development creating or enlarging a large internationally drawing NP destination to protect Mother Nature's favored region "native and unspoiled for future generations." I write this book in semi-retirement from a career in international mega construction on every continent but Antarctica, plus several major islands (mainly in Indonesia-New Guinea) that brought me to live and work 17 years in Africa, 14 in Muslim countries.

That's in Africa where I hunted in East Africa, yes but thereby became interested in protecting endangered African wildlife and such native tribes as the DNA special Kalahari Bushman in human evolution, a true endangered HUMAN species (more details below). I write this book as a retired-hard-nosed-construction-stiff engineer-cum-mega Project Manager key man with more than 35 years of mostly international overseas mega project involvement. That was with US giant Bechtel's engineer-constructors where I bid (contracted) or managed huge construction development projects including the feasibility study for the GoM awarded 914 Sq Mi wildlife-botanical CPD-NP in MZB. That's as one who was a key man on a laundry list of several other high-profile-world-class-beachhead-no-existing-infrastructure-cum-turn key-grassroots-construction projects. That's at worldwide—mostly remote—locations on every continent but Antarctica. That's plus on several Indonesian major islands years living and working in Muslim countries. Our family roots and career odyssey theme was of my (2015) published third book. This 4th book is now a how-to create, enlarge or improve three specific NPs cum-wildlife sanctuaries in Africa and Alaskan USA, places where I have lived and worked, thus have specific knowledge and experience.

My 2015's book number three dealt with documenting, sharing, some of the more colorful incidents that evolved from such projects, R&Rs (with Bechtel only post 1974) or other outside of pipeline work visiting adventure travel destinations worldwide. That year 2015 book dealt with these three green causes sagas which here are revisited with a how to approach their needing to be done, not just talked about such as was stepping stone subjects in a world odyssey scope or saga. Now the approach is how to "save native and unspoiled for future generations" these sites via mankind's NP way. That's as National Parks (NPs) the internationally accepted way. My first two books in 1992 and 2007 were African 'green cause' efforts, fact vs. fiction, nonfiction as is this book more as a lead into two specific African and one Alaskan wildlife sanctuaries or NP development feasibility studies. My first book dealt with African native peoples–the Kalahari Bushman–by DNA human mankind's oldest still surviving (barely) legacy. That is the now few surviving Kalahari Bushman along with their God given now endangered African wildlife in their fragile Kalahari Desert 'thirst-and-thorn' was homeland ecosystem survival on which traditional land they are now being dispossessed of, which anthropologist have called `death by dispossession'. That is while being treated more as useless Stone Age embarrassments by their Government of Botswana (GoB).

That's vs. the world class treasures in mankind's evolution that they are as per the 2002 book THE JOURNEY OF MAN, A Genetic Odyssey (via DNA) by Brit DNA scientist Spencer Wells. There are more details below. That's Bushman as pre Agricultural Revolution hunter-gatherers now replaced by Johnnie come lately `more advanced' or `civilized' black African `cattle people'-cum-current rulers. That first book was a "the rest of the story" sequel for those having seen the circa 1986 English version of the earlier South African original of The Gods Must Be Crazy movie. That whole saga was briefly revisited in book three (2015) via Chapter 32 an odyssey's happening or stepping stone international odyssey saga. But be ready for much more (a solution) herein via increasing the whole western Botswana's Kalahari Desert into a single expanded-united Kalahari NP for both endangered African wildlife, plus near extinct Bushman as a best economic and ecological (cash cow) competitive Botswana `thirst and thorn' Kalahari Desert land use. My second 'green cause' book (Mozambique Elephant Coast NP in 2007) detailed my key man involvement in the creation of a for GoM feasibility study for an offered 63 Sq MI Mozambique Indian Ocean coast MZB President Chissano's Machangulo Peninsula `dream' development that in 10 months evolved into a huge 914 Sq MI Government of Mozambique (GoM) awarded wildlife-botanical-CPD-NP-develop-and-operate-99-year-land-lease concession on MZB's S of Maputo then native, unspoiled Indian Ocean Elephant Coast.

This MZB President's dream project which serendipitously evolved to be (via surprise divine intervention) entirely within a UN designated Rio 1992 Earth Summit created Center of Plant Diversity (250 CPDs worldwide 84 in Africa). What better than an a combined-endangered-botanical-African-wildlife NP to protect it all "native and unspoiled for future generations." Then when that 914 Sq MI version phase fell in a crack, then and now trying to revive and expand it to a resurrected 4000 Sq MI now version NP (still all in UN designated CPD territory) development. That's when its New Orleans American `developer' who turned out to be a sick bait-then-switch nonperformer along with his project sabotaging Machiavellian New Orleans lawyer (NOL) intentionally failing to develop and protect it "native and unspoiled for future generations" as UN mandated and to GoM contracted and promised. That is what should have been built out per the 1992 Rio Earth Summit UN Center of Plant Diversity (CPD) via International Biodiversity Accord mandate and New Orleans `developer' 1996 contract with GoM.

My year 2015 third book germinated out of an original lifelong evolving to lingering desire to document to thus save and pass on to my now and future Perrott family generations our family history—roots—of our tribal clan with its French Huguenot Protestant name and northern California `save the redwoods' historical memorial plaque awarded activities. That's Huguenots back in 16th century epoch when France had 16 million Catholics, only two million 'new religion' Protestants. That's a saga that starts in the epoch of France's 1572 Saint Bartholomew Massacre of European Christian religious wars. There were family members who escaped to England then for several generations to live in the Cork southern Ireland region with dim to now no surviving details. That is until when a single male Perrott sailed from Cork, Ireland to America in 1823 well before the Irish Potato Famine of 1845-52 with now reasonable documentation. Then was when an orphaned next Perrott male generation mostly went west from Michigan to California in gold rush days. That's to then establish our Federal-Land-Grant-family ranch on Table Bluff in Northern California's Redwood Empire in 1865 in the Civil War (Lincoln assassination) epoch. That's where I was raised as a Perrott 4th generation launching pad for my to be world odyssey.

Then a story unfolds of our family's key and early involvement in saving Humboldt County's Sequoia Coastal Redwood forests. That's in saving some of the world's tallest trees native, unspoiled for future generations as in the prime now surviving Rockefeller Forest Redwood State Park part of the since 1960s Avenue of The Giants in southern Humboldt County CA as an international tourist redwood trees destination. This family root's history I became more aware of then interested in only later in my career. That's after my Botswana and Mozambique green cause `shared' experiences (in two books). That's when one could no longer discover or to document more of our roots with any still surviving earlier Perrott generations. A next generation would find it much more difficult to impossible to find even that diminished level of historical detailed record. So to retain—safeguard—as much `history' as possible was a main objective of my 2015 3rd book's publication. That's to document what is known of our family's historical roots or where we came from which is a large part of who we are. That's info—roots—which younger people are often not yet as interested in until much later in their too short lives or often after it's too late.

That book three being more a complete odyssey `tell it-all' book had passing chapters on Botswana Bushman and Mozambique's Elephant Coast CPD-NP saga, and Alaska's ANWR. That's which this book focuses on as now unfinished business, as a determined Sagittarian try TO DO IT stage. In 1995 my key man involvement in the MZB Elephant Coast feasibility study which won a GoM's 99-year-land-development-operate lease to create then operate the 914-Sq Mi-wildlife-botanical EC CPD-NPon the MZB Indian Ocean coast. But which MZB project sadly fell in a crack to the sorrow of GoM, world environmentalist's, NGOs et al. That's when my 2007 book with the 914 Sq Mi plan's history with a revised new plan towards resurrecting then enlarging the CPD-NP to a larger MZB National Park development of 4000 Sq Mi. It had a then current reasons to (1) save more CPD territory plus (2) rescuing 5000 neighboring Kruger National Park (NP) elephants scheduled for euthanasia for `over grazing' their NP short term but longer term safeguarding that additional huge MZB Maputaland Center of Plant Diversity "native and unspoiled for future generations" as UN mandated as a fall out of the International Biodiversity Accord as was signed by the World's Heads of State at the 1992 Rio first Earth Summit and (3) joining up with the by then 38,500 Sq Mi GLTP. Herein (Cpt 3) is a further focus on that MZB found (created) then lost exciting 914 Sq Mi-cum-4000 Sq Mi MZB CPD-NP herein again proposed project.

My herein 4th book is organized more with bullet point facts up front of why the `green cause' developments make the best competitive land wildlife NP use choice good sense. Then that's with the more detailed `how to' following. That's devoted to endangered mainly African (but world including Alaska) wildlife and native peoples (Kalahari Bushman) favoring audiences and NP destinations. But also to the black governments that have the final say. That's those who might see these efforts opposite to their views, even intrusions into their homeland's affairs like they did my bleeding heart 1992 `for the Bushman's salvation' book. It was to some black Botswana types in my opinion of typical African Tribalism of their treating the Kalahari Bushman as stone age embarrassments vs. as an endangered (DNA) human species or thus an asset to intrigue international tourist to come to Botswana to see Bushman now that they are more universally known from their mid-1980s Gods Must Be Crazy movie introduction. I believe that international enlarged NPs in MZB or Botswana would be a huge cash augmentation to those two countries GDP and thus bush dwelling citizens' drastically improved welfare. This 4th book will be what it is to different readers especially who haven't been there to be acquainted with the landscape and all, or so be it.

The philosophy of this book is `Be who you are and say what you feel because those who do matter don't mind while those who do mind don't matter' that's unless they are the local black inhabitants who have to be advised of (convinced) these green causes are the best GoB or GoM land use for them. This `how to' saga creating green cause wildlife sanctuaries somewhat follows Walt Whitman's advice "Do not go where the path may lead, go instead where there is not a path and leave a trail." That's more, bigger, better "native and unspoiled for future generations" Mother Nature's blessed sites or wildlife sanctuary NPs. So there you have it. This is a serious attempt to save (or upgrade)two-African-green-cause sites and to get international tourist access to the ANWR one in Alaska. That's which are major international projects, but still no more or less. That is to persuade the regional owners (like GoB or GoM or Alaska) of their environmental while win-win cash cow merits or rewards of their very best competitive land use via international class feasibility studied development plans and options then funds to create them.

2

Kalahari Wildlife-Bushman National Park

Land locked Botswana was Britain's S African colony (Bechuanaland Protectorate) until independence in 1966. Botswana's W 70% is Kalahari Desert `sands' which continues on S and W into South Africa, but mainly W into Namibia. In British days a string of wildlife sanctuaries were created to essentially defined the E border extent of the Kalahari Desert SANDS. Britain left this string of wildlife sanctuaries on the desert's E border within Botswana stretched some 700 miles from South Africa's border in S Botswana N to Botswana's border with Zambia. Or the E Kalahari border (wildlife fence) at 700 MI from Werda town (or E) on the Molopo River on Botswana South Africa border rather than further W. This British string of wildlife sanctuaries (from Werda vs. Gemsbok NP too far SW) essentially defines the Kalahari's E-border between Kalahari Desert W and more verdant beef cattle pasture of the E 30% of Botswana as none desert running N-S on Botswana's E border with South Africa in the S and Zimbabwe in the N. The Brits left only four hiatuses short of a continuous string of the Desert's E border defining wildlife sanctuaries (mostly independent unconnected). That's to define the E edge of the Kalahari Desert within Botswana from S to N. Everything further to the W was essentially `thirst and thorn' Kalahari Desert best left to wildlife. That's except the few circa 1950 rediscovered Bushman earlier thought to have been massacred to extinction in southern Africa by the 1870s. This chapter's proposal is to get GoB to fill in those four hiatuses (from E of Werda N) then declare everything W as an enlarged single NP in Botswana (W of that fence line an enlarged-consolidated Kalahari Desert endangered wildlife-Bushman watching' international Kalahari NP destination.

That's all to be restocked with wildlife thus developed as a combo wildlife-Bushman sanctuary in the now age of `wildlife-watching-tourist' destinations. That's no longer a forgotten off limits semi-desert, now a significant GoB cash cow GDP contributor IF developed as an international `wildlife watching' destination. That's where the Brits were headed before leaving in 1966. That's to save previously thought extinct Bushman, their God-given now endangered African wildlife, Kalahari fragile ecosystem et al with world class unique Okavango Delta (world's largest desert oasis) saved "native and unspoiled for future generations." That is to develop (protect) it all as a sole homeland for Bushman, their wildlife NP. That's for Bushman who are mankind's oldest surviving tribal people. That's sharing their DNA with all the rest of us white, brown, red, or yellow skinned folks worldwide except `never left' black Africans. That's leaning to evolution as per Spencer Well's book THE JOURNEY OF MAN, A GENETIC ODYSSEY (2002) to save these still pre Agricultural Revolution people massacred by later white, black people in Africa, thought late 1800s extinct, but on their way there unless there is a drastic change soon. Who are they? A comical movie was the entire world's introduction to that query which the Brits had surmised before they left now Botswana in 1966. The *Gods Must Be Crazy* (1986 USA version in English) movie was something else!

It was one of the most enlightening ever providing our modern civilized world an insight into an endangered nearly extinct Botswana (a few more in Namibia) Kalahari Bushman, the "coke bottle people" to many enchanted international movie goers. The movie provided a glimpse into who most of we `modern' humans are, where we came from since well before the start of the Agricultural Revolution some 10,000 years ago. That's much earlier to when we were all still simple African hunter-gatherers like still Kalahari Bushman, Australian Aborigines or a few others remote area people still are. That's we few walked out of Africa (OOA), to evolve by learning to domesticate wildlife (animal husbandry), to cultivate wild plants (agriculture). So who are the few surviving Kalahari Bushman? Via DNA they are us, a few surviving nomadic hunter-gatherers Bushman are mankind's now oldest extant human legacy on earth. That's this white-faced-blue-eyed-Amero African found their movie exciting as an epiphany in discovering my African roots. Adding to why I'm now interested in endangered African wildlife, dispossessed-still-tribal-African peoples, unspoiled ecosystems as Tanzania's Serengeti NP, Botswana's world unique Okavango Delta, our world's 2nd ever created South African Kruger NP. I NOW herein propose an enlarged consolidated NP of a TOTAL Botswana Kalahari Desert of W Botswana of a still extremely low human population density W of the cattle herding E 30% of Botswana. That's with the E 30% of Botswana's none desert only as right for Tswana beef cattle. So how did this world's humanity (mostly outside of Africa) take The Gods Must Be Crazy movie?

The Gods movie didn't play in the USA's big movie theaters, only in smaller community movie houses. But it was so popular it played longer than any movie ever had. No big advertisements, just by word of mouth. People JUST told friends, family "you've got to see it." That was to see our roots, where we came from in Africa. What does an enlarged consolidated Botswana NP entail? That's a larger than any now sanctuary for endangered African wildlife with their historic owners, hunter-gatherer Bushman. The Brits before they gave their Bechuanaland Protectorate independence as Botswana in 1966 had created a series of several independent unconnected wildlife reserves. A major one was a Bushman homeland bigger than Switzerland now renamed the Central Kalahari Game Reserve (CKGR) which Bushman have been since independence ejected from. This string of Brit created independent game reserve sanctuaries is like a string of pearl necklace of independent reserves that very closely define, constitutes some major length of the E border of SANDs or of the Kalahari Desert's E limits vs. the more verdant cattle pasture lands of E Botswana in a N to S band between GoB's E neighbors South Africa in the S, Zimbabwe in GoB's N.

That's where Botswana's sparse (humans per Sq Km) ruling Tswana tribe population live. The Kalahari Desert W is the other 70% of Botswana's total land mass. That's only 32% of Botswana now NPs excluded from the W desert or the herein proposed ENLARGED-CONSOLIDATED one Kalahari NP. As you get back onto your chair, additional facts to consider unique to Botswana are that support for making 70% of W Botswana one larger consolidated endangered African wildlife NP-cum-wildlife watching DESTINATION-sanctuary for beleaguered Kalahari Bushman as their protected homeland. Where the Brits left it in 1966 the string of desert border NPs already made up 38% of all Botswana. Develop the remaining 32 % farther W of existing NPs, or 70% of Kalahari (semi) Desert of all Botswana. Not as big a deal, mostly already done, then amalgamate it all developed as one wildlife-watching destination, with lodges for international tourists to stay nights, restocked with wildlife to compete with South Africa, regional neighbors. That's with Bushman employed in THEIR traditional wildlife's Management and PROTECTION is a plan that protects the unique Mother Nature's Kalahari Desert ecosystem "native and unspoiled."

To over simplify, that's for GoB to have themselves, ruling Tswana beef cattle owners to the E, Kalahari Bushman historic `wildlife owners' to the `thirst and thorn' W (all Kalahari Desert) where now few to no Tswana live, but where the last surviving Bushman are but few. The bullet points (paragraphs) that follow define the situation that would feature for facts in a next needed international class feasibility study to make GoM aware of their wonderful opportunity to develop a total Kalahari Desert W into the largest consolidated NP in the world for endangered wildlife (simultaneously) a Bushman homeland which it was in the past. But now with the evolution of the international wildlife watching industry craze, a CASH COW GDP enhancer for GoM vs. a current `thirst and thorn' essential Kalahari wasteland. A tourist destination draw that will outdo UAE's Dubai at dimes on their dollar development cost in a now wasteland for a world class international wildlife watching destination development.

(1) This NP proposer's herein's background is in real DESERTS vs. the only semi-arid marginal desert that is the Kalahari Desert where wildlife and Bushman have long (few still do) survived. I've lived several years in the North African Sahara (Tunisia, Libya, Algeria, Sudan) where it is useless, barren Sahara Desert except for some crude oil underground. That is where it was more like 100% useless arid desert except for a thin coastal Mediterranean strip or a bit more Atlas Mountains coastal strip in Algeria and Tunisia. That's with huge expanses with not a blade of grass, not a bush or tree, or desert water hole oasis with date palms mostly a very sparse myth. That's with wildlife nonexistent, even camels very few. While in Botswana its Kalahari 70 % to the far W is mostly only semi desert with vegetation enough to support the hardier wildlife, plus surviving Bushman. Add a la ETOSHA NP (Namibia) windmill water holes to developed this region further as an international wildlife watching expanded NP to be an ever more cash cow for GoB. There are variations of `desert' with Botswana's Kalahari 'light or semi' desert with tasama melons, buried tubers , scattered green vegetation as grass, bush and tree ground cover.

(2) That's for herbivores to graze or browse on. That's while the Sahara and Saudi Arabia are essentially vegetation less `deep desert' with much less to no rainfall. Scientists now tell us if you increase the greenery, rainfall will also increase. Humans cluster on coastal ocean areas while Botswana is land locked. Then Botswana has the Okavango River from Angola which empties into its Kalahari's Okavango Delta. That's a very unique largest desert (or semi desert) surrounding an oasis in the world that supports African wildlife. Botswana's population is only some less than two million people one of the lowest population densities in our world (few are lower). Botswana is 224,607 Sq Mi which is order of magnitude 84% the size of for instance USA's Texas (268,596 Sq Mi) with a TX's population of a fairly uncrowded 25 million but which still offers vast USA areas of open territory. So Botswana has lots of room (extreme low population density) to consider increasing to some 70 % of their country as one big NP including the few surviving Bushman in their Kalahari Desert region via restocked wildlife especially with creating a la Etosha NP in N Namibia's wildlife water holes paradigm with drilled wells with windmill pumps. It is proposed herein the semi-desert 70% of Botswana be international class feasibility studied to see if it can be dedicated to the world's largest endangered African wildlife plus traditional historic `herders' the Kalahari Bushman as GoB's very best competitive land utilization for this their `thirst and thorn' Kalahari semi-desert for wildlife-watching.

(3) That's while in N Africa the Sahara `inland' percentage of land S of the Mediterranean coast strip (yes a bit more in Algeria-Tunisia) is essentially useless. Be aware that 38 % of total Botswana's western Kalahari Sands portion is already dedicated to NPs or wildlife sanctuaries. Only 32% of all Botswana is Kalahari not yet so already dedicated to wildlife via NPs. Only 30% of Botswana is E of Kalahari `sands' as more verdant cattle pasture but even that is very low population density (2014) at 3.4 persons per Sq Km. Worlds' lowest is Mongolia (Gobi Desert) at 1.89 per Sq Km. So Botswana is really a low population density country. That's of major continental land locked nations, scarce of rivers with no coastal populations or few to no big urban cities. Outer Mongolia is the most sparsely inhabited in its Gobi Desert. I've visited there via Russia (Moscow) curious to see where Genghis Khan came from. Industrialized USA with much coastline, large cities, rivers has 33 inhabitants per Sq Km with many urban areas. Botswana's already sparse population is concentrated in the S to N eastern strip 30% of non-Kalahari sands up against its SAouth African and Zimbabwe E borders where its cattle herding Tswana people live. That's where bride prices for a groom's family are or were in heads of cattle. That's 38% of total Botswana is already dedicated to wildlife NPs all created by the British in the then Bechuanaland Protectorate before 1966 independence well before a now booming of international wildlife watching destinations in Africa evolved. It's time to test dedicating more territory to wildlife. The nature of the semi-desert ecosystem indicates to increase the wildlife NP `cash cow' GoB enhanced GDP. The Critical Path is to provide GoB such a feasibility study.

(4) See the Botswana sketch map (Pg 16) of these long-time already-existing wildlife sanctuaries from Botswana's SW corner border with South Africa to its border with Zambia to the N. That's with existing wildlife sanctuaries E border essentially inside the E limits of the Kalahari SANDS border like a string of NP pearls which needs an electrified wildlife fence between cattle country E with territory semi-desert Kalahari `sands' W only suitable for hardier African wildlife. That's with vegetation and water suitable for evolution's `mollycoddled' beef cattle only in a 30% strip N to S to Botswana's E against their border with SA-Zimbabwe. Enlargement to a consolidated NPs would all be W of this mostly already E border (established string of Brit NPs) in what except for by a few resident Bushman is considered useless `thorn and thirst' uninhabited country. It's where for centuries endangered African wildlife survived `owned' by Bushman the only humans that had managed, thus chosen in modern times to survive there. That's the few that avoided the African massacre of Bushman in the rest of southern Africa from the Dutch creating Cape Town on the S Atlantic coast of South Africa in 1652 with the 1st coming of Europeans. The Bushman were universally considered extinct in Africa by America's time of Custer's Last Stand in 1874. That's from all of southern Africa but a few survived `out of sight out of mind' in the deep Kalahari, only rediscovered in circa 1950 as no one had bothered to go far W in this semi desert Kalahari wasteland.

(5) By 1870s then thought `extinct' Bushmen became more appreciated as their rock wall paintings were discovered as at Botswana's Tsodilo hills (now called the Bushman's Louvre). But that's in what is now Botswana there was still a bounty paid until 1923 for a pair of Bushman ears as payment for killing useless varmints. Not unlike how white Australians were treating their still hunter-gatherer Aborigines (or America their Native American Indians). Then the affluent American Marshall family rediscovered still surviving Bushman (urged on by curious

Harvard anthropologists) in post WW II 1950 in the avoided Kalahari for lack of 4x4 vehicles or camels or any reason to go there. The Marshalls (other anthropologists) wrote exciting books about Bushman survivor's rediscovery with copious pictures. That's where Dr Jack Wheeler took us to visit a rediscovered few still then nomadic hunter-gather people in 1988 as reported in our (my authored) BUSH FOR THE BUSHMAN (1992) book. That's hunter-gatherer people with no home but a for the moment camp fire until nearby gathering was depleted, or due to seasonal rains wildlife meals had migrated elsewhere so they searched a new campfire location (home).

(6) African bush hunter-gatherer people's campfire was mainly to ward off carnivores like lion, leopard, and hyena at night from their `temporary' or seasonally changing campsites. They in their game skin only clothing on their backs for day and night survival, no closets for changes of nonexistent other wear, or any tools like pots or pans, knives or spoons, scissors or anything such. Thus that's people that could break camp and leave in 90 seconds, with no baggage, just the hunter's game skin shoulder bag for arrows or making a fire by twisting a stick (like boy scouts do for a merit badges), bare footed despite huge scorpions, bush and tree thorns that will puncture vehicle tires. There are frequent encounters with poisonous snakes like our three run-ins with puff adders in our one week's visit in their remote `thirst and thorn' Kalahari bush vicinity in 1988. On living simple, these people didn't have tooth brushes, combs, pocket knives, needle and thread, you name it. They were without such by living very simply but happy, lacking most of what we modern civilized people think we cannot do without.

(7) In 1993 at a Florida book convention I gave Margaret Thatcher a copy of our Dr Jack Wheeler groups' BUSH FOR THE BUSHMAN (1992) book where she was the featured speaker per her just published own biography. I enlisted her help for the Bushman with "In your other British Commonwealth countries in Australis in the 1970s they gave Aborigines back Kakadu NP and Ayers Rock, other former Aborigine lands. At about the same time in Canada they gave your Inuit back Canada's Arctic Circle lands on N. Botswana needs to do the same for the Kalahari Bushman instead of still treating them like Stone Age embarrassments." She agreed to help. This book's chapter herewith proposes enlarging the scattered Brit NPs already in the Kalahari to make all of the Botswana Kalahari W of those British created wildlife sanctuaries to their deeper Kalahari W an enlarged all Kalahari one endangered wildlife-Bushman NP to protect both wildlife, human species "native and unspoiled for future generations." That's a bottom line message of this Botswana chapter. Help Botswana to improve their view of Bushman in line with what has transpired in white Australia, Canada and America, Bushman now as tourist assets.

(8) That's the entire background `skinny' on our herein proposed plan of getting an international top level FEASIBILITY STUDY to present to GoB as to establishing one enlarged consolidated Botswana W Kalahari expanded NP enclosure from Botswana's now S and W border with South Africa then N to its international N border with Zambia via the E boundaries of the mostly UK created like string of existing wildlife sanctuaries. That's with four yet needed to fill in hiatuses E of Werda town S to Zambia N. That's everything to the now isolated W (deep Kalahari Desert). To if deemed economically feasible (via feability study) to create a solid continuous E boundary of existing consolidated NP(s), then fill in the far W expanse as NPs with the S plus W boundaries with South Africa and Namibia. That's with essentially near half that proposed enlarged NP's E border (to be wildlife fenced) already established by scattered Brit NPs. That's like half of that NP's E boundary length with Botswana beef cattle country in four only still now remaining missing hiatuses (additional wildlife sanctuaries) E extent of NP to be officially established on the ground (maps) as the to be FEASIBILITY STUDY territory on which for GoB to make a GO or NO GO decisions. Probably best the S most `hiatus' to be E of Werda N to CKGR vs. a more W Gemsbok NP.

(9) A listing of established plus to be established E border NP(s) (hiatuses) is as follows S to N. That's first on paper, for the limits of a feasibility study on the ground if GoM agrees to consider completing where the British left off in 1966 (50 yrs ago). To describe the proposed feasibility study limits-cum-enlarged NP. We start at Botswana's S border with South Africa (Werda town or E) vs. the southern Gemsbok NP too far W (a 1st hiatus) NE to the large CKGR. That's start S of the CKGR near (E of) Werda town at Botswana's S with SA border. From the CKGR's SE most E protrusion, it's then near due N. Then the 2nd hiatus is N to connect up to the Makgadikgadi Game Reserve. On to the 3rd hiatus to small Nxai Pan NP. Then a 4th hiatus to Chobe NP with a reported 50,000 surviving elephants up to Botswana's N border with Zambia. Fill in these four hiatuses in the expanded Kalahari Desert NP's E wildlife fence along Chobe NP's E border to the Zambezi River and Zambia. Then extend the one NP

status W to the SA's border in the S, then W, mostly Namibian border N of that. It sounds like a lot, but its already 38% of Botswana in Kalahari `sands' NPs, just 32% to add. The final reach W from a now established E NP boundary (wildlife fence) is 32% more of Botswana's deeper W Kalahari to now be feasibility studied toward creating the rest of the world's largest wildlife NP. That's some order of magnitude four times the now largest NP which is the three nations GLTP at 38,500 Sq MI (2002-3) of wildlife-watching-international-tourist destination.

(10) This total Botswana proposed NP E border of mostly now smaller independent British created existing game sanctuaries with four hiatuses filled in would establish the one now to be essentially consolidated Kalahari Desert NP W with an order of magnitude 700 miles of length (N of Werda). The inside of or W of this now complete NP border (electric wildlife fence with solar generators) would establish the new consolidated Kalahari wildlife and Bushman homeland NP's E border. It would simultaneously by its choice of location be essentially an E extremity of the Kalahari SANDS vis-a-vis Tswana beef cattle `pasture' further to the E to border South Africa-Zimbabwe. To create what? Four times the largest African wildlife sanctuary in the world. That is order of magnitude four times the 2002 creation of the Great Limpopo TransFrontier Park (GLTP) in NE South Africa (Kruger NP), SE Zimbabwe (Gonarezhou NP), newly created `mirror-image' E in MZB Limpopo NP wildlife sanctuary. This 38,500 Sq MI three nation GLTP wildlife sanctuary is the handy work of South Africa's Peace Parks, their new paradigm of Trans-Frontier Parks with the GLTP International boundary fences within removed to increase the wildlife's range, ability to migrate for mating, seasonal changes in available water, vegetation or protein (wildlife meat) for carnivores. Again who is Peace Parks? It was created by South African breweries billionaire Dr Anton Rupert with his two cofounders then President of South Africa Nelson Mandela, Crown Prince of the Netherlands.

(11) What's W of this proposed enlarged-consolidated Kalahari Desert African Wildlife-Bushman haven NP's now established continuous some E 700 mile border (from Werda or E). In this otherwise `thirst and thorn' semi-desert virtually unoccupied wasteland there is found one of Mother Nature's greatest gifts to mankind the Okavango Delta which is already partially developed (NE corner)as an International wildlife watching destinations reached via Maun the E entrance to that unique wetland (largest desert oasis in the world). It gets its annual wet season water resupply from the Okavango River that flows SE from Angola to the now Okavango Delta. That's rather than flowing on W to the Atlantic Ocean which scientist tell us it did way back in `dinosaur days'. The Delta's NW, W, S shores are largely under developed for wildlife tourism. There is another smaller town Ghanzi SW of the Okavango Delta which could be fenced off (surrounded) by wildlife fence to keep hyenas from attacking their garbage at night. Otherwise the territory is `mostly thorn and thirst' Kalahari semi-desert where generally no one lives but the few surviving Bushman, their God-provided hardy arid region wildlife, where humans other than Bushman couldn't or didn't want to try to survive there. It is generally considered a useless huge region by others like the Tswana cattle herders of GOB's to Botswana's 30% E more verdant beef cattle region.

(12) There's Maun as one fairly large town W of the herein proposed E enlarged NP boundary. It's the entry W now to the huge Okavango Delta wetland especially Moremi Game Reserve (I visited in 1983) where the Okavango River from Angola dumps not W into the Atlantic Ocean but curves around SE into the SAND SEA of the Botswana's Kalahari Desert. Everything W of the proposed one enlarged all W Botswana Kalahari is where the few surviving Bushman are found. GoB could (should) make it something no other country can, the world's largest Wildlife sanctuary (the cake) but with the added international draw of the `Gods Must Be Crazy' Kalahari Bushman being saved and employed in the game management and protection (the frosting) for an unmatchable GoB cash cow international endangered African wildlife, accompanying Bushman haven international tourist destination. Development cost to be a few pennies on the dollar what UAE's Dubai is now spending on making their tourist destination on the Persian (Arabian) Gulf that can't hold a candle to what Mother Nature's international tourist draw would be in "native and unspoiled wildlife" international tourist destination draw in Botswana's huge consolidate NP. Botswana can contribute the `worthless' land and find international partners et al to restock it with wildlife, create tourist lodges and the access to get them in and the garbage out. Put in the one story guest lodges and logistics for the tourist there for a small share of the cash cow income from international tourism.

(13) The entire Kalahari sands area as a potentially enlarged W Kalahari NP is unsuitable for the Tswana beef cattle. It's to them a `thirst and thorn' wasteland that could, SHOULD be developed as one enlarged, consolidated endangered African wildlife-Bushman (few surviving) hangout, especially in light of the current booming `African

wildlife watching' tourist industry plus additional unique draw of the internationally now known of Bushman to be employed for extra international NP fame and kudos thus tourist draw since THE GODS MUST BE CRAZY movie in the mid 1980s as an absolutely best competitive LAND USE possible (to be proven by international feasibility study) thus GoBM international wildlife watching destination cash cow vs. a huge region that is currently considered a mostly nothing but useless `thirst and thorn' wasteland GoB dumping grounds for the few Stone Age surviving Bushman, but which can be superbly developed, restocked with wildlife as a world class wildlife watching destination. That's converted from `thirst and thorn' wasteland to a GoB international wildlife watching (cash cow) GNP enhancer by developing it so as to save it "native and unspoiled for future generations."

(14) So my even if it's a wild idea is to add that some further W 32% of all Botswana semi-desert to its already declared NP roll, or the whole Botswana Kalahari portion as the basis of an international class impartial FEASIBILITY STUDY for GoB's edification. That's added to NP status to the already 38% of Botswana dedicated to wildlife NPs since before 1966 independence. I predict that GoB will be surprised at the `golden egg' they have waiting to be developed into a top international wildlife watching destination. That is made up of the several individual now unconnected existing Brit created wildlife sanctuaries forming already existing some 50% of the E fence length of a new enlarged NP's E border then W of it the already deeper Kalahari Desert surrounded world class Okavango Delta wetland-cum-wildlife sanctuary. That is to create or develop the whole of now Botswana's 70% W land mass that is Kalahari Desert (semi-desert supports wildlife) into an enlarged wildlife watching destination, to be the world's by far four times largest. That's which development would involve Kalahari Bushman as not only their now official homeland but with them heavily involved participants in `their' God-given wildlife's management, protection from poachers et al in the now enlarged gigantic Kalahari Desert W one NP.

(15) Yes let the very few older Bushman still hunter-gatherers still hunt like we found them in our 1988 visit per our book BUSH FOR THE BUSHMAN (1992). That is bagging now only excess (redundant) male wildlife with their traditional bows and poisoned arrows or an added international tourist draw like the one that caused us to be curious to visit them in Botswana in 1988 per the `GODs' movie. Also see my Cpt Five herein to discover that for most wildlife species males are largely redundant, not needed for their species survival, just the females and a very few `survival-of-the-fittest' males as breeders. So simply let a handful of still traditional Bushman male hunter gatherers family clans camp out to hunt male only herbivore wildlife as an added to the NP international tourist `Bushman watching' tourist draw. Then educate a younger generation of Bushman to speak English or other European or worldwide languages as guides or armed game guards thus an increased international tourist draw.

(16) Then arm some of the younger Bushman males or even females (per women's liberation) and as the military in Israel with GoM's guns against poachers (another important tourist draw saga). What's the bottom line of all this? It's that Botswana has a world's best opportunity to create a huge enlarged-consolidated international wildlife watching destination one NP cash cow for Botswana's GDP via their absolutely best competitive Kalahari LAND USE. Call it divine intervention with all the making of the via GoB provided international class feasibility study like the one Bechtel-WATG-Horwath and I provided GoM in 1995 that lead them to award the Elephant Coast Wildlife-Botanical CPD-NP (914 Sq Mi) 99-year-develop-and-operate leases with all land being GoM Marxist-wise nationalized (more on MZB 1995-6 NP development next Chapter).

(17) What's in a `naming' rights of tourist destinations? Like in the US, when professional sports teams (football, baseball, basketball) get big companies to compete in naming rights `auctions' (as AT&T, Airlines, et al) to pay big prices to get their names on new stadiums. Not to get ahead of ourselves, but would GoB choose a fetching name for the overall whole Kalahari Desert W Botswana NP to compete with well-established destinations like Serengeti in East Africa or Kruger in South Africa. That's call it like the XYZ Kalahari Wildlife Bushman-land NP. A juicy name to entice wildlife watchers to want to `curious' visit the now proactive vs. `passive' new international wildlife watching destination. Let XYZ pay an annual fee and advertise. Let the already established NP elements like the Gemsbok NP, Chobe, the Okavango Delta proceed as they are, or can be encouraged to choose to participate on any newer approaches, but keep their individual names within the overall new XYZ named overall Kalahari Desert NP umbrella. The feasibility study would be based on an overall development of the new 32 % of the newly added larger NP now total Kalahari Sands NP. Overall `development' features would include restocking that new NP portion with wildlife. That's providing a la Etosha NP in N Namibia created wildlife water holes.

(18) That's with windmill pumps to increase water available to expand the list of wildlife species that are to be restocked thus international draw as a wildlife watching destination is increased. That's toward offering the African big five, elephant and buffalo (in Chobe, Okavango), rhino (black and white), lion and leopard. The last two carnivores are there, can be augmented with more herbivores to eat, water holes to drink at. A larger Kalahari sands NP is desired by wildlife lovers. That's to turn around the threat of extinction of endangered African wildlife plus accompanying Kalahari Bushman (by DNA our world's oldest surviving mankind's ancestors) per scientific DNA studies. That's via the book by British DNA scientist Spencer Wells titled THE JOURNEY OF MAN, A GENETIC ODYSSEY (2002). Now there are many spread out isolated GoB NPs. Consolidate them into one big NP that is now too much for poachers. That's with all NP regions joined together, now with funds for staff to take strong action vs. poachers. As plenty of armed wildlife protectors with vehicles, helicopters, radios. That's so black and white rhinos, elephants et al can survive vs. not go the way of the southern African zebra like quagga (1870s), flightless dodo bird (17th century-Mauritius) for a gigantic win-win. That's a now vast fenced well protected NP so poachers don't dare venture for fear of being shot. Large and affluent enough to have helicopters, all the latest anti-poaching gear paid for indirectly by international `wildlife-watching' tourists. Not to get into the CREATION vs. EVOLUTION squabble but that's via DNA scientist Well's scientific discoveries. I'm for the bumper sticker solution: IN THE BEGINNING GOD CREATED EVOLUTION in the direction that great debate is now trending.

(19) How could this enlarged-consolidated W Kalahari NP be CREATED? There are many world endangered wildlife saving NGO organizations who would be all for it plus those several international charitable organizations that support saving endangered humans species (specifically the world renowned most everybody's roots–via DNA– Kalahari Bushman. As UK's Survival International, USA's Cultural Survival, Ecoterra (HQ in Kenya). Who has to be convinced are Tswana of GoB in spite of tendencies toward outdated `African tribalism' as looking down on still hunter-gatherer tribal people.   There is the organization Peace Parks who are action oriented especially in increasing African wildlife NPs especially TransFrontier wildlife NPs across international borders taking down border fences in NPs to give wildlife larger ranges vs. seasonal droughts, needed seasonal access to vegetation like in the Serengeti's Tanzania to Kenya and back annual wildlife (wildebeest and zebra) world famous migrations as a tourist draw destination. 38 % of Botswana is already NPs or wildlife reserves but in isolated under developed sites. It takes 32% of Botswana yet to be made NP, then developed to add all the Kalahari to wildlife-watching.

(20) HOW TO proceed? Get interested entities (a charitable billionaire?) involved to fund hiring a top international firm of tourism feasibility studies like our London's Bechtel-WATG-Horwath did in MZB (1995). I was the New Orleans `developer's' key man in MZB on that successful effort.  GoM's President Chissano shanghaled my `developer' offering a beautiful unspoiled MZB Indian Ocean peninsula of 63 Sq Mi for development a larger than but like San Francisco (47 Sq Mi) Peninsula. The Bechtel team and I (et al) in our 10 months on site effort won GoM's 99-year-lease-develop-operate the 914 Sq Mi awarded Elephant Coast CPD-NP land lease concession. It's big factors were in the feasibility study of the whole 914 Sq Mi was its (1) renovating the adjacent shot out by Cuban Army 273 Sq Mi Maputo Elephant Reserve (MER-1932) , (2) the `divine intervention'  discovery of a then 914 Sq Mi to be NP protected `native and unspoiled' EC south was a big chunk of the Maputaland CPD as created under the International Biodiversity Accord by the world's Heads of State at 1992's Rio Earth Summit. There were 250 CPDs (unique botanical sites) designated worldwide, 84 in Africa. But developer NOJim was mentally, physically ill, failed to perform, died, lost our project. His Machiavellian lawyer (NOL) sabotaged the project via hid `terms -conditions' different from GoM accepted per our feasibility study 99 year lease award (see MZB Cpt 3).

(21) The Maputaland CPD's existence news was tons in convincing GoM to give my New Orleans `developer' his 99 year develop and operate lease contract with land free as the then post-independence MZB was Marxist. With independence from Portugal in 1975, GoM nationalized and owned all MZB's formerly private land. There was no longer private land after the Portuguese left in 1975. In land development GoM took only 10% of the Developer's shares for 99 year leased development or budgeted free land. Our 1995 feasibility plan got New Orleans what turned out to be the 914 Sq Mi Indian Ocean Elephant Coast NP (forever thereafter wildlife and botanical preservation). Bechtel team's, my et al total cost to New Orleans for 10 months was a relatively insignificant ONE MILLION only dollars for the GoM award of what was a when built out to be $800 million project. Details of that happy-cum-sad saga are in the next chapter. Bottom line this type development process is in line, now very timely

in Botswana per the now booming, wildlife-watching craze paradigm of international tourist destinations in southern Africa (ecotourism). Think of hundreds of JNB 747s with happy international tourist with their cameras.

(22) That's as this new booming tourist industry paradigm is much more proven now than it was in MZB in 1995. What a positive change in 20 years. An international level feasibility study now will take `wildlife watching destination' (ecotourism) into account, is more apt to be positive on a feasibility study outcome than two decades ago in MZB. Now as times move on African wildlife-watching destinations are booming businesses. It is amazing such an opportunity still presents itself in Botswana, a large half developed region where wildlife have always been, in what is otherwise considered a wasteland, to be a GoB cash cow. Put in Etosha NP Namibia like wildlife water holes, restock with more species than in former days. Better so developed now late than never as NEVER is FOREVER. The Botswana Kalahari ecosystem's unique `green cause' virtues cries out to be developed to then guard "native and unspoiled for future generations" mantra as a large GoB GDP `cash cow' Kalahari Sands NP.

(23) Unfortunately in MZB my NO developer boss was in over his head. He should have taken in moneyed partners. He told me to follow my so such suggested approach of getting Bechtel as development contractor to so search. But his NO lawyer (NOL) was anti-Africa investment. Then NOL prevaricated to my New Orleans developer that Bechtel and I were trying to steal NO's GoM awarded project. But our NO developer was mentally, physically ill. It was his lawyer who stole (sabotaged) our 914 Sq MI CPD-NP project. Thus NOJim failed to perform, as our NO-developer had a substance abuse problems which frailty his Machiavellian (slimy self-serving) NOL used to run Bechtel and I off, sabotage this near billion dollar Elephant Coast NP project in 1996. But our international feasibility approach, lessons learned in MZB should now be used to alert (advise-convince) GoB of their cash cow best land use is via an enlarged-consolidated NP for Botswana's Kalahari to guard it "native and unspoiled for future generations" developed as a wildlife watching destination under an ecotourism umbrella or mantra.

(24) That's provided with wildlife windmill water holes, restocked with otherwise endangered African wildlife, outfitted with overnight tourist lodge facilities, but not overcrowded in them. That's kept in scattered light bed numbers to not become another Kenya's Masai Mara `too vehicle crowded for photography' conundrum. My experience on international mega construction projects, the MZB saga creating a wildlife-botanical NP, the now booming wildlife watching industry the herein proposed plan for Botswana is the way to go for a win-win for GoB as (a) saving endangered African wildlife, (b) saving endangered human species Bushman from extinction (as a created tourist draw or asset). Then (c) creating a cash cow for GoB's GDP and (d) saving the unique ecosystem Mother Nature `green' "native and unspoiled for future generations." That's (e) creating an in-country market for Botswana beef in providing international wildlife watching tourist high protein meals on Botswana beef steaks.

(25) Why such an optimistic projection? A big fact, the center of wildlife watching is Africa where most of Noah Arc species now reside. In-Africa the wildlife watching tourist industry has moved Kenya East Africa to Johannesburg South Africa. At Johannesburg airport the lineup of 747s for WILDLIFE WATCHING (cameras not guns) is staggering. This is mainly because in southern Africa there is a new paradigm in wildlife-watching. That is with smaller-stay-several-nights lodges where a limited number of beds puts a tourist lodge size limit on the then competing lodge's guided 4x4 vehicles taking pictures of wildlife in a designated region exclusive to that lodge. That's not Kenya's Masai Mara NP where the gate to the too small one sanctuary is wide open so it's over crowded with too many zebra stripped tourist VW mini buses so a tourist can't get uncrowded photography shots of a lion kill without several surrounding vehicles in the picture. Bah Humbug. In South Africa such low profile thatched roof lodges with names like Mala Mala, Londalozi, Singida, Phinda there is the new paradigm that would need to be utilized in the upgraded development stage of a W Kalahari NP development as envisioned and proposed herein.

(26) Another development innovation for the arid semi-desert Kalahari NP region is to adopt the N Namibian Etosha NP paradigm of giving each overnight lodge a territory with several created water holes with drilled wells, windmill pumps. With water available the species list for a region to be restocked with then many more species toward or well beyond the African big five international tourist wish to experience. If the Kalahari water table is too deep in some regions for windmills, lay water mains from the Okavango Delta wetland S, W, N or E to supply the created wildlife water holes with water seasonally or full time as needed. So with this new wildlife watching paradigm, then in 2002 adding to Kruger NP the GLTP three country international TransFrontier Park concept.

Then next in 2005 a BIGGIE was when for the 1st time ever in South African history the GDP derived from tourism (wildlife-watching) replaced previous GOLD mining as the number one South African GDP contributor. This is an undisputable litmus test indication of the growing strength of world wildlife watching paradigm which is now centered in southern vs. formerly East Africa. This exploding wildlife watching tourist market can be satisfied only in equatorial or southern Africa where a Noah's Arc of exotic African wildlife exists. Botswana's vast wildlife under developed Kalahari Desert-cum-proposed enlarged one Kalahari Desert NP as the cake (if properly developed).

(27) That's the Kalahari Bushman now as a GoB asset vs. `what-to-do-with-them' GoB problem. The Bushman are special to the world if not yet to GoB or Tswana cattle people. Scientists consider they're our earth's oldest surviving humans. If you trace our roots back as far as you can go (via DNA) you end up with these few surviving Kalahari Bushman. See the 2002 book THE JOURNEY OF MAN, A Genetic Odyssey by Spencer Wells. In modern times Kalahari Bushman are now an ace card international tourist draw asset via THE GODS MUST BE CRAZY people of late 1980s overwhelmingly popular movie. GoB's now Bushman problem should be converted into an international tourist draw destination asset. This can make a Kalahari NP one or more up on their Southern Africa or East Africa's Kenya Masal Mara NP or even real competition with Tanzania's Serengeti, Ngorongoro Crater, Lake Manyara wildlife watching destinations. These others would be substantial competitors to GoB. Still Botswana would get their `growing market' share. But in competition between wildlife (Masal tribe) of East Africa, Botswana with its Okavango Delta, the rest of the West Kalahari NP wildlife (restocked with water holes then wildlife) and its Bushman, Botswana could expect fully booked a year ahead for their NP tourist beds with the NP development in the now new southern Africa Mala Mala et al model of world-wildlife-watching destination paradigm.

(28) From Botswana's S border (Werda town E region) N to Zambia international borders (filling in the four gaps or hiatus in length (some 355 Mi) in between already existing NPs total enlarged Kalahari NP wildlife fence length order of magnitude some 700 Mi with only four hiatuses to be filled in. That's in Brits string of E edge of the Kalahari string of already existing underdeveloped NPs (wildlife sanctuaries). The so created-expanded NP (to the W) is in uninhabited but for a few surviving Bushman's et al space. That's who are on the edge of extinction but not favored by ruling cattle owning Tswana-cum-GoB. Bushman could be converted to an added international wildlife-Bushman tourist draw as a GoB asset vs. problem. Bushman should be treated as GoB assets as tourist draws vs. treated more as problems (or as Stone Age embarrassments). As in America, on about spotted owls or snail darters with no knowledge of or charitable care for our same DNA threatened human endangered roots Bushman? The Kalahari supports hardier wildlife, could support even more wildlife species if waterholes are added in the development stage like Etosha NP in Namibia (also semi desert like) which I visited in 1988 after our Dr JW's Kalahari Bushman visit. Botswana's Kalahari Desert is a world class unique situation. That's in Botswana with such a large land mass, small population vis-a-vis the world demand for wildlife watching destinations. It's simple supply and demand. Limited world supply, exploding demand. Hello Kalahari sands expanded NP development.

(29) In this generally human over populated world, where there exists this unique opportunity to make such a large essentially otherwise worthless `semi-desert' into the largest wildlife sanctuary (GoB cash cow) in this our world. It needs a feasibility study. Here's some population densities, the lowest is Outer Mongolia at 1.7 persons per Sq Km. Botswana is 3.4 per Sq Km with USA 33 per Sq Km with India at 368 per Sq Km. If the powers that be (GoB et al) after an encouraging enlarged Kalahari NP feasibility study should declare everything W of the already nearly complete string of pearls existing Brit unconnected wildlife sanctuaries as one enlarged consolidated W NP as proposed. That's to define or separate the `Kalahari  sands' region out W from the more verdant E Botswana `cattle pasture' (wildlife fence). Then from British days created sanctuaries (NPs). Then declare everything W of that completed E Kalahari now border fence a wildlife enlarged-consolidated NP at four times the now largest such (the three country GLTP). The Kalahari sands continue due S into South Africa. Optionally declare GoB's enlarged one NP fence starting it E of Werda town on Botswana's S border with SA on the Molopo River. Make the NP's S border Botswana's South African border which is the Molopo River E up to the Werda town vicinity. Then N up to Kutse Game Reserve extending S from the CKGR. Then the E border of the CKGR to its E most extension. Then near due N to Chobe NP, its E border to the Botswana-Zambian border N. That's a shorter (Werda) some 700 miles of existing NP E border (electrified wildlife fence) Werda to Zambia with filled in hiatuses. See the sketch map on the next page as a first `cut', for starting limits of an international feasibility study for Gob's NP decision. Get GoB thoughts as to their `cash cow' and GDP improvement of a total W Kalahari sands enlarged NP proposal.

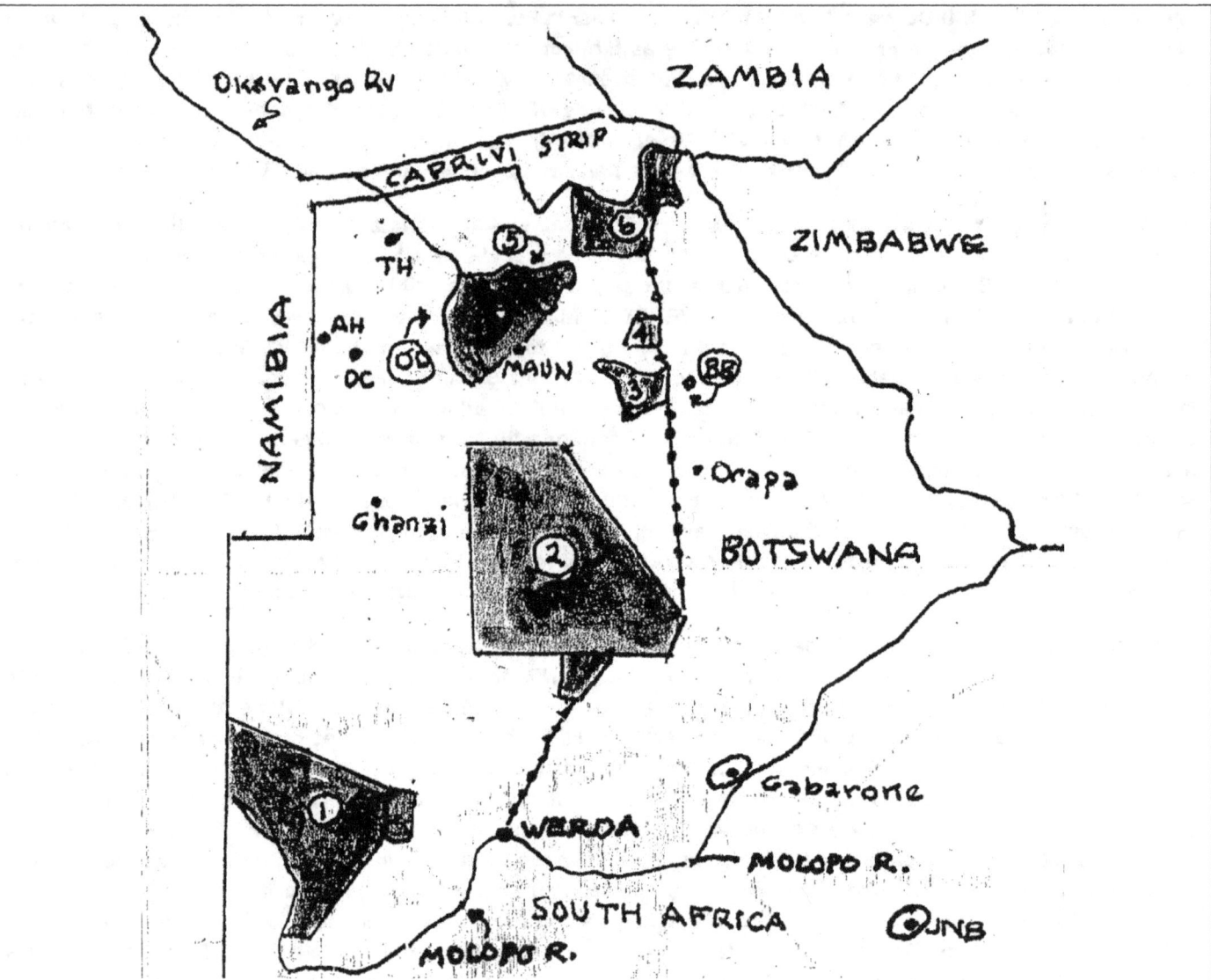

Above is a sketch map of all Botswana with the proposed electricified (solar powered) wildlife fence of the herein proposed all Kalahari NP's E boundary with wildlife W of the fence, beef pasture to the E. The existing wildlife preserves, NPs are the numbered dark land areas. Existing wildlife sactuaries are: (1) is Gemsbok NP in Botswana. It is joined by a smaller South African version of Gemsbok NP to its W (not shown dark). The two are now the Kgalagadi Gemsbok Trans Frontier Park with Botswana-South Africa border fence removed. The E edge of the Kalahari sands cross over S into South Africa E of border Werda village. (2) is the Central Kalahari Game Reserve (CKGR) which is larger than Switzerland. Then (3) next N is now the Makgadkikgadi Game Reserve. N (4) is Nxai Pan NP. Well E of a NP wildlife fence is (5) Moremi Wildlife Reserve within the NE of the larger Okavango Delta (total Delta is black).   N is (6) Chobe NP to the Zambia border. AH is Aha Hills. BB is Banes Baobabs. DC is Drotsky's Caverns. TH is Tsodilio Hills (Bushman's Louvre). Towns are Gabarone (capital), Ghanzi, JNB (Johanesburg in SA), Maun, Orapa, Werda. The Molopo River (Botswana's SW border is mostly a dry river bed, only runs wet to the W sporadically when there are rains. The Okavngo River from Angola flows SE into Botswana's (5) the Okavango Delta. The Zambezi is Botswana's N border in it's NE corner. Victoria Falls is on the Zambezi River between Zambia and Zimbabwe just downstream of where the Zambizi River leaves Botswana flowing E. The Limpopo River is Botswana's SW border W of Gaborone flowing E. The Chobe River is the Capri Strip's (Nambia's border with Botswana) until it flows into the Zambizi. The only nonborder river in all of landlocked Botswana (84% the size of Texas) is the Okavango River in Botswana's NW corner. Botswana has a population of less than two million, Texas has 25 million for a population density comparison. Botswana is near a world low.

(30) The Grand Limpopo TransFrontier Park (GLTP) three country joined NPs idea was via Peace Parks. The GLTP joins three NPs or in NE South Africa (Kruger NP) then Gonarezhou NP in the SE corner of Zimbabwe, then recently in (2003) now new created a `mirror image' of the first two long existing wildlife sanctuaries to their E in MZB via newly create MZB's Limpopo NP. The total size is 38,500 Sq MI (border fences removed). It's the world's largest wildlife sanctuary. It gives wildlife freedom to migrate seasonally within the entire GLTP. This GLTP was due to the lead of Peace Parks created by South African brewery's billionaire Anton Rupert. His two Peace Park cofounders were Nelson Mandela, then Crown Prince of the Netherlands for a wonderful addition of NP land for endangered African wildlife use or many more, better choices of wonderful destinations for a fairly new now emerged booming African wildlife-watching industry. It's hauling them in to Johannesburg via a gigantic plethora of 747s bringing in mostly wildlife watching international tourists. Get Peace Parks active on convincing GoB of the merits of a W Kalahari enlarged NP. Peace Parks was the catalyst for now Kgalagadi TransFrontier Park of removing an international border fence between SA and Botswana adjoining versions of Gemsbok National Parks with border fences removed or adjoining SA and Botswana Kalahari Gemsbok NPs now better Kgalagadi TransFrontier Park.

(31) Back to the Gods Must Be Crazy Botswana Kalahari Bushman. They were massacred in southern Africa starting after `1st white people' Dutch created Cape Town in 1652. Then by `advanced' cattle raising blacks migrating S took their turn. Bushman were thought to be extinct by the time of USA's Custer's Last Stand in 1876 by paralleling developments in native America's west. The Bushman were caught in a pincher between Europeans in SA in 1652 on then by black Bantu Africans moving S as Zulus et al into the Bushman's former bailiwick tandes later. When Dutch arrived there were only two African peoples that far S or the two click speaking tribal tan skinned (vs. black) people. That's cattle herding Hottentots, then still hunter-gather Bushman. The Dutch got along with the Hottentots to marry some of their women (offspring) to later be given the title of `coloreds' in post 1948 South African apartheid, distinct from SA's vast majority blacks, Zulus et al. Dutch rode out, killed game or Bushman's `cattle' so the battle was on between Dutch and Bushman. Some Dutch were killed by Bushman's poisoned arrows. The later arriving S blacks like the Zulus et al joined in to massacre Bushman when Zulus et al migrated S into traditional Bushman territories decades after Dutch arrived to create Cape Town (1652).

(32) In 1950 came the American Marshal family on the urging of rumors some Bushman still existed. Their efforts rediscovered surviving Bushman in remote Kalahari Desert (now Namibia) and Bechuanaland Protecterate (now Botswana) W border. That's which was off limits back then to other African residents black or white before 4x4 vehicles or with no camels to penetrate into the heart of the Kalahari Desert where a few Bushman out-of-sight-out-of-mind survived. Thus most of the few Bushman that had survived are in the Botswana's W and a few on W into Namibia. It is all what I call semi-desert, with enough foliage to support the hardier of African wildlife. The Kalahari sands region could support more if water holes were created, with wells drilled and provided with windmill pumps like in Namibia's ETOSHA NP in neighboring Namibia which I `curiously' visited in 1988 after our Dr JW's in Botswana Kalahari Bushman discovery visit. I then also visited the Makgadikgadi wildlife reserve E of the Okavango Delta in Botswana to see white men shooting zebra there out of racing vehicles for their striped skins to realize Botswana then (1988) at least was not much into protecting their wildlife sanctuaries from illegal poaching. That was a similar arid semi-desert but with sparser trees and foliage to support wildlife seasonally.

(33) Wildlife restocking in southern Africa as a Kalahari expanded wildlife sanctuary is now old hat, an established South African industry. Like the wildlife preserve created `overnight' surrounding Sun City (SA's Las Vegas gambling). The Pilansberg NP N of Sun City is circa 200 Sq MI. During apartheid post 1948 start of apartheid the Afrikaners (Dutch) did not allow gambling. But an entrepreneur built Sun City (gambling like Las Vegas) in a black `dumping ground' homeland as part of apartheid that the apartheid central SA government could cry out about but not stop. Then next the enterprising developer wanted an adjacent wildlife sanctuary to increase the tourist draw. That's like to see wildlife in the day, gamble at night. Pilansberg NP was created from scratch. I visited it in 1995 preparing our MZB Elephant Coast NP feasibility study where we would restock with African wildlife from annual auctions when NPs et al sell off their surplus wildlife. Pilansberg NP was quickly created `overnight' with wildlife solar powered electric fences, restocked with surplus NP wildlife NPs sold at annual regional auctions to stock Pilansberg NP N of Sun City. That's inext in Botswana in current unconnected large and small (Brit) NP's in varied sites vis-a-vis the advantages of one interconnected whole Kalahari sands NP to avoid wildlife overcrowding, over

grazing in several smaller unconnected NPs of wildlife as browsers (trees or bushes) to grazers (grass) in wide ranging seasonal changes in wildlife 'pasture'.

(34) In neighboring SA are wildlife PhDs that as a first step in a potential NP development feasibility study decide which species that fit the botanical carrying capacity of different NP region's terrain, the botany, numbers of chosen species that are supportable. The not yet NP W Kalahari in recent years has become sparse of wildlife due to lack of interest, no wildlife management, no restocking, essentially only the harvesting of wildlife, despoiling trees, botany that supports wildlife herbivores (then carnivores). Wildlife would have to be restocked to be a competitive international wildlife watching destination which is a major while unproblematic undertaking. In the past the W Kalahari supported more species, herd numbers, but has been shot out without the protection of such as a NP fence, managed wildlife protecting status or any game guards with helicopters, vehicles, radios. My 1965 Kenya pro hunter besides hunting in Kenya, annually (seasonally) he also international safari hunted in the Kalahari too (then big lions). GoB's Kalahari is a fairly arid-semi-desert of low rainfall. But it's far from barren as `not a blade of grass' of the Sahara Desert or Saudi Arabian deserts with neither greenery nor any existing wildlife.

(35) The logistics of getting tourists there needs development. A possalbility is by rail. If so, put rail in early as a method of `boxcar' transporting restocked wildlife in from SA. Then later to get tourist to their reserved overnight lodges. A best control over uncrowded wildlife watching is to have tourist in their overnight lodges' 4x4s vs. tourist's own driven vehicles to control numbers of vehicles, their respect for wildlife watching good manners so tourists get good photo opportunities as is the newer paradigm of top lodges in SA with names as Mala Mala, Sabi Sabi, Singida, Londilozi W of Kruger NP, or Phinda in Natal. In the logistics of getting there, it should be provided by the lodges or NP, vs. have (or need) tourist or third party tours to find too many vehicles in too small a viewing area. Proven are airstrips at lodges then viewing in lodge provided 4X4 viewing vehicles. Rail should be investigated in the feasibility study. In MZB (1995) rail was our main people moving means after crossing water to Elephant Coast's peninsula by air or water from Maputo, then S to lodges by rail.

(36) In details of a GoB enlarged NP development my first book BUSH FOR THE BUSHMAN, Need "The Gods Must Be Crazy" Kalahari People Die (1992) alerted the world of the Bushman's `death by dispossession' threatened extinction enigma. See internet site www.savethesan.org. Then in 1995 in MZB I got stuck into African wildlife NP development thus to published my MZB how to book of SAVE MOZAMBIQUE'S ELEPHANT COAST, Recreating Mother Nature's Wildlife Wonderland Africa (2007) with internet site www.savemec.org. Both books are IRS 501 (c) (3) not-for-profit net sites owned books. Over the years thinking of Bushman, our failed MZB Elephant Coast NP, looking at the Botswana map, the existing near complete E Kalahari border the Brits left in 1966 of several existing smaller wildlife sanctuaries was like divine intervention. I was struck by what an opportunity Botswana was missing in the by then international endangered African wildlife watching destination craze, with simultaneously to save the Bushman from extinction a double barreled to be win, win for GoB.

(37) Over the years thinking of the Bushmans' plight; our shot down MZB Elephant Coast NP, looking at the Botswana map, there was an existing near complete E Kalahari NPs border necklace' of several already existing smaller wildlife sanctuaries (Brits provided divine intervention). Having camped out with `wild' kBushman (1988) I was struck by the opportunity Botswana was missing in the world's endangered African wildlife-watching-destination craze, plus simultaneously saving Bushman from extinction, then help on increased anti-elephant and rhino horn poaching.. What more was needed? I had a vision of what could be. That's first do an international feasibility study. GoB has to be made aware of what the international (this world) possibilities are, given a chance to make an `informed' development decision of what a total Kalahari wildlife-Bushman (homeland) NP offers. That's an objective decision, based on a detailed top international professional feasibility study. That's advised of the unique opportunity that the enlarged far W Kalahari Desert offers. Like the London Bechtel-WATG-Horwath international team that enlightened GoM of what an opportunity they had for their MZB Indian Ocean Elephant Coast NP at 914 Sq MI (1995). In a 10 months MZB time, for a nominal cost to their (my) NO developer of only one million US $s. Then somebody like Peace Parks GoB knows and trusts to introduce this process.

(38) Then a big boy like my international Bechtel (or equal) to find development entities for money to proceed. An international professional approach to make GoB aware of what an undeveloped gold mine GoB is largely

otherwise unaware of via an initial feasibility study step. In MZB 1995 GoM shanghaied NOJim. They wanted a feasibility study. NOJim was ready to fund it. It might take somebody like Peace Parks to open the feasibility study door, to get GoB interested vs. politicians suspicious of outside interference. Now you have my Nick Nobody From No Where's enlarged Kalahari NP idea. Get Peace Parks to present it to GoB, then get GoB interested enough to `allow' a free (to them) feasibility study?  That's to find a door opening way (via this how to book) or any others (as Peace Park et al) to get GoB's ear to then bring GoB to realize what an opportunity they have to be proved by an international-`bankable'-feasibility study by established international pros that GoB's best competitive LAND USE is to develop what is otherwise `thorn and thirst' or regarded as useless waste land to develop it to become an international-wildlife-watching destination via developing it with windmill water holes, restocking it with endangered African wildlife, developing low density low profile lodge wildlife watching tourist beds for a world class endangered top African wildlife destination. An opportunity the likes of Dubai wish they had with Mother Nature gift tourist draw, stamp of approval at GoM bargain development costs.

(39) That's where international wildlife watching tourists would get good photo opportunities, not Kenya Masai Mara NP too many tourist, vehicle overcrowding, lacking overnight beds. The feasibility study would look at the needs for air and ground (road or rail) transport to move tourist in and out, food and fuel for lodges, garbage out. That's developing it as an enlarged NP produces the overall umbrella to plan, provide for such logistic needs to guarantee a highest quality international-wildlife-watching destination. Rail access to the region is `need to study' as a key to logistics.  Especially for transporting `rail boxcar' wildlife restocking with economically first, later times for moving tourists in and out, and offering `for the day only' rail tours of the enlarged NP. In our MZB's Elephant Coast NP plan we had an antique steam engine passenger train to deliver tourists to their wildlife watching lodge accommodations S (another bell and whistle) to add tourist draw.   It fits the Kalahari terrain with no need for expensive bridges and tunnels in real flat railroading country. That's to connect up to the existing rail systems of the southern African region. That's thus to attract wildlife watching railroad buffs while as a basic logistics tool, while as an added international tourist draw bell and whistle, like where's yours Dubai?

(40) There is a real opportunity to increase the quality and interest in the already 38% of Botswana dedicated to wildlife NPs and sanctuaries some mostly undeveloped and unmanned (lacking lodges). That's pull them together like the Gemsbok NP in GoM's SW, the Okavango Delta in the middle, and Chobe NP in the N. Investigate the rail approach to draw two types to visitors. Those that are being delivered to their lodges for like an average three overnights of 4 x 4 guided tour wildlife watching, then those that are only the day visitors game viewing from railroad coaches. Only both wanting to also have a glimpse of some still native hunter-gatherer Bushman, the enchanting "The Gods Must Be Crazy People" which movie would play in wildlife-watching lodges for a younger generation or any who have missed it. Or other anthropological like themes that have played on world TV's of the Bushman's story as per the movie version of the book THE JOURNEY OF MAN, A Genetic Odyssey. Or fill in the evenings with African wildlife movies like which are shown regularly on US, European wildlife channels et al.

(41) A unique big feature of the enlarged Kalahari NP would be with the endangered Bushman now gainfully employed (a unique strong tourist draw) to safeguard wildlife as an otherwise endangered human species is the by far best competitive land use of what most GoB Tswana regards as largely useless 'thorn-and-thirst'-arid acreage. The remaining 32% of all Botswana's Kalahari sands awaits being developed or guarded as a huge international wildlife watching NP destination as a win-win for (a) GoB developed as an international-wildlife-watching destination cash cow-cum-GDP enhancer, (b) endangered Bushman for their chance to survive as an oldest-DNA endangered-human species, their unique DNA (ours), and (c) a greener wildlife world, significant region designated and designed for being a world class wildlife haven now being poach protected huge region for endangered African wildlife and (d) a new exciting wildlife-watching destination for international humans hungry for such international wildlife watching tourism (the craze), now BIG and exploding international industry.

(42) That's to protect "native and unspoiled for future generations" Botswana's 'diamond in the rough' precious endangered ecosystems Kalahari sands home of our world's very few barely surviving still hunter-gatherer-nomadic Bushman with their God-given-endangered-African wildlife (restocked) in the fragile Kalahari Desert ecosystem. That's surrounding the Okavango Delta swamp-wetlands, world's-largest-desert-super oasis plus added windmill water holes throughout to increase wildlife carrying capacity. Make the Kalahari NP compete with what has

transpired in Australia, where there is much less wildlife (no other continent has Africa's gift) but there are Aborigine hunter-gatherers with their centuries old rock paintings. In Botswana, the Tsodilo Hills `Bushman's Louvre' would be a good `inside the NP' secondary day visit destination, or like the historic Banes Baobabs, or Gcwihaba Caverns all three sites I managed to visit during our Dr Jack's Kalahari Bushman visit in 1988.

We now stray from our enlarged-consolidated-Kalahari NP pitch. That's to share with readers the interesting Bushman homeland theme. The original classic very popular GODS (Bushman) movie was done in South African in Afrikaans in 1980. It was redubbed in English, released in America in 1986. It was to alert out `modern' world of these unique barely surviving endangered human species Bushman thought extinct by the late 1870s until a few hidden away in the remote Kalahari were rediscovered in 1950 by the American Marshall family plus follow on glee of international anthropologists. That's by DNA our world's oldest still living humans (relatives). In America the `GODS movie never played in big USA theaters, only in smaller community theaters. But by word of mouth stir of "You've got to see it" demand by people referring to it as the-`coke-bottle movie' so eventually it played longer than any movie ever had in America! It's now a popular established classic. In that world-falls-in-love-with-the-Bushman epoch I discovered Dr Jack Wheeler to make three international trips as twice to Tibet first in 1986 then 1987 then the North Pole in early 1988. During all this time Jack was cooking up another over-the-top adventure travel trip to the Botswana Kalahari Desert to camp out in remotest desert bush near a small family Bushman clan.

That's of never-visited-by-whites-before Kalahari Bushman. What an experience! It was like a magic time machine effort to go back to see where we came from. Our initial curious purpose was to see among other things if the movie about 'The Gods Must Be Crazy People' or 'coke bottle movie' was authentic or what. Curiosity killed the cat. Jack's August 1988 Bushman trip was hard to organize as few of the desired still-hunter-gatherer Bushman are still nomadic or are then changing camp location with seasons or rains, or game movement. That's where would they be camped in their Kalahari encampment when we got organized to finally arrive in Africa to visit them? Dr Jack made an earlier 1986 clandestine trip into Angola to visit anti-Angola-Marxist-Government-(post-independence from Portugal in 1975) pro-western (anti-Marxist) Angola rebel Jonas Savimbi deep in remote Angolan bush. To get there Jack entered Angola illegally via chartered air from Botswana. Jack's tour organizer was a young South African couple Peter Comley, his partner Salome Meyer. They were HQed in Maun E gateway to the Okavango Delta plus servicing other international-wildlife-viewing Kalahari region destinations.

Since early 1986 Jack had worked with Peter and Salome to organize Jack's (our) 1988 Kalahari Bushman visit. First to support our now total Kalahari NP proposal herein let's look at the big Bushman picture. That's aside from the USA 1986 version of their movie a distinguished author said the following of our Bushman friends: "At the dawn of history Bushman possessed all the land or bush in the whole of southern Africa. They viewed their bush like water and air as their gifts from God or inappropriate for individual or private ownership. But then it came to pass more 'advanced' people (both white then black) who thought differently arrived armed with guns." These others killed, dispossessed Bushman with their guns vs. Bushman armed only with bows and dreaded poison arrows. Bushman lived in small family clans. They didn't have anything like armies. They were peaceful, not into African tribal wars to control vast land regions (like later Zulus et al). Today Bushman people have none of even their thirst and thorn Kalahari `last stand' bush left. In 1652 Dutch first established in what is now Cape Town to resupply Dutch ships to Indonesia (Dutch Spice Islands) their colony which Dutch lost in WW II to the Japanese.

The UN kicked the Dutch out in 1949 after they tried to repossess Indonesia post WW II in 1949. Post WWII the winds of independence blew in Africa and elsewhere. Cape Town was Holland's 1652 on S tip-of-Africa-resupply station for sailing ships going to and from their spice islands in now Indonesia. The Dutch established Cape Town with domestic cattle to provide beef, fresh produce and potable water for passing Dutch ships. The new white settlers had time on their hands. Dutch men rode out on horseback to shot African wild game. Resident Bushman saw this with anger considering all African wildlife their community's gift from God or their equivalent of owned European cattle. Bushman retaliated by killing some Dutch and their cattle. In the ensuing skirmishes some Dutch died by poisoned Bushman arrows to be the Dutch's enemy or savages to be exterminated. In earliest historical references by J Wintervogel in 1655 three years after the Cape Town Dutch arrival described the strange Bushman "...as a certain tribe very low in stature and very lean, entirely savage, without any huts, cattle or anything in this world clad in little skins". That's people the Dutch called "Bosjeswmans."

This was Anglicized to Bushman for hunter-gatherer people who resided nomadically in the bush without any dwellings, just an anti-carnivore campfire. The Bushman were closely related to the only other small stature click speaking people which the Dutch encountered on arrival in 1652 called Hottentots as pastoralists or cattle herders. That's who called themselves the Khoi Khoi. The Bushman had no name in their own click language for themselves. They were called San by their cousin Hottentots meaning aboriginal hunting people in the Hottentot language. Their combined click language group is now called Kholsan by scientists of Khoi Khoi, San (Bushman) together. San is the current more used 'scientific name' for Bushman with anthropologists if not recognized or accepted by the Bushman for themselves. Hottentots or Khoi Khoi had been there a long time too, were friendly Bushman's neighbors as their Hottentots cousin none hunters with their post-Agricultural Revolution domesticated cattle herds. Hottentots got along better with the Dutch. The Dutch being short of females had early unions with Hottentot people's women. Then later under apartheid their semi-Dutch-Hottentot offspring became known as 'coloreds' vs. blacks in eventual official South African apartheid (1948-1993) as one of its four apartheid ethnic classifications treated a step above Bantu African blacks in the complicated apartheid segregation-separation.

That's with four separate rest rooms, other facilities in schools, medical facilities, housing, transportation and at four isolated different Durban Indian Ocean public beaches. As separate facilities for (1) whites, (2) Indians or British people imported from India, (3) coloreds or mixed Dutch Afrikaans with Hottentot Africans then (4) majority black tribal Africans who migrated S from Central Africa only well after the Dutch first arrived in 1652. It was well after the Dutch arrival that larger more aggressive pastoral cattle tribes like Zulus migrated S from more equatorial Africa. Bushman by Custer's Last Stand in Montana in 1876 were essentially all gone from South Africa or exterminated. Bushman everywhere were wiped out in a pincer between Dutch working N with other Europeans, black Zulu et al descending slowly from more equatorial Africa S claiming the former Bushman haunts. Bushman were then extinct, to be forgotten. Then their haunting rock art painting on rock walls were discovered. Who or where were these people now? They became more appreciated (cherished) as a unique, now gone peoples.

But only a few Bushman had survived mostly in the remote unvisited western Bechuanaland or now-Botswana, or in now Namibia W in the Kalahari Desert in regions generally avoided by Europeans and other blacks before the time of four wheel drives or without camels so the few still surviving Bushman could survive fairly undisturbed in their thirst-and-thorn Kalahari remote regions which Europeans and other black Africans avoided. Namibia was formerly SW Africa a German colony until they lost WW I. There are many parallels between what was happening to the Bushman in southern Africa with Native American Indians or Australian Aborigines in timing and shoot-the-heathen treatment. That's from the first European African settlements in the mid 1600s on. Or the native people's demise by the late 1800s was on four continents. That's including Central and South America by the Spanish. In Africa as in America there were different tribes like America's Sioux, Apache, Comanche, Blackfoot, Crow, etc. The Bushman we visited were Kung as was the main actor in *The Gods Must Be Crazy* one Nixau. That's who was a Kung Bushman from nearby now Namibia. An arbitrary European border fence between Namibia and Botswana divided the Kung's historical tribal area. That's into two different international countries. That's with different governing more advanced European people's bureaucracies and strange new `civilized' policies.

Other Bushman tribes in Botswana with slightly different languages were Naharo from further S of the Kung near Ghanzi, Xo of western Botswana S of Ghanzi, Gwis and Ghana from E of Ghanzi in what was first created by the British as their Bushman Reserve before Botswana's Independence. That's which since became the renamed Central Kalahari Game Reserve (CKGR). It's a huge area 20% larger than Switzerland at 20,400 Sq Mi or one sixteenth of Botswana's land mass. We visited Kung Bushman in Botswana's NW Kalahari in August 1988 in the cul-de-sac region NW of the Okavango Delta with Namibia to the W and N. That was in southern hemisphere winter. Via DNA research there was strong evidence that Bushman are earth's oldest surviving humans. Thus according to Darwinian evolution (now DNA) they are all our `walked out of Africa' mankind's oldest living relatives. On page one of my-green-cause book titled *Bush For The Bushman* (1992) I stated "This clan represents the most primitive people remaining in the world today. Genetic research at University of California Berkeley (my university degree) via blood sample DNA fingerprinting had recently announced these Kung Bushman as the oldest surviving humans as restated in this book. UK DNA scientist Spencer Wells provided further evidence 10 years on. Princeton Press outdid Berkeley with Well's book *THE JOURNEY OF MAN, A GENETIC ODYSSEY (2002)*.

This scientific study used mitochondrial DNA's new genetic techniques in evolutionary genetic anthropology for real science. That was by using the Y chromosome of males only. Science has been able to locate our real ancestors living long before biblical Adam and Eve. This is to back up archeological finds in Africa by the Leakey's Olduvai Gorge in Tanzania, Lucy in Ethiopia, elsewhere all to support a 'we-all-came-out-of-Africa' theory of our human evolutionary story. Well's 2002 book added scientific credence to evolution vs. creation via mitochondrial DNA. That all now living humans relate back to people who departed out of Africa in a secondary ultimate migration 60,000 years ago. They crossed from now Somaliland in NE Africa to Yemen. That was in ice ages when seas were lower or frozen, easy to cross the Red Sea Africa to Yemen.   Then over centuries they gradually multiplied to emigrate further to spreading out over a world well beyond Africa. They eventually replaced their also-from-Africa forerunners or Neanderthal Man who were in Europe 350,000 to 600,000 years ago. Scientific theory is Neanderthals walked out of Africa from Egypt to Sinai (if it was there then) then eventually W to Europe, NE to now Persia. They spread along the S Mediterranean shore into SW Europe, also E to Persia or today's Iran.

So Neanderthals in their W range disappeared as long ago as 30,000 years ago. Those in Eurasia are believed to have died out at 50,000 years ago. Was there interbreeding between earlier Neanderthal and us as Homo sapiens (more modern man)? Genetic evidence suggests (still debated) that a very few disappearing Neanderthals mixed with the expanding Homo sapiens for 1 to 4 % of the genome of people from Eurasia now having some Neanderthal genes. Wells's book is a leg up for evolutionist vs. biblical creationist. All cultures had youth asking "where did we come from?" Different stories are given in different cultures (religions). As a spiritual leaning engineer I go with scientist. Strict Creationism is in trouble via scientific facts. Or in explaining Smithsonian Natural History Museum's evolutionary display of dinosaurs et al in Washington DC a favorite haunt of mine. Biblical authors were not yet aware our world was round, that there were dinosaurs on earth from 235 million years ago until their extinction 65 million years ago.   Then recently some religions, other peace makers have come up with the intelligent design theory. Saying evolution was not just helter-skelter Darwinian natural selection.

But rather evolution was intelligent design by a religious Almighty. This leads to the bumper sticker compromise: IN THE BEGINNING GOD CREATED EVOLUTION. Through DNA every extant male excluding more recent Africans who arrived by slave ship outside of Africa has a glitch in their DNA record carried out of Africa some 60,000 years ago. Thus an ultimate second wave (us) with our same Y chromosome glitch from Africa as we humans slowly spread N to get to Australia. Then others traveled NW skirting around to the W of the Himalayas to Siberia then across the Bering Strait to Alaska crossing during an ice age bridge. That is eventually they (we) walked or rowed S to Argentina and Chile. There were eventually late second arrivals in Europe to replace the earlier "we-walked-out-of-Africa-too" Neanderthals. Our OOA ncestors were probably more advanced than Neanderthals in the first use of fire, advanced language thus communications, other evolved skills. For Wells and scientists somebody was left behind in Africa with the same DNA glitches as those second waver African-world-wide emigrants who left Africa some 60,000 years ago second wave OOAers. Scientist checked the Pygmies, tall cattle owning Watutsi, shorter sodbuster Bantu Hutus of Rwanda, Zulus of Natal South Africa, Masai cattle owners of East Africa, et al.

Scientists finally found a match for our OOA DNA glitch carried out of Africa eons ago only in still-in-African Bushman. That is our barely surviving relatives still in Africa now concentrated in the remote Kalahari Desert. So who are the Bushman we visited? Per Wells they are US! Our 1988 Kalahari visit awakened us that our by DNA relatives are now an *endangered human species*. They're currently in risk of dying out! While most naïve uninformed tree huggers, environmentalists, bleeding heart liberals worry about spotted owls, snail darters with no regard whatsoever for our (their) earliest human legacy the endangered now few still left Kalahari Bushman! Our visit was to Botswana a flat country, with a low population density, western 70% written off as useless Kalahari Desert 'thirst and thorn' country.   But that's where Bushman, their wildlife have survived together for near `forever'. Shouldn't that be a NP? Botswana's W 70% is the Kalahari Desert where the few Bushman who have survived live. Who were rediscovered in circa 1950 and where a very few are now still found. Botswana is 84% the size of Texas but has only less than two million population compared to 26 million in Texas. Botswana has a very low population density of 3.4 persons per Sq Km; Outer Mongolia is low at 1.7 per Sq Km, USA mid pack at 33 per Sq Km. Botswana's ruling Tswana tribe who took over from Britain have a saying "beef is our currency." Their tribal bride prices are in heads of cattle. Ruling-GoB Tswana (1966 on) are cattle people. But the W 70% of Botswaa is the semi-arid Kalahari Desert which is is too arid for genetically evolved mollycoddled grazing beef.

Botswana's main low human population is thus restricted to the E 30% of their country E in Kalahari sands. Botswana's more fertile-N-S corridor is up against its E border with South Africa (S) and Zimbabwe (N). The people density in the W or Kalahari is very low which leaves it open to wildlife NP development avenues not open to population dense, urbanized China or India or UAE with its Dubai as a glitzy human created international tourist destination. A sad fact for Botswana since our 1988 Bushman visit. That's the world epicenter for the HIV-AIDS virus is in nearby Swaziland. That is followed closely by regional countries as Botswana, South Africa, Zimbabwe, Malawi et al. This has taken a toll on all their life expectancies. Botswana's life expectancy was 45 years in 1958. It then improved to one of Africa British Commonwealth countries highest in 1988 at 60 years. Then with HIV-AIDS by 2003 it tumbled back to 40 years! It was estimated in 2006 that 24% of all adults in Botswana were infected. But then GoB took strong, positive measures to improve this situation. Not arguing it didn't exist like in SA.

That's by GoB from 2003 on providing free medicine and treatment. Unfortunately dispossessed Bushman (as those removed from the CKGR) were in reservations or what some referred to as concentration camps where alcoholism, prostitution, HIV-AIDS thrive for a further blow to the endangered-Bushman-human species' survival. Our Bushman visit was to Botswana's NW corner a geographic cul-de-sac W of the Okavango Delta. It's relatively arid while not nearly as devoid of trees, vegetation as the Sahara Desert or Saudi Arabia where I have lived. The Kung Bushman we visited were in a geographical-political-cul-de-sac in Botswana W of the Okavango Delta and river. The Delta is one of Mother Nature's gifts to Botswana in a precious wetland ecosystem populated by a Noah's Ark of African wildlife otherwise completely surrounded by more arid Kalahari sands. The Okavango Delta is fed annually by seasonal flooding via the Okavango River flowing SE out of Angola. It's one of a very few major rivers in the world that does not empty into a sea, ocean, or lake. The Okavango Delta wetland is the largest desert oasis in the world, officially the world's largest inland delta as a seasonal-wetland W of the herein proposed E enlarged NP wildlife boundary wildlife fence surrounding the (a) semi-desert Kalahari Sand Sea on to their W.

Everything W of the proposed one enlarged all W Kalahari NP E border (fence) is where the few surviving Bushman are found. GoB can make it what no other country can, the world's largest wildlife sanctuary (the cake) but the added international draw of Kalahari Bushman being saved and utilized in wildlife management-protection (the frosting) for an unmatchable GoB GNP cash cow opportunity (a big deal). That's via development cost of pennies on the dollar what Dubai is spending to make a tourist destination on the Persian (Arabian) Gulf that can't hold a candle to what Mother Nature's international draw would be as a `native and unspoiled' international-wildlife-watching--ourist destination. Botswana can contribute the otherwise useless land and find international partners if needed (after an international feasibility study) to restock with endangered African wildlife to have put in one story thatched roof guest lodges, road, rail, aircraft logistics to get tourists in and out for a small share of the cash cow income expected from being a world class tourist destination. The Kalahari region is unsuitable for beef cattle. It was tried and failed. This to GoB (Tswana tribe) is a `thirst and thorn' wasteland that an international feasibility study will most surely prove that can and SHOULD be developed as one enlarged consolidated endangered African wildlife and the few surviving Bushman's homeland sanctuary-cum-tourist draw destination.

That's in light of the current booming African wildlife watching industry plus the additional unique draw of the endangered Bushman employed, involved for extra international kudos and thus international tourist draw since THE GODS MUST BE CRAZY movie in the mid 1980s as the absolutely best competitive LAND USE possible thus international wildlife-watching destination proven GDP cash cow. Usually deltas are the mouths of rivers emptying into an ocean like the Amazon, Nile or Mississippi. While the Okavango Delta jewel here ends up against the dry Kalahari sand sea. Water evaporates so the Delta or wetland water level varies seasonally. The Delta occupies 5800 Sq MI of fragile, precious wetland ecosystem, already a top tier international African wildlife watching tourist destination (I visited it in 1983 on R&R from Saudi Arabia). The Kalahari is classed as a major world desert on its low annual rainfall. But it is not near as dry. arid or barren as the bigger than USA's lower 48 states or North Africa's Sahara desert which stretches S to near the equator. That's with next to no plant or tree ground cover. That's outside a very few and far between oases with date palm trees. But N Africa does not have equatorial Africa's and on S's Noah's Arc of African exotic wildlife the rest of the world is goofy to see. Rather the Kalahari has reasonable vegetation, ground cover in grass, bushes, and scattered trees unknown to the Sahara or Saudi Arabia plus the African WILDLIFE. Then again still resident few Bushman with their exotic DNA.

The Kalahari supports eland, greater kudu, wildebeest, zebras, giraffe, lions, leopards, hyenas, jackals et al. What brings International `wildlife watching' tourist to Africa? It's Noah's Arc's long list of African wildlife species. What most International tourists want to see are carnivores. That's African lions, leopards, cheetah, wild hunting dogs, hyenas and smaller Jackals. Then there's the African `big five' of elephants, rhino, Cape buffalo, lion and leopard. The Kalahari is famous for big male lions in past decades. They have been there in good numbers. They still are and can be restocked to tourist drawing numbers like in the Serengeti or Ngorongoro Crater NPs in East Africa. For an enlarged Kalahari NP increase to higher species numbers to be restocked it takes water (wildlife water holes). There is enough Kalahari `greenery', just increase the wildlife water holes thus the wildlife species list to restock with. Put in some a-la-Etosha NP wildlife water holes and drilled wells with windmills to increase the African wildlife species list via a-la Etosha NP paradigm in neighboring Namibia like giraffe, ostrich, warthogs, springbok, and comical baboons et al to be restocked. In the feasibility study process PhDs would visit the varied vast Kalahari regions to produce a list of what species are to be restocked via number for different regions.

That's in differing regions with appropriate numbers for each region based on their carrying capacity (vegetation and waterholes). That's where to put lodges, their exclusive wildlife viewing areas. Then lodge sizes (tourists beds) or number of competing wildlife viewing 4x4 vehicles so that there are not too many to result in poor to unacceptable photographing conditions with too many vehicles `at a lion kill' like in Kenya's Masai Mara NP of the upper Serengeti ecosystem. In the Mala Mala, Singida, Londolozi, Phinda in the SA paradigm where viewing vehicles have radio contact to alert other vehicles when an interesting photographic situation turns up. But then only two or three vehicles approach any to be photographed wildlife. The others hang back until they are called forward. That's to insure excellent photographic conditions are intact. In new portions of any enlarged Kalahari NP such a paradigm would be expected to be adopted by new tourist lodges. What of the wildlife viewing lodges in e several established NPs like Chobe or the Okavango Delta's wildlife Moremi reserve? That's let them be as they are unless they choose new innovations offered by the new secondary development of newer portions of a now not yet Kalahari NP not already designated or developed as a wildlife-watching destinations.

The not yet 32% of all Botswana as Kalahari NP vs. the 38% of Botswana that was `created' (not always developed) by the Brits before the Bechuanaland Protectorate became Botswana in 1966. We now go back to the lost Bushman homeland-cum-Death by Dispossession of these (by DNA) oldest living human survivors on our human family tree. Yes long after dinosaurs had come 235 million years ago, became extinct 65 million years ago. That's The Gods Must Be Crazy people, their now few survivors. That's people Dr Jack Wheeler took us to meet in remote Kalahari (semi-desert) in 1988. Where more `civilized' people are now encroaching, trying the survival chances of a last stand for Bushman and their endangered wildlife. Can our ideas, impressions from our brief 1988 Kalahari (Bushman) bush camp out visit, now 30 years ago, a generation or later more still be valid? Or has civilization, the times gone off and left us, with climate change, a Kalahari region been invaded and despoiled beyond repair? Despite its low population has Botswana since more so invaded the Kalahari? Wildlife and ground cover (trees, grass) may have diminished? The EC wrongly encouraged the introduction of beef cattle to destroy wildlife and the Bushman's domain. But still humans come to cut (rather than plant) trees and ground cover.

Land owning is a major human desire and drive. Human populations are increasing from 300 million at the birth of Christ to over seven billion today (or 23 times). Vacant land with trees and plants (convertors of carbon dioxide to oxygen) are less as they are replaced by civilization's `asphalt jungles'. Botswana is one of few places that can add land (space) for African wildlife use vs. needed for peoples low populations. The Kalahari question with its already NPs and wildlife sanctuaries there is still too little land for African wildlife. But where else is there a suitable wildlife land where there is Africa's Noah's Arc diversity of African wildlife species? Luckily places like Yellowstone, Serengeti, Kruger, and Kakadu were saved "native and unspoiled for future generations." Then we zero in on should the remaining 32% of total Botswana's Kalahari sands be developed as a wildlife NP and Bushman homeland? One would hope so, as it is such a unique wildlife ecosystem and only home of Bushman via DNA our oldest living human tribe that with Botswana's low population density GoB would fit to finish what the Brits started there in the Kalahari sands W. Dr Jack, we six others in our Kalahari Bushman 1988 visit's main observation were: (1) domestic beef cattle should not be there, (2) Bushman should have a homeland in the Kalahari as via DNA the oldest survivors on mankind's family tree, all we (our) `out of Africa' peoples' roots.

1988 Maun, Botswana boarding the Islander twin engine aircraft to fly NW to a dirt strip at Xai Xai to start our week Bushman visit. L to R our group of seven is Dr Joel, Dr Jack, Wally, Jim, author, Bud, Tom. Xai Xai was W of the Okavango Delta, a half hour N of our encampment within a quarter mile of the 11 member two Bushman hunter brother's camp which was essentially only a campfire to ward off lions or other carnivores. Jack's trip was to see if smash hit movie The Gods Must Be Crazy about Kalahari Bushman was for real or maybe a Hollywood hoax.

1988 Xai Xai dirt strip where the Herrero cattle people have one well driven out of SW Africa by the Germans who lost it in WW I. Herrero adopted European wear visor bonnet caps, long dresses very different from usual black attire in Africa. Bushman Ma and child lower R.

1988 Herreros' one community well at Xai Xai is barricaded to keep cattle out. Herreros were the one exception to cattle in W Botswana Kalahari with low density humans beside few surviving Bushman in the `thirst-thorn" Kalahari where others can't survive.

1988 Bushman clan Kalahari encampment on their day's food gathering. Note the gal's wildebeest skin garment, this day its back legs are tied over her L shoulder, the tail is up on the food receing drape or 'back pack' of her single large wildlife skin one and only every day garment.

1988 Bushman gals display for us whites their tasama melon dance. Note the older gal this day had same wildebeest one game skin garment but this time the animal's tail of skin is down worn opposite today.

1988 our Bushman visit the younger of two brother Bushman hunters makes a meal of a tasama melon. Melons are their and wildlife's main source of moisture or essential water in the otherwise arid-thirst-thorn Kalahari Desert where no others chose to or can survive.

1988 day of hunt with Kalahari Bushman, half-Bushman Kieme with pocket knife which Bushman don't possess works to remove a thorn from the younger of two Bushman hunters foot who are barefooted vs. thorns, scorpions, poisonous snakes.

1988 Bushman campsite, Bushman mother's profile
with 'backpack' drape in her one game skin 'dress'.
They have a simple life, the men hunt, bring in the
occasional meat. The women raise the kids, but go out
daily to 'gather' melons or other tubers, botanicals.

1988 Bushman boy studies whites having heard they
collected a bounty for a pair of Bushman's ears
as late as 1923. What do they now want, what's that
thing (cameras) they keep pointing at us. They have
never ever had close contact with whites before.

1984 Gemsbok NPs in SW Botswana and South Africa
were later amalgamated, fence removed in the recent
past. Gemsbok are one of the most adaptable to arid
conditions. Develop the total Kalahari into the bigger
Wildlife-Bushman NP of the whole of W Botswana.

1988 Kruger greater kudu. Botswana has kudu in
their W Kalahari. Develop the whole western Kalahari
into the enlarged total W Botswana Wildlife-Bushman
NP, increase water for wildlife via a-la-Etosha NP
water holes with drilled wells and windmill pumps.

1988 Bushman camp baby rolls *a* tasama melon while keeping an eye on us white faces with thing (cameras) they keep pointing at us thinking "why aren't they sun tanned brown like we all are. They look bad, unhealthy sickly white to me. And then they wear such really weird stuff vs. our skins."

1988 at the Bushman camp this pensive mother may be thinking "If you whites want to help us Bushman get Botswans' pols , everybody else to quit taking away our home, this thorn-and-thirst Kalahari Desert where we've lived `forever' but no one else wants to or knows how to survive out here except for us, our God given wildlife."

At Bushman campfire site mother prepares her babies meal from ubiquitous tasama melon. They dug a hole to catch any rain but there was none, so they had to depend on melons for their only moisture.

1988 Bushman encampment where we interfaced with them. The little guy was a great target for photos. He always had his eagle eye on us "those white faces and that thing (camera) they always all had pointed at us."

1988 Bushman's campsite, a guinea hen. We asked, they showed us snares for guinea hens beyond only bows and their poisoned arrows to produce protein .

1988 Bushman's campfire site. My Hasselblad had a Polaroid back. The boys are intrigued at seeing a Polaroid photo of themselves in the remote bush.

1988 the clan's two Bushman hunter let us join them on an all-day hunt where they left us in their dust with our water bottles, energy bars. They showed us the bush, roots from which they get a grub to poison their arrows. Note their comparative small stature to JW.

1988 on Bushman's hunt older hunter had only a hide loin cloth, his shoulder gear, was bare footed vs. snakes (two run ins with puff adders on hunt), ubiquitous thorn, scorpions, et al. They survive where no others can or care to try in their remote-harsh-thorn-thirst Kalahari.

1988 Tsodilo Hills or Bushman's Louvre where several thousand ancient Bushman rock painted images have survived. We visited Tsodilo after a week of our camp a 10 minute walking distance from the Bushman clan's established campfire site.

1973 myopic rhinos Ngorongo Crater TNZ now unknown in W Botswana. Create proposed all W Botswana Wildlife-Bushman NP Park as a survival haven vs. rhino horn poaching, extinction, Bushman to shoot poachers.

Tsodilo Hill 1988. Several resident boys showed up to have their picture taken. It's easier with the color image, but from front the 2nd, 5th look to be Bushman, first and third more black Bantu, African 4th half and half. Bushman are not Bantu blacks.

1988 after Tsodilo Hills we descended Okavango River in dugouts as above to spend a night with a 'river Bushman' to end Dr Jack's tour. Some of us then went on to Chobe NP, Victoria Falls. I added Makgadikgadi, Banes Baobabs , Etosha NP NW Namibia for more background.

By 1966 Independence the Brits had created 38% of Botswana as wildlife-Bushman homeland NPs sanctuaries. We herein now propose all of the remaining 32 % of all W Botswana in Kalahari sands be added as NP fragile semi-desert as more Mother Nature's ecosystem developed as a wildlife-watching destination. International tourists will come from around our world to see endangered African wildlife. Beef destroy such as a fragile ecosystem. GoB may best developed the whole Kalahari sands guarded "native and unspoiled for future generations" if they had done an international feasibility study to ascertain that's their best competitive land use rather than a short sighted Europeans introducing of beef cattle into an arid semi-desert. This's what we found to be transpiring in 1988. Is it too late to make it all a Kalahari sands NP to save what is still then possible? Is it now too late to go wildlife-Bushman vs. beef and a despoiled Kalahari sands 70% of Botswana? That's to now still be a cash cow wildlife watching destination saved "native and unspoiled for future generations" to enhance GoB's GDP. What's different now 30 years later? African wildlife watching tourism is now a more booming industry. A feasibility study now would show the way to go for GoB to be so convinced to let it be so developed. This unique `diamond in the rough' region is best to be guarded "native and unspoiled for future generation." Such is still herein hoped for.

The Europeans encouraging (1980s) GoB to introduce beef cattle into the Kalahari was an ecological travesty. The Kalahari is far too arid or fragile for domestic cattle which have been only mistakenly introduced there since Botswana's Independence in 1966 by misguided European Community (EC) bureaucracy (see below). For our Dr JW's 1988 visit with the Bushman clan Peter established our tented camp about a quarter mile from the nomadic-`can-disappear-anytime in 90 seconds' Bushman clan campfire of a two brother family plus two single adult women others totaling 11 with wives and children. Peter organized critical communication links over the months in contacting them, keeping track of their seasonal movements. Contacting them go between was a more civilized relative Kieme with a Tswana (major tribe of Botswana) father and Bushman mother. He thus spoke Setswana the tribal language of Botswana plus the Kung-Bushman-click language. The Bushman we visited conversed only in their click language. Thus our contacts and communication with the clan was thru half Bushman Kieme residing with the clan during our visit. Kieme then talked to Tswana tribe member Shylock staying in our camp in Setswana. He talked to us in English for a double level of translation. We learned more by looking than talking.

We were seven Americans including Dr Wheeler. Organizers Peter, Salome were joined by Map a white European resident of Botswana and Salome's sister Liza plus a couple of their Botswana black native camp hands. Well organized Peter and staff had our Hyena tented camp set up within a few minutes walking distance of the Bushman clan's campfire. A hyena had devoured a porcupine leaving its calling card plus a pile of porcupine quills to name our site Hyena Camp in a grove of shade trees. We overnighted in JNB to then fly to Gaborone capital of Botswana. That's to then fly on into Maun on the SE edge of the Okavango Delta wetland from Gaborone to Maun on scheduled tourist flights. We flew on NW or W of the Okavango Delta to Xai Xai with a dirt landing strip N of our Bushman visit encampment on our chartered dual engine Islander. Xai Xai was a one-dug-well-remote-bush village. Its single well is a big deal in arid Kalahari or the reason a small band of Herrero cattle tribe refugee people lived there. They were run out of now to the W then German South West Africa (now Namibia) pre WW I. Herreros were one of the few people beside only Bushman in this remote western Kalahari Desert region of Botswana. From Xai Xai it was a half hour S to the Bushman's camp via Peter, Map in two 4x4 pickups on the only regional N-S desert track past our Hyena camp in a shade-providing-grove-of-pleasant-Kalahari-apple-leaf trees.

In camp before our first interface with the shy clan Peter, Map warned us eager beaver Yanks to go slow as these were nomadic so called '90-second people' could vanish. They could decide to abandon their simple camp fire protection from lions to vanish into the bush without prior notice or delay. That's which idiosyncrasy lead to them being called the "90 second people" by scientists. This concerned Peter, Dr Jack that the Bushman very well might just vanish, their escape for being unused to curious camera-toting-question-asking whites should we not click with them. We were forewarned to approach the clan warily, politely, to be subdued not to spoil our unique opportunity. Bushman were still shot in the Bechuanaland Kalahari as late as 1923. You brought Bushman's ears in to be paid a bounty for exterminating vermin. Luckily for us times had changed but we learned we were the first whites to interface with this few and far between still nomadic Bushman clan so they were white-face wary. Contact with the clan was thru half-Bushman Kieme recruited by Peter. Kieme had been enticed to go out on a limb to organize our unusual bush camp out encounter with his cloistered nomadic Bushman clan relatives. Thus there was room for expected error or misunderstanding in our two layers of bush language translations.

This also tended to put the Bushman clan off. The Bushman were uneasy or they couldn't imagine why we white faces were there or so interested in them? That is like we might be facing an IRS audit or worse. These remote bush nomads had no previous personal contact with whites but the history of Bushman being ethnically cleansed by whites was in their campfire lore. They had not a clue about the *God's Must Be Crazy* movie and all that as the neon light that had attracted us inquisitive white strangers to visit them as `noble savages'. They were puzzled why we'd come to this remote uninhabited place in their native-and-unspoiled bush to gawk, query, photograph them. They were at first wary, subdued, ill at ease, suspicious or confused as to our intent. We quickly reverted to observing with our eyes, limiting our oral questions to put them more at ease. Later the younger brother did admonish us with "You can see with your eyes so why ask so many goofy questions?" Everything they did or knew they had learned from birth in the bush as survival bush lore. What little they had was bush provided, nothing store bought, in a box, can or bottle. That's we had not been so educated in their harsh Kalahari' survival knowledge and wanted to ask lots of to them dumb things. They didn't see a difference between prying or for information queries.

Questions coming from them were nil or scant queries came only from the two mature brothers. The women and children, the two-other-single-unattached-adult women never initiated any queries or if so they were channeled thru the two Bushman brothers spokesmen. They hadn't had previous contact with whites so this was a big deal occasion for them. Eventually over several days we went on a full day's food gathering with the whole clan. It was like a remote-bush-Easter-egg hunt. They found, dug up food we couldn't imagine existed. Then we went on an all-day-on-foot hunt with the brothers which taxed our ability to keep up. Having hunted in Africa I would never have allowed a gaggle of us seven, two translators, Peter and Map to haunt me on a hunt, no way. The clan eventually good naturedly went along with it. At the far end of the hunt they took us to a known-only-to-them-specific bush. They dug up from its buried roots the grubs with which they poisoned their arrows with divulging to us this unique element of their survival or hunting with poisoned arrows. On the day of the hunt we had two encounters with poisonous puff adders. We had a third travelling on foot between their campfire and our camp all in one week. This was almost as many puff adders as I had had encountered in five years in East Africa.

Puff adders have a cytotoxic poison which is not immediately lethal as the neurotoxic black and green mamba poison which causes death in an hour. Puff adders are more apt to cause gangrene requiring amputation of foot or leg. The danger is puff adders are big, lethargic, well camouflaged with yellow-brown color. They are prone NOT to move, to be stepped on then strike. More lively poisonous snakes move off if not cornered. Back in their camp their younger gals showed us their midday melon dance. We were honored to be invited to observe their after dark spiritual healing dance around their campfire. On inquiry they showed us how they set snares for guinea fowl. They showed us how they `twist a fire' or start a new fire by rapidly twisting a round stick in the hole in a small flat piece of wood which we'd learned to do as boy scouts for merit badges. Despite puff adders, five inch scorpions, or ubiquitous tire puncture thorns the clan were all barefoot. That's with hunters travelling long distances daily, gals out in bush gathering Mother Nature's fare to dig up or collecting surface melons.

Bushman and many other bush (vs. urban) Africans do not wear footwear vs. the many hazards. Part of Bushman being 90 second people they have little but what they wear like any shoes (vs several pairs). They have no wardrobes or suitcases, or changes of animal skin wear, or things like combs or tooth brushes, knives, scissors, or you name it, they didn't have it. After seeing them live happily with so little, I was embarrassed we have so much. For clothing wear men had an animal hide skimpy loin covering. That was it. That's naked head to toes but loin brief. The women were outfitted with a single larger animal skin with two legs, front or back tied over one shoulder with a thong tied around their waist as a belt to keep their animal skin `garment' doubled or overlapped or closed in front. They created a drape or back pack in the animal skin in back above the waist thong. The created drape above the waist thong was for carrying veggies they gathered back to camp against their bare back skins. We observed animal skin garments with tail up and tail down changing from day to day. We concluded they took the skin `dress' off at night to use it as a blanket, and wore its leg tie wildebeest tail up or down next day, not to worry. For women there was no indication of breast wear, maybe a loin skin for what we call underwear. They had one flimsy tent like open fronted stick frame with grass covered structure near the camp fire probably for shade for the still crawling baby's nap. The 90 second people could leave their campfire site very quickly to leave scant evidence of their having been there. They had no luggage, just what `skins' they wore.

1988 Victoria Falls on the Zambezi River between Zambia and Zimbabwe. It's generally considered the biggest fall (flow) vs. Iguazu in Brazil-Argentina. In the God Must Be Crazy movie it's where the Bushman went (edge of the world) to throw his `bad' coke bottle away.

1988 Makgadikgadi Pan Game Reserve E of Okavango Delta, still in Kalahari Desert. I visited it with Peter, saw vehicles chasing zebra for their striped hides. It needs game protection to save Botswana's wealth as a top international wildlife-watching tour destination.

1988 Banes Baobab was painted by him in 1862 in route to Victoria Falls on foot. It is E of Okavango Delta (Maun) should be included in nearby game reserves to protect it from civilization's encroachment as a rare surviving site as an exquisite gift from Mother Nature.

1988 Banes Baobab grove, the 'fallen' baobab. This area has a surrounding lake during the rainy season. It's an internationally famous site. Include it in nearby game reserves as an additional international tourist-draw-destination with no nearby civilized structures.

1988 Etosha NP in now N Namibia I visited. It is in an arid region like Botswana's Kalahari where they created waterholes with windmill pumps, restocked with game, for a strong international tourist destination, a plan that Botswana could follow for a huge Kalahari West NP.

1988 Etosha zebra at water hole with snag tree colony weaver bird nests. The Etosha model of water holes with windmill pumps to support wildlife could be copied in Botswana's Kalahari W to create the largest wildlife NP in the world as their best choice land use cash cow.

The Botswana's Kalahari is lion country. My Kenya pro Ker and Downey hunter (1965) went there seasonally. He verified it supported big male lions. Lions are on the endangered list from over hunting, loss of range to humans. Add windmill pumps at created water holes, restock with the huge W Kalahari wildlife-Bushman NP with restocked endangered African wildlife to develop it as an international wildlife-watching-destination-tourist draw as a best chosen land development option to joint that craze.

When it got warm midday the gals undid their wildlife-skin-shoulder-leg tie. This let the full animal skin garment drop to double down at their waist over their thong belt. They were now bare breasted, not to worry. Thus exposed were lots of ostrich egg chips necklaces as heirlooms passed down from how many generations? See cover picture of our 1992 BFTB book (Pg 41). For the Bushman clan our visit was very out of their ordinary. That's vis-à-vis their remote bush cloistered still hunter-gatherer survival in their remote thorn-and-thirst Kalahari. For them it was a first contact with whites, up close and personal for a week. From our standpoint they did not pull their '90 second' disappearance thing to flee to be rid of us, all our questions and photographing as we had been warned could happen. The bottom line of our interface with them we learned about ourselves, our roots. For us a LIGHT came on. We had a discovery epiphany of "they aren't different; they are just STILL like we were a few centuries back." That's before our Agricultural Revolution some 10,000 years ago for our departure from being simple hunter-gatherers too. That was by our human evolution since domesticating wildlife or animal husbandry and cultivating plants and trees for our agriculture. That's with most humans evolving to private land ownership.

Bottom line of our interface with the Bushman clan was we learned through them a lot about ourselves for an epiphany. Our curiosity led to the discovery these Stone Age remote bush people were US visited by a magic time machine taking us back into our deep past to visit our roots. That's that post Agricultural Revolution (vs. still being nomadic) we have transitioned or evolved (evolution) into having fixed locations (an address) to be with our plants (agriculture) or livestock (animal husbandry) and now even transitioning far beyond that. Not to oversimplify as there are now still people in our `civilization' without addresses, sleeping under bridges. We arrived to that the Bushman are us (what we used to be)--our African DNA match thus--that we are them. They were the starting point of our (or any) search for `our roots' in any determined roots search. We observed these people. Then a light went on for us. We then universally said "They 're not different they are just STILL like we were many centuries back" before we went thru our Agricultural Revolution starting 10,000 years ago to transition from being hunter-gatherers by domesticating wild animals and cultivating plants then settling in fixed locations (probably near water) and creating shelters. They now lived in an arid Kalahari native and unspoiled wildlife ecosystem not one fit for domestic beef cattle. Cattle had mistakenly been EC ntroduced to SPOIL that fragile ecosystem.

But we red-meat eaters wanted to see this their Kalahari Bushman land preserved for these Bushman with their God given wildlife to survive for our more 'advanced' future generations to be able to enjoy them as all our human roots "native and unspoiled for future generations." In the years since our Bushman visit whenever I go into a crowded Safeway grocery store (HEB in TX) or a Wal Mart I think of our Bushman clan. In our grocery store they would be frightened by all the shelves with mysterious things they have no need for. They might be calmed only slightly in our fruits and vegetables section where they could relate to their daily bush food gathering. After our several delightful adventure days with the Bushman clan Peter took Jack's crew N from our Hyena Camp to Tsodilo Hills called the Bushman's Louvre for its prehistoric eons of their rock wall paintings. The Kalahari is relatively flat with but very few Tsodilo Hills like rock outcroppings. Tsodilo however is a substantial rock hill where Bushman came in prehistorical times to do their vertical rock wall art. Scientists have inventoried several thousand painted mostly wildlife figures there. It is amazing they have survived sun, wind, rain for so many centuries.

Peter then led Jack's party SE from Tsodilo down the Okavango River in dugout canoes for an overnight camp out to visit a 'river Bushman' to top off Jack's exquisite Bushman adventure. Several of us then visited Chobe NP (Chobe River front elephant herds et al) in Botswana's NE border then nearby E to visit Victoria Falls on the Zambesi River on the Zimbabwe-Zambia border. I then hung on in the region to do a loner visit with Peter to the Makgadikgati Pans wildlife area E of the Okavango Delta and visiting famous Baines Baobabs a grove of baobab trees which artist Banes painted while walking N with David Livingston to Victoria Falls (1862). I next went to Etosha NP four days in the N of South West Africa (SWA) or now Namibia. Etosha is an arid area like the Kalahari. The interesting thing they have done is create water holes, drilled wells and pumped water via windmills. Why not do this in a Kalahari NP's further development? That's which I now strongly propose herein. With such available wildlife drinking water the number of species that can be restocked in Botswana's Kalahari is substantially increased. Success as a wildlife-watching destination is more wildlife species despite the somewhat restricted vegetation in the semi-desert Botswana Kalahari. With water there would be more herbivores. If you have plentiful herbivores there will be carnivores. Lions and other carnivores is a large part of what African wildlife-watching destinations consist of. But is it too late already? I believe if there is a human will, there is a human Kalahari way.

The encroachment of cattle, botany despoiling and wildlife killing on the fragile Kalahari took its toll. It's a fragile ecosystem that heals slowly. Where if there is a decrease in ground cover, it leads to reduced rain. A good example of that is the barren Sahara, a real desert. In early historical times Greek and Romans report that the now barren N Africa Sahara was once green, the home of African wildlife. An opinion is that as Muslim Arabs spread their religion (7th century) W across N Africa their goats killed off ground cover. Today it has devolved to a grass blade barren desert. If so the Kalahari might be headed to such an unsavory outcome in the matter of decades or a very few centuries. The Sahara saga is hard to believe but otherwise where did the Romans get the lions to turn on Christians in Rome's coliseum? Not from equatorial Africa. Or where did Hannibal from Tunisia's Carthage get elephants to attack Rome before Christ? Making the Kalahari sands a tourist developed NP would stop such a downward spiral. But it may be too late to get GoB politicians et al interests in developing an entire region expanded Kalahari NP as proposed. Let an international feasibility study tell its story. My 1988 Etosha visit was by flying JNB to Windhoek then driving 260 MI N. That's for three nights in Etosha NP wildlife lodges.

That's in an exciting wildlife safeguarding place despite its Kalahari like semi-desert-arid nature. I was sizing up this southern region vis-a-vis my then better known (1965-1973) E Africa NPs looking for ideas of how Botswana could save its entire W 70 % essentially whole of Botswana's Kalahari as an endangered wildlife-Bushman bigger NP. That's filling in the hiatuses (wildlife fence) between now UK created 'stepping stones' smaller independent NPs as Werda town (or E) on Botswana's S border N to Chobe NP in the N with other existing NP or game refuges in between. That's to create an E border of a huge wildlife-Bushman NP to the W of a now 'completed' S to N necklace of already existing Brit wildlife refuges as the already there outlines of the herein proposed total W of Botswana Kalahari amalgamated wildlife NP (creating world's largest) as discussed in more detail herein. I'd spent several years in E Africa visiting wildlife and native people's ecosystems plus hunting, but lots of serious wildlife photographing in E African better NPs. That's Tanzania's Serengeti, adjoining Ngorongoro Crater NP and Lake Manyara NP both on Serengeti's SE flank. The Kalahari was always a place of wildlife. They were always there (in Bushman rock paintings) but without the protection as a wildlife sanctuary and wildlife management, the density of wildlife has been substantially diminished by encroaching `human civilization'. The Kalahari's wildlife has survived greatly diminished. See map pg 16 for start of S end of enlarged NP's E fence near Werda (or E).

That's as an unprotected wildlife place as the Kalahari was off limits to most as a `thirst and thorn' region except by its `they-survived-there' Bushman. Our world cries out for more land dedicated to wildlife, not less. The full Kalahari is a leading candidate to be recreated (restocked) as a wildlife sanctuary or official NP. 38% of all Botswana is already NPs or wildlife reserves since the days before the Brits departed in 1966. My proposal adds the other 32% (of all Botswana) more interior W Kalahari sands not yet protected as the Okavango Delta is on W of the string-of-pearls (with four E Kalahari sands border hiatuses to fill in) of already wildlife sanctuaries defining the E boundary of a Kalahari.sands NP. Where to route a wildlife fence to let all know? The legs and limbs are there already, just add the body and heart (the interior Kalahari W). Make the whole Botswana Kalahari an official enlarged and consolidated NP (biggest in the world). Create, manage it as a NP by wildlife restocking, in its development to then be thus NP protected "native and unspoiled for future generations." That's for an ever more developed NP as a wildlife-watching-international destination-cum-added cash cow element of GoB's GDP, country's `developed' wealth. That's before it goes Sahara Desert like the Greeks and Roman historians say it did not that many centuries ago. That's the North African huge Sahara from green to barren not-a-blade-of-grass sands!

I am not alone in worrying it may already be too late to save the Kalahari. Michael Main published his book KALAHARI, Life's Variety in Dune and Delta (1987) a year before our Kalahari Bushman visit when the ejection of the Bushman from their Brit created homeland (now CKGR) and European politicians urging GoB to make the arid Kalahari sands beef pasture. Main's is a brilliant, detailed book that gets into details that far back then that give pause for the Kalahari being a follow on of the N African Sahara. We saw indications of a downward spiral in the fragile Kalahari then despite the Brits having already protected 38 % of to be Botswana in a good encouraging direction as NPs and wildlife sanctuaries. In visiting then SW Africa's (now Namibia's) to see the Etosha NP wildlife water hole with windmills paradigm was positive. I was now developing a second love for southern Africa vis-à-vis African wildlife in East Africa. This was further advanced years later with my near year's tour in MZB to create (via feasibility study) the Elephant Coast CPD-NP concept (914 Sq MI) as awarded by GoM in 1996.

Then when it cratered, I had the audacity of trying to resurrect it at 4000 Sq Mi due to improved regional changes plus wildlife-watching-destination craze-cum-market. That's in my book SAVE MOZAMBIQUE'S ELEPHANT COAST. (2007) but my boss (New Orleans USA entrepreneur-developer) failed to carry out the wonderful 914 Sq Mi project then he died. I then proposed in my book *SAVE MOZAMBIQUE'S ELEPHANT COAST (2007) with details see* www.savemec.org) to expand its 914 Sq Mi coastal site W of the Maputo River, then N to Kruger NP's latitude to 4000 Sq Mi to connect to (by then) Grand Limpopo TransFrontier Park (GLTP) the already (then) largest wildlife sanctuary in the world at 38,500 Sq Mi. This was the handiwork of South African breweries billionaire Dr Anton Rupert of South Africa's (his) Peace Parks Foundation with his two cofounders South Africa's `prison-to-President' Nelson Mandela and then Crown Prince of the Netherlands in the early 2000s. That is in MZB I was not building pipelines my back then usual career bag but organizing a world class project (via international feasibility study) to create a 914-Sq-Mi-Elephant-Coast-botanical-wildlife CPD-NP (1995-96) in Mozambique (MZB) (Cpt 35 of my 2015 book) as awarded by GoM to my New Orleans developer-boss NOJim. He who belonged to a then "invest when there is still blood in the streets" ilk who I'd come to know on a Dr Wheeler adventure travel spring visit to the North Pole earlier in (1988). New Orleans failed to perform in MZB, but then the GLTP was created in 2002. This new African-wildlife-watching-destination craze was dawning, then positively exploding.

In my 2007 MZB NP book I proposed with `how to' details of increasing our MZB Elephant Coast project from 914 Sq Mi (approved) to a resurrected 4000 Sq Mi. That's increasing our 914 Sq Mi NP plan to W of the Maputo River to MZB's W (Swaziland) bordera0 then N to connect to the GLTP thus protect the by then known Maputaland CPD all within the limits of a now proposed MZB 4000 Sq Mi version of the Elephant Coast NP addition. That's to protect the Maputaland CPD-NP "native and unspoiled for future generations." The words used by the UN to mandate how all the 250 worldwide CPDs (84 in Africa) were to be so protected. That's CPDs as per the International Biodiversity Accord as signed by the Worlds Heads of State at the 1992 Rio Earth Summit. Above you've seen a sketch map (page 16) of my version of such a similar proposal to make near all the Botswana Kalahari Desert an endangered wildlife-Bushman-homeland NP. That's by providing to GoB what was their competitive best land use via a professional international feasibility study. That's to protect the Kalahari sands from intruding humanity and its asphalt jungle `civilization' rather to guard it "native and unspoiled for future generations" as an enlarged GoB Kalahari NP cash cow GDP enhancer vs. being a `thirst and thorn' wasteland with changing times. That's by restocking the enlarged Kalahari W NP, developing it as a world-wildlife-watching site.

That's with endangered African wildlife by adding windmill pump water holes as is so successful in likewise arid African wildlife ecosystem Etosha NP in N Namibia. International tourist would eat Botswana beef from E Botswana's traditional `beef cattle pasture'. I am not subjectively anti beef cattle. I grew up 4th generation on my family's 1865 Pacific view cattle ranch in northern California. But we had 40 inches of rain, thus greenery to support beef ranching. That's developing an enlarged Kalahari NP international-wildlife-watching destination with other ideas borrowed from our 1995 MZB NP feasibility study my year 2007 SAVE MOZAMBIQUE'S ELEPHANT COAST book. This MZB saga is revisited in this books next chapter as a still candidate for NP resurrection. That project should have been developed in 1996 on when the time was ripe with an awarded MZB 99 year develop and operate lease. MZB has devolved into problems since then to make its resurrection (despite its UN CPD land status) a now longer shot for success. That's with several years African wildlife tourism experience, background.

That's knowledge of East Africa's best in wildlife watching destinations to apply in a proposed increased 'the rest of the MZB-CPD NP expanded to the N. Now before it is too late, or blocked by GoM despite the clock running out. Why not give GoM an updated feasibility study to know what their more CPD-NP development MZB GDP enhancement opportunity still is (in Cpt 3 next). Back to GoB's Kalahari case, that's by filling in between the already 'stepping stones' of existing Brit Botswana NPs, finishing where the Brits were headed. Start with an international feasibility study done for GoB supported by the world 'green' cause organizations as Peace Parks, UN, World Bank, US and European Governments, green NGOs et al. All the best current know how would be reintroduced into the enlarged W Kalahari NP concept and cause toward investigating upgrading the Kalahari into a top international-wildlife watching destination enlarged Botswana NP via a starting point international class land use feasibility study of the now Kalahari and what could be to alert GoB and the world's environmentalists of its potential worth as a world class international wildlife-watching destination saved native and unspoiled.

That's as a perpetual Botswana upped GDP raising NP cash cow from tourist out drawing such as Dubai in UAE. That's as tourist excited by a more Mother Nature's international-wildlife-watching destination. That's with a development cost of nickels on Dubai's billions of dollars expenditure trying to make Dubai a proverbial `silk-purse-out-of-a-sow's-ear' top international tourist destination via stacked glitz. What is needed 1st is a for GoM 'bankable' feasibility study by top pros like the Bechtel-WATG-Horwath study I was the site key man for in MZB for NOJim (developer). That was in 1995 that in 10 months at the NO developer's cost of only one million dollars GoM award us a 99-year-develop-operate-land lease 914 Sq Mi CPD-NP. Post 1975 independence from Portugal all MZB `nationalized' land is now GoM owned. That's as in creating our 914 Sq Mi Elephant Coast CPD-NP concepts (1996). It's now a similar Botswana Kalahari effort to-prove-a-NP developed wildlife watching paradigm as GoB's by far best-land-use for Botswana's huge enlarged W Kalahari Desert NP E border fence from near Werda town (or E)N to Chobe NP enlarged NP E 700 Mi boundary by filling in between some already smaller Brit NPs.

That's Brits almost established an enlarged W Kalahari NP's essential E border of the Kalahari sands. Next with an international feasibility study done for GoB supported by the world 'green' cause organizations as Peace Parks, UN, World Bank, US and European Governments, green NGOs et al. All the best current know how would be reintroduced into the expanded W Kalahari NP concept-cause toward investigating upgrading the Kalahari into a top international wildlife watching destination enlarged Botswana NP via a starting point international class land use feasibility study of the now entire Botswana Kalahari region. That's via an international feasibility study to alert GoB, the world's environmentalists of its potential worth as a world class international wildlife-watching destination to save Mother Nature's diamond-in-the-rough-wildlife-watching jewel (via NP) native and unspoiled for future generations as a perpetual Botswana cash cow to outdraw such as Dubai as an international tourist destination. That's with a significant development cost of coins on Dubai's billions of dollars. Or that's like South Africa's proven Mala Mala, Singida (S of Kruger) or Pinda (KwaZulu Natal) wildlife lodges which are all fully booked up a year ahead status of international best wildlife-viewing destinations vs. the Kenya Masai Mara NP overcrowded disappointing NP visit of "you can't-get-a-lion-kill image-for-too-many-zebra-striped VW mini buses."

So our Kalahari Bushman 1988 visit bottom line was like we'd gone on a magic time machine voyage back to visit—guess what—ourselves! It was an adventure to discover who we were (or are) and where we came from (our roots) or a glimpse of bush living sites to eventually evolve into extended family clan sites then villages of several families, then towns, then cities. That was our Dr Jack's Bushman visit epiphany. They gathered their 'organic' food fresh each day straight from nature. They dig up tubers from underground. A mainstay is their tasama melon as food and moisture. I muse how Bushman would become claustrophobic, frightened of our modern grocery stores as I even sometimes am. That's in our grocery store aisles with all the mysterious cans, boxes, plastic bags, glass and plastic bottles, or that strange coke bottle featured in THE GODS MUCT BE CRAZY movie. When I head for the produce (fruits and vegetables) section, I think maybe only here could the hunter-gatherer-Kalahari Bushman be at peace with it all in what is our modern civilization. That's which to them would be a frightening horror story. But is for us too, with FDA, Monsanto's `gone mad' via genetically modified crops like corn, soy et al.

What is needed critical path 1st is a 'bankable' feasibility study (billionaire financed?) by top pros like our MZB (1995) Bechtel-WATG-Horwath study I was site key man for that in 10 months at a developer's cost of ONLY one million dollars got GoM to award a 99-year-develop-operate-land lease—post 1975 independence all MZB GoM owned `nationalized' land—in creating the 914 Sq Mi Elephant Coast CPD-NP concept (1996). That's a similar Botswana effort to-prove-an enlarged, amalgamated NP via developed wildlife watching paradigm is GoB's by far best-land-use for Botswana's huge enlarged W Kalahari Desert NP full S near Werda village (or W) N to Chobe NP enlarged NP E fenced boundary. That's by filling in between developed as an international wildlife-watching destination a new African tourist draw. Who else has such a low population country and Kalahari wasteland that qualifies, is already headed in a wildlife watching direction via Brits before Botswana's 1966 independence? Brits left the 'stepping stones' of existing Botswana NPs essentially `Kalahari sands' E border of an all Kalahari sands NP. The next step, give GoB an international feasibility study to be supported by the world 'green' cause organizations as Peace Parks, UN, World Bank, US, European governments, a long list of green wildlife NGOs et al. All the best current know how would be used into a W Kalahari NP concept. That's for GoB to yah or nay on the whole Kalahari W NP wasteland into an enlarged top international wildlife-watching destination.

A study to alert GoB, world's environmentalists of the potential worth as a top international class wildlife-watching destination to save Mother Nature's diamond-in-the-rough-wildlife-watching jewel-cum-NP. That's "native and unspoiled for future generations" as a perpetual Botswana cash cow GDP enhancer to outdraw such as Dubai as an international tourist destination. That's with a development cost, yes but of nickels compared to Dubai's billions of development dollars. That's expenditure to make Dubai a proverbial silk purse out of a sow's ear international tourist destination by spending billions on producing offshore islands, then adding cement, steel, plastic, glass in skyscrapers to convert Dubai's bare desert (camel pasture) into an international tourist destination. That's what Mother Nature has already gifted Botswana's Kalahari region with. Add the finishing touches to develop thus protect it as a more wildlife international tourist draw destination with thatched roof one story tourist overnight lodge destinations to photograph reintroduced endangered African wildlife with Etosha like windmill pump wildlife water holes. Or lay a water mains from the Okavango Delta as a second source of upgrading the W Botswana NP to an Etosha like water hole system. Add water holes, roads, rail and air access (logistics) to get tourists there with beds, meals for overnights for their stay in single story thatched roof lodges.

That's with beds numbers per game lodge site design limited to insure good low density excellent good photographic opportunities the gold standard that has been proven in South Africa. That's like South Africa's proven Mala Mala, Londolozi, Singida (W of Kruger) or Phinda (KwaZulu Natal) et al which are booked up a year ahead international best wildlife viewing destinations vs. the Kenya Masai Mara overcrowded case of "you-can't-get-a-lion-kill-image-for-too-many-zebra-striped VW mini buses." So our Kalahari Bushman visit bottom line was like we'd gone on a magic time machine voyage back to visit–guess what—ourselves. It was an adventure to discover who we are and where we came from (our roots). That's a glimpse of how it was before the Agricultural Revolution evolved with a miniscule world population but when we were transitioning—evolving—to be more than nomadic family groups living around campfires like the clan we visited in 1988 still was. Humans tend to settle in locations with water for our livestock or places to plant crops to avoid carrying water long distances as is often still the case in bush Africa. We're spoiled now by running water, flush toilets, electricity the Bushman don't know.

That was our Dr Jack's Bushman visit epiphany. But there was another immediate conclusion of our visit. The Bushman by DNA are the oldest surviving humans. But they since independence in Botswana have become again an endangered human species. Generally GoB post 1966 independence treats their Bushman more like Stone Age embarrassment problems vs. what they really are to the rest of the world as indicated by the success of the GODS movie. The American English 1986 movie version set world attendance. records. It is still very popular. That's as a potential draw to an international wildlife-watching destination with Bushman involved therein as game management, guides, an added tourist draw. Now GoB just has to be made aware of their world class opportunity with Bushman as an extra draw via a feasibility study. More details of our visit (our Bushman epiphany) are available in our 1992 book. That's which I wrote as our group effort with copious photos. Our book's aim was to alert the world to the `rest-of-the-Bushman's-story' beyond the internationally popular mid 80s on movie teaser THE GODS MUST BE CRAZY. As an engineer I was trained more into dealing with numbers and engineering-construction issues than with literary talents (inexperienced author). Help came from Wheeler's literate group.

Our Kalahari `magic time machine' visit back to well before the Agricultural Age saga is titled BUSH FOR THE BUSHMAN, Need the Gods Must Be Crazy People Die? (1992). It's now out of print but there are used copies on Amazon et al. Our Bushman cause on the internet is at www.savethesan.org advising of this human endangered species (via DNA our distant relatives) or where-we-came-from, our roots. Jack's 1988 adventure trip was on the sort of "let's go see these people" (off our Gods Must Be Crazy movie introduction). Like do such people really still exist? Yes, they do as we found them in 1988. But they are now an endangered human species, but unappreciated or not treated as such. But should be (with our shared DNA) as the assets they are. Combine them with restocking the W Botswana Kalahari with wildlife. Botswana is one of the lowest population countries for their size in the world. The Kalahari is only a semi desert. It's a Garden of Eden compared to such as the real deserts of North Africa's Sahara or such as Saudi Arabia. Give GoB an international class `bankable' feasibility study. More details of our visit (our Bushman epiphany) are available in our 1992 book. Our book's aim was to alert the world to the `rest-of-the-Bushman's-story'. That's beyond the mid 80s movie teaser THE GODS MUST BE CRAZY. An engineer I was trained more in engineering-construction issues than with literary talents.

I was encouraged by the rest of Dr Wheeler's literate group. Our Kalahari `magic time machine' visit back to before the Agricultural Revolution saga book is now out of print.  There are used copies on Amazon et al.  It's about a human endangered species (via DNA our relatives).  Where we-came-from, our way back roots.  From our visit our book tells `the-rest-of-the-story' beyond the light hearted, comical 1986 GODS movie that but a few such precious people still do exist. Our 1992 BFTB book is a semi travelogue but as green cause (book) alerting mankind of an impending endangered human species extinction travesty. Botswana's has a classic chance to `out Dubai' the rest of our globe via creating an international wildlife watching destinations.  Our book's aim was to alert the world to the-`rest-of-the-Bushman's-story' beyond the internationally popular mid 80s movie teaser THE GODS MUST BE CRAZY. What would now help Bushman? Add an all Kalahari NP, restocked with wildlife drinking water.

By creating an enlarged Kalahari NP of the whole (rest of) 70% W of Botswana that the Kalahari sands occupy. That's adding 32% W to already existing now 38% of all Botswana in Kalahari NPs or wildlife refuges. That's for GoB to ride the tsunami tidal wave of international-wildlife-watching industry (an African thing) by developing the remaining otherwise `thirst and thorn' Kalahari waste land into an endangered African species plus the human Bushman as employees in game management, poaching protection, tourist guides in an developed-all-W-Kalahari NP. The initial critical path progress issue is to provide GoM with an international grade 'bankable' feasibility study borrowing on Etosha NP's approach of wildlife water holes with windmills vs. Etosha's similar to Kalahari's arid territory. That's wildlife with drinking water will support more varied wildlife. Then that greater herbivore wildlife population will attract, support carnivores to now have an international wildlife-watching destination. Put in wildlife water holes with windmill pumps. Restock the NP with African wildlife (a now thriving African industry).

For GoB what other competing land use `cash cow' is there to significantly enhance GoB GDP? That's with a relatively low development cost tourist draw, mostly already provided by Mother Nature. That's the ecosystem that has been a wildlife haven in the past (subject of Bushman rock wall painting back to prehistory). Then via DNA GoB has the oldest living human tribal clan species. Who would come as ecstatic wildlife watchers in all the now lined up in JNB 747s. People whose way back parents 60,000 years ago walked out of Africa but we now find out have DNA matching only the Bushman who still exist (barely) in Botswana (a few W in next door Namibia). There are lots of choice destinations for wildlife watching in southern or equatorial Africa. But who but Botswana can develop their huge Kalahari sands W with more NP Sq Mi that has a double barreled draw with some restocking of wildlife plus utilizing of the Bushman (problem-cum-draw) in an expanded NP operations. Thanks to global popularity of the Gods Must Be Crazy movie, GoB's advertising (international tourist draw) is already done for them. They (GoB) has a unique `diamond in the rough' situation to decide to augment the size or extent of developing their all 70 % of W Botswana in an enlarged, consolidated largest in the world African endangered wildlife plus Bushman homeland NP. The key to this puzzle is to get an international feasibility study that alerts GoB et al.

That's to GoB's unrecognized treasure-cum-development avenue (favored inside track) in the now booming African wildlife watching destination paradigm. Botswana has a classic opportunity to `out Dubai' the rest of our globe in a world class tourist destinations vs. the rest of the African wildlife watching destination in Eastern and Southern Africa in the quality of product in wildlife, ecosystem with a Bushman frosting on their wildlife cake that no one else can offer or call it GoB's unique `tourist draw'. A subject of world discussion is creation vs. evolution. I was brought up via Christian religious bible training. But my later education was a background or belief in science or a knowledge (belief) in anthropologists reported history of whom we are and where we all came from which is without my question Africa. An Adam and Eve creation story was derived at a biblical time when people didn't yet know the world was round or that dinosaurs ruled the earth like from 235 million years ago until they died out 66 million years ago. Knowledge of the existence of DNA is very recent. Having read UK DNA scientist Spencer Wells's book THE JOURNEY OF MAN, a Genetic Odyssey (2002) et al makes me lean (if I had to choose) to vote for science's evolution over biblical creation. Wells gave us what I call accepted modern science. That's the basic theme that the second human wave (us) out of Africa happened approximately 60,000 years ago. Those people were of Bushman DNA (who we visited in 1988). To anthropologist the now Kalahari Bushman are DNA special. I have to admit that to me they are also VERY special. That's more after visiting them than before, now knowing more `facts' about them, our human family tree (evolution) based on their DNA as reported by DNA scientist Spencer Wells et al. That DNA fact of the God Must Be Crazy people in not yet widely known or appreciated.

BUSH FOR THE
BUSHMAN

by John Perrott

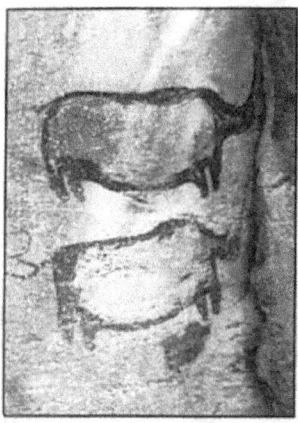

Need "The Gods Must Be Crazy" Kalahari People Die?

This 1992 book was donated to (is owned by) the US IRS 501 (c) (3) charitable nonprofit. See details at www.savethesan.org. The single adult Bushman gal's wildlife skin garment is folded down to her waist thong (belt) in the mid-day warmth exposing her many necklaces, no breast wear which is fairly customarily in bush Africa. Her short hair is fairly typical of females in Africa. By tribal choice, some African males have longer hair. An unanswered query of mine, Bushman females without scissors, knives, how do the women keep their hair short?

1988 author at the top of Tsodilo Hill rock outcrop where Bushman came for eons to rock paint now called the `Bushman's Louvre'. Botswana is very flat with few such rock outcrops. Tsodilo Hills is a key tourist draw in a bigger W wildlife-Bushman NP.

1992 Florida book signing in one of 332 events (TV, radio, appearances, news media) to publicize the Kalahari Bushman death by dispossession of their Kalahari Desert homeland plight. Herein we go the next step, create a W Botswana wildlife-Bushman NP.

1992 Margaret Thatcher as key note speaker at a FL book seller's conference. I gave her a BFTB book, enlisted her Commonwealth help on the Bushman's behalf in Botswana vs. their threatened extinction in the Kalahari Desert homeland without NP protection.

1988 Kalahair Bushman visit, a hunter's shoulder bag often of a warthog skin. His only other attire is a small game skin loin cloth as he is barefooted despite many tire-puncture thorns, scorpions and poisionous snakes like especially puff adders in the region. On a hunt the scantily dressed two borther hunters left us in their dust despite our water bottles, energy bars and all the rest.

Our 1988 visit-cum-book tells `the-rest-of-the-Bushman's story' beyond the light hearted, somewhat comical 1986 GODS MUST BE CRAZY movie that a few such precious people still do exist even if now threatened with extinction. Our 1992 book is a semi travelogue but as a `green' cause (book) alerting mankind of an impending endangered human species extinction travesty. Botswana now has a classic opportunity to `out Dubai' the rest of our globe in world class tourist destinations plus the rest of E and S Africa by creating an enlarged Kalahari NP of the rest of the 70% W of Botswana (add 32% NP W) to the already existing now already 38% of Botswana in Kalahari NPs or wildlife refuges. Finish creating NPs Brits were in route to do. That's to now ride a new tidal wave of international wildlife-watching industry (an African thing or destination) by turning the now `thirst and thorn' Kalahari otherwise waste land into an endangered African species destination (including endangered human Bushman) as employees in game management, poaching protection, and as tourist (draw) guides in an expanded development as an all W Kalahari NP. Yes the real-surviving-in-the-bush-still-hunter-gatherer Bushman lived up to a wonderful untainted utopian vis-a-vis `pre-civilized' people as depicted in their GODS movie as a healthy, happy variation of the noble savage, then to us as our roots (via matching DNA). That's when I think of our stresses vs. their simple, healthy, happy lives if not suffering `death by disposition' (loss of their home land) with only sunlight as their clocks.

Our rest-of-their-story bottom line is to alert mankind that the few surviving Bushman now face death by loss of land dispossession-cum-extinction at the hands of more-evolutionarily-advanced-so-called-now-civilized humanity. That's we Europeans and local ruling black Tswana tribe who are more into their cattle wealth than anthropology. Botswana is seen as one of the better evolving black African nations. Their Pols are more charitable, less into buying Mercedes and opening Swiss bank accounts. But they are generations behind in African tribalistic not appreciating their Bushman as living museum pieces vs. defeated lowly redundant Stone Age embarrassments. By we so called `more advanced' world citizens Bushman should be considered a human endangered species being ignored while we carry on about spotted owls and snail darters, or into such unproved mental dead end cul de sacs as global warming or climate change dogma. We accept that there were ice ages so there is climate change. But being `politically correct' or global warming? Yes there is a 'climate change' as well excepted past ice ages.

In high school basic biology we learned that trees and plants take in carbon dioxide while giving off oxygen. So shouldn't we humans be planting more trees vs. cutting them for fire wood (especially in Africa) and all. A scourge of the fragile Kalahari ecosystem is killing off endangered wildlife, stripping the fragile ecosystem of its already meagre trees, bushes, and oxygen producers while claiming `global warming' via carbon dioxide. World change could be in Botswana the Tswana cattle people's GoB tends to look down on Bushman bureaucratically to thus treat them as Stone-Age embarrassments vs. the roots of our more advanced peoples (read DNA scientist UK's Spencer Wells THE JOURNEY OF MAN, a Genetic Odyssey). GoB's policy is like a wish that Bushman would just die out so the world's bleeding hearts would make no more tear jerking movies about Bushman like that internationally popular *The Gods Must Be Crazy* movie. But in doing so GoB misses a huge opportunity of harnessing their Mother Nature's provided gift of a unique exotic but fragile ecosystem to produce an international tourist destination cash cow GDP enhancing return if the Kalahari sands are developed as for endangered African wildlife with now Gods movie and DNA internationally known Bushman's participation as assets vs. problems.

That's Botswana's best competitive alternate land use option for their REST OF 70% arid SEMI desert of W Botswana Kalahari is to create a wildlife-watching-international-tourist destination-cum-wildlife Kalahari NP GoB cash cow GDP enhancer at a peanuts development cost vis-à-vis Dubai or what the international-wildlife -watching destination GoB cash cow would return forever more. Could Tswana come to except harnessing their Bushman `asset' as tourist draws, to increase the `cash cow' nature of their enlarged W Kalahari NP in competing with other southern African (or East African) wildlife watching destinations? GoB is now politically or bureaucratically on a course to ignore or destroy their Mother Nature's precious gifts to themselves rather than conserving, safeguarding it, developing it, harnessing it as an eternal-cash-cow-international-wildlife-watching destination "native and unspoiled for future generations" as was our plan for a somewhat similar coastal, UN Center of Plant Diversity (CPD) region in MZB (1995-6) in which I gained `been there' key man experience (next chapter). Both with wildlife, MZB with a CPD, GoB with their special human DNA carrying Bushman as living museum pieces, and thus harnessed exotic curious international tourist draws. Is unaware GoB now headed toward turning their back on Mother Nature's extraordinary gifts of the Kalahari and Okavango Delta plus their Bushma? That's plus an entire fragile W Kalahari by NOT joining a current international-wildlife-watching craze-cum-tsunami.

That's which could make GoB a top international-wildlife-watching-Kalahari destination. Or that's to otherwise risk having nothing but a despoiled Kalahari ecosystem as an environmental, human (Bushman), endangered African wildlife tragedy vs. safeguarding it all as a precious native, unspoiled now and future generation's wildlife-watching destination as a challenge to the Serengeti, Kruger, or Dubai et al. But GoB could be one up on those others by saving from extinction their ace in the hole Bushman as assets vs. to be disposed of as a problem. But this isn't so different from what we Americans did to our Plains Indians or Australians did to their Aborigines or Spanish to their native people (Incas, Aztec or Mayan) of Central-or South America all in the same epoch in recent past centuries. Those early mistakes have now been somewhat realized, corrected in America, Canada and Australia several generations too late. Or travesties been over corrected as Native American's gambling law gifts. That's to assuage lingering USA `white guilt' several generations too late (wrong generations). Or Australia turning their international destination Kakadu NP in Australia's Northern Territory plus Ayers Rock et al back over to their Aborigines in the 1970's, good news. That's to atone for earlier ethnic cleansing travesties vs. their aboriginal people. In Canada in a same 1970 s time frame, Canada returned northern lands back to their native Inuit. That's most of their northern-inside-the-Arctic-Circle (and more) land rights to their Inuit native Canadians. Now such a change is overdue, but yet to come in Africa for Kalahari Bushman vis-à-vis their last homeland while they barely survive on the edge of a death by land dispossession-cum-extinction.

In writing my 1992 save Kalahari Bushman's green-cause book I did considerable Bushman research. I borrowed scientific facts from international anthropologists et al who had spent years with Bushman so our 1992 book was more than our one 1988 visit's travelogue. It was sprinkled with anthropological facts our Bushman clan would not known about their own roots without any reading, writing or formal education or access to Bushman history (except their campfire yarns-cum-roots memory). In our 1992 Bushman book we did take on the then GoB Bushman poor treatment. That's for then Tswana-tribalistic "our-cattle-come-first" treatment of Bushman or what is bureaucratic despoiling of mankind's fragile, unique Kalahari Desert sands ecosystem in W Botswana by then unsuccessfully introducing beef cattle (while ejecting Bushman from their now CKGR Brit created homeland) or missing the Kalahari region's now unique potential as an international wildlife-watching destination while not saving the oldest surviving DNA links to most of the rest of the human race via links with GoB's few surviving Bushman. That's by proceeding to develop the Kalahari as a NP as British left 1966 as a `half-haven'. That's for GoB's otherwise unprotected endangered wildlife vs. their unable-to-survive-there-long-term mollycoddled-domestic cattle while destroying a prized unique potential international wildlife-viewing destination plus GoB cash cow vs. guarding it native and unspoiled for future generations as a GoB's very best possible competitive profitable land use choice enlarged NP. Visiting world anthropologists were wary of finding fault (in print) in Botswana.

 That's of GoB's officially unstated Bushman 'death-by-dispossession' policies. That's as taking away Bushman's British created CKGR as a Bushman home land. Or such anthropologists could end up as persona non grata as the American Owens couple (tell-it-as-it-is authors) did. That's for mentioning wildebeest dying up against hoof-and-mouth-cordon fences (more below) part of EC's `subsidized beef' folly thrust on GoB. Our pro-Bushman book was discussed in Botswana's parliament in 1992. It was taken as unwelcome foreign intrusion into Botswana's affairs. That's vs. objective-foreign advice not to despoil their Mother-Nature's-GDP cash-cow-international-tourism-destination Kalahari treasures. When Botswana received its independence from the UK in 1966 the traditional-cattle-owning top politicians tended to do the then African thing they'd seen many other African politicians or too many others `whites' worldwide do. To over simplify it was for some to buy a Mercedes, open a Swiss bank account. Was it just common learned (observed) human nature? In Botswana's defense they were less like this than most other new African countries. But that's who didn't have GoB's diamond-in-the-rough gifts of the Okavango Delta ecosystem wetland surrounded by wildlife's Kalahari home with resident endangered human species Bushman (DNA). That's plus still hunter-gatherer Bushman, only humans able to survive there. Worldwide humans are now in love with endangered African wildlife. They see the Noah's Arc of endangered African wildlife as assets, while native Africans too often view wildlife more as common competitors for their land use, as an ordinary thing or African's land use competitors. That's the wildlife asset non-Africans pay dearly to photograph as a main reason for huge lineups of 747s at JNB airport bringing foreign tourist to SA for wildlife-watching. Since WW II with black African countries independence ex European countries African governments were not as aware of Africa's wildlife's draw as an asset rather than almost as a problem except for maybe first Kenya.

Think of this, Kruger NP was the second NP in the world (1898) after USA's Yellowstone NP (1874). Who created almost all the African wildlife sanctuaries? It was white Europeans (in Africa) before post WW II black African nation's independence. Like Brits created Botswana's now 38% of total surface dedicated to wildlife NPs before they left. Africans are generations slower in coming to regard land dedicated to African wildlife as a special, unique ASSET. Then Africans to regard the Kalahari semi-desert and still hunter-gatherer Bushman as cash cow draws as international tourist destinations or competitive land use assets-cum-eternal cash cows. While in 2005 for the 1st time ever wildlife tourism became SA's top GNP contributor! That's vs. forever before gold mining was their GDP number one. Times change, the places largely remain the same if not despoiled by `civilization'. Worldwide now endangered African wildlife is something special. African's are slower to become aware of their improving asset. African wildlife is a too common or even enemy to them. Like me I grew up in the world's tallest trees in the heart of CA's Coastal Sequoia Redwoods. To me they were so what `common'. It wasn't until I'd travelled the world that I came to appreciate them as an international tourist destination, world's tallest trees at up to 379' tall. Botswana has been one of the few judged better economic successes of Africa post-independence from `white' Europe in post WW II. No wars, politically stable, economically sound. That's partially due to their natural resources vis-à-vis low population density but unlucky for their more recent late 20th century HIV/AIDS experience. As to wildlife sanctuaries the 38% NPs in Botswana were created by Brits before leavomg in 1966.

Now comes me Jonnie-come-lately proposing that GoB create another 32% (rest of Kalahari sands) as GoB's best competitive land use choice. I propose our world somehow (billionaire?) give GoB an enlarged NP feasibility study to be made aware to consider it. That's to protect Botswana's unique Kalahari ecosystem "native and unspoiled for future generations" as GoB's best competitive land use asset choice, now, especially for ever more. Think ahead 50 or 500 years. Will the world's population be tired of photographing African wildlife? Not a chance. Thanks to cameras, photography, new generations. Forget hunting African wildlife with guns, or relegate it to a minor reason for internationals coming to Africa. New African nation Botswana did as too many now newly independent black nations were doing. As tribal people they looked out for their own tribe or to hell with such as their still-extant-Stone-Age-hunter-gatherer Bushman tribe (The Gods Must Be Crazy people). They went thru a phase that white nations went thru—some still are. Unfortunately the GoB rulers probably don't yet appreciate they could have a gold-mine-cash-cow-tourist destination far beyond their now Okavango Delta and other UK created wildlife NPs (already 38% of their land mass) by expanding on that now international wildlife-watching destination avenue of land development (wildlife NP). That's make Botswana's all W (Kalahari Desert sands) an enlarged (32% more of Botswana) African endangered Bushman-wildlife NP cash cow land use GNP enhancer like South Africa's of wildlife-watching vs. gold post 2005. That's all W of Botswana's now existing E facing limits of their `already 38%' dedicated to Kalahari wildlife sanctuaries (not yet fully developed). That's an enlarged Kalahari wildlife E border fence from S near Werda town (or E) then N via the CKGR then almost due N to well E of the Okavango Delta to the existing Chobe NP on Botswana's N border with Zambia. That's via already existing NPs but are they fully developed? No! Then now fill in with the other 32% of all Botswana's Kalahari with updated NP.

That's the rest of Botswana's Kalahari W of the existing string of NPs or rest to wildlife sanctuaries W-of-this-Brit NPs border line with more-wildlife NP (see per schematic map pg 16) with resident Bushman now fully involved as caretakers (thus 'The Gods Must Be Crazy' tourist draws harnessed as an ASSET not a GoB PROBLEM via the now booming African wildlife watching destination double barreled with the draw of Gods Must Be Crazy People positively utilized. Get Peace Parks et al, wildlife and native culture NGOs, nature loving bleeding hearts et al on this pro-larger-NP bandwagon. All to help fund, provide GoB an international bankable feasibility study to prove an enlarged Kalahari sands NP endangered African wildlife restocked is the best competitive land use for this special Okavango Delta desert surrounded region W of which Brits nearly completed creating its E border (wildlife fence) string of wildlife sanctuaries. Fill in four hiatuses (355 Mi in 700 Mi—ex Werda (or E) in the S in enlarged NPs then the rest to the far W. That is of the rest (32% more of all Botswana in Kalahari sans) considered useless semi-desert. How is this? Make the whole 70% of Botswana's Kalahari a NP. Repopulate the Kalahari W with wildlife (the Bushman's' favorites in Tsodilo rock painting) eland antelope et al. Or S of where we visited our Bushman clan other elk sized herbivore the majestic gemsbok antelope in the SW Kalagadi TransFrontier Park) et al where in 1984 I camped out there to hear nocturnal lion-hyena serenades (SA side). That's a serenade to bring international tourist to Africa. Copy Etosha's paradigm of adding scattered water holes with drilled wells with windmill-pumps.

Replant trees, bushes and open grazing areas (Bushman work) to increase oxygen producing green ground cover and to encourage increased rainfall (opposite of Sahara per Greek historians). That's all to increased wildlife species that can adapt to the otherwise Kalahari's now marginal arid semi-desert ecosystem with added surface water for more greenery and herbivore species to then support the carnivores that water and increased population of herbivore will support. That's which will then in turn attract international tourists with their cameras. Harness the now booming international wildlife watching industry which in 2005 in South Africa passed up previously their gold as their top annual gross domestic product (GDP) producer. Get this all started by providing GoB a top international guru feasibility study development plan to prove such a wildlife watching destination is the ultimate best alternate land use cash cow into future generations.

That's like the process we (with Bechtel) did in MZB in 1995 which got GoM approval of their then 914 Sq Mi Elephant Coast CPD-NP in 1996 of UN Maputaland CPD territory see (www.savemec.org). Bechtel London et al clinched-the-deal-of a create-operate-feasibility study. It was a bargain 10 month one million dollars only order of magnitude saga by my New Orleans boss. That's get South Africa's Peace Parks (internationally-known-respected entity) to take the whole NP-wildlife-watching tourist industry evolution news to GoB. That's with windmill water holes to enlarge animal species to restock with as proven in Etosha NP in N Namibia. Create a world cash cow wildlife watching destination vs. GoB letting their Mother Nature's gift be destroyed vs. protecting it by dedicating it to wildlife-Bushman that have survived there together near forever. Let Mother-Nature's-provided-international-wildlife-watching-tourist-destination's draw be GoB's partner vs. not having to spend billions on making an international tourist `glitz' draw out of camel pasture as Dubai (UAE) is doing.  That's to dredged up offshore islands, add boring cement, glass, steel, plastic skyscrapers, other expensive `glitz' attractions that can't compete with Botswana's wildlife-Bushman double barreled tourist draw. That's with GoB's terrain already developed for an international wildlife-watching-destination with Mother Nature's-ecotourism-destinations appeal.   Restock W Kalahari with `all-we-need-is-a-little-water wildlife' like or with eland, wildebeest, zebra, springbok, giraffe, impala, Cape buffalo, elephant, endangered black and white rhino, sable, roan, greater kudu, lion, leopard, cheetah wild hunting dogs, hyena, baboons. warthogs et al that's which international tourists are goofy to photograph.

That's with individual species numbers as recommended by South African wildlife PhD gurus (as we did in MZB in 1995) now around created water holes. As a fall back if the water table won't support windmill-water-holes in any of these Kalahari W Botswana regions we pipeliners will lay water lines from the Okavango River and Delta as needed anyplace to the N, W, S or E as relatively inexpensive old technology (like any urban city's water systems). Unfortunately vs. this GoB cash cow paradigm avenue into future generations instead GoB's leaders have been misdirected toward Kalahari beef cattle not adapted to the arid-W-Botswana-Kalahari-Desert ecosystem to risk environmentally despoiling it with Mother Nature's unique priceless (Dubai's wish they had them) gifts or international tourist draws despoiled. GoB's leaders are unknowingly permitting destruction of their Mother Nature's gifted fragile Kalahari, its endangered African wildlife, plus draw of their now internationally famous Gods Must Be Crazy Bushman Kalahari with special DNA. That's who have `been-there-forever' Bushman residents.

It's an ecosystem developed wildlife watching international tourism option that in 2005 in South Africa made wildlife tourism South Africa's top GDP earner over always previously gold mining. That's in South Africa with its African continent's top national GDP despite others with huge crude oil deposits like Angola, Nigeria, Libya, Algeria, and Sudan proving the competitive real world worth of developed wildlife watching destinations. But what will it be in 100 or 500 years as earth's population yearns more for 'green' vacations. GoB is also permitting the extinction of their endangered-human-species Bushman with the Bushman's accompanying God given African wildlife while destroying their fragile Kalahari thorn-and-thirst ecosystem vs, their best possible alternate land use would be to keep it "native-and-unspoiled for future generations" as a huge wildlife-Bushman ecosystem. Adopt a development plan that adds low-construction cost-rustic-wildlife-watching facilities (tourist overnight beds).That's for a win-win-enduring-gold-mine-cash-cow-wildlife-watching destination into forever future generations. The combination of wildlife-cum-happy Bushman with the international wildlife watching craze is a to African only unique. It's an African international-tourist-destination draw choice or a best low-development-cost-high-return cash cow type competitive development GoB land use 'diamond in the rough' to compete with the likes of Serengeti NP. Tourist will come to see endangered African wildlife, their Gods Must Be Crazy Bushman tenders.

That's as added frosting on an international tourist destination cake choice. No one will come to see a fragile Kalahari destroyed by beef but will with a wide choice of otherwise endangered African wildlife destinations over Dubai like `asphalt jungle' glitz. This unique best-land-use choice can all be created by Botswana's developers (partners) spending only nickels and dimes on dollars of what Dubai is investing trying to create an international tourist destination of real no vegetation desert camel pasture in UAE. But in GoB's case Mother Nature has gifted Botswana with a ready made Kalahari semi-desert surrounded Okavango Delta ecosystem as a potential world class tourist draw ecotourism destination but more so with the endangered human species (Gods Must Be Crazy) Bushman's involvement. Yes like Australia in turning their Kakadu NP et al over to their Aborigines but continuing to manage and operate it for and with them. That's which drastically increased the draw of international tree huggers (like me) to visit Australia's Kakadu (1989). From my experience in our 1995 MZB Elephant Coast (914 Sq MI) wildlife-botanical NP development feasibility study-cum-99-year-lease-develop-operate concession award by GoM (1996) this is a very doable create a world class NP tourist cash cow-GDP plus development project.

Mother Nature has provided Botswana a diamond-in-the-rough Okavango Delta in the Kalahari that needs to be NP fence protected then the whole-region-properly developed with a keep it "native and unspoiled for future generations" mantra to appeal not only to today's international tourist but future more environmentally concerned `crowded-earth-asphalt-jungle' generations. That is in a keep-it-native-unspoiled mode for a GoB perpetual economic cash cow. That's the whole Bushman-land Kalahari W of Botswana is potentially a top drawer world wildlife-watching-tourist destination with Bushman involvement as frosting on the then perpetual-Botswana-cash-cow cake and GoB enhancing GDP. A big ongoing current thorn is the Central Kalahari Game Reserve (CKGR). Noted South African author Van der Post (he was mentioned by Margaret Thatcher in my chat with her in Miami FL in 1993). He grew up in South Africa with a Stone-Age person (Bushman nurse) as his mentor. Van der Post thus took a special interest in Bushman. He wrote two of his laundry list of international best seller books about these special Bushman. That's as VdP's *LOST WORLD OF THE KALAHARI* (1958) then HEART OF THE HUNTER (1961). In my Miami conversation with Margaret Thatcher I gave her a copy of our Bushman visit book at a Miami book fair (1993). She said "Yes I know the Kalahari Bushman from reading Van der Post books.".

I'd approached her as a world-key-person decision maker `heavy' in her British Commonwealth.  That's to get her Botswana GoB to do like Australia had its Aborigines or Canada inside the Arctic Circle had their Inuit when newer generations took over in the 1970s.  That's for Bushman to have their Brit created `thirst and thorn' Kalahari homeland (CKGR) given back to them. Treat them as the human anthropologic jewels they are. That is correcting the sad saga of `death-by-dispossession' vs. Kalahari Bushman in UK Commonwealth Botswana plus next door neighbor Namibia vis-a-vis the Bushman's fragile Kalahari wildlife ecosystem. That is like her Commonwealth members had in Australia (Aborigines) and Canada (Inuit) in the 1970s. My query was "How about B for Botswana, N for Namibia next for the Bushman and Kalahari's fragile wildlife ecosystem?" She kindly promised to include her supporting voice. Prior to Botswana's 1966 independence Van der Post influenced the British to create a refuge (official homeland) for Botswana's Gwi and Gwana Bushman tribes (CKGR). They were Bushman who'd lived in that S central region E of Ghanzi for eons. What is now the CKGR refuge was originally created in 1961 five years before then approaching Bechuanaland independence from the UK as Botswana in 1966. It was at first called something like the Central Kalahari Bushman Reserve.

But those were South African apartheid days. It was considered by some politically incorrect or pejorative to create what smacked of a hated South African Afrikaner 'homeland' (dumping ground) for South African blacks under apartheid (or Bushman in Botswana). This was an illogical argument for the Botswana's Bushman reserve. But despite the facts the refuge was renamed the Central Kalahari Game Reserve (CKGR) as besides Bushman the CKGR had the Bushman's cattle (wildlife).   That was their God-given-looked-after-by-Bushman-surviving-endangered-African wildlife. But later others unaware of this history or not appreciating the Bushman's very hunter-gatherer nature (as now Stone Age embarrassments) complained the Bushman (humans) were killing wildlife in a sanctuary (Bushman reserve now misnamed a game reserve). The accused Bushman had done so for centuries looking after their God's given wildlife (their 'cattle'). Yes, eating an occasional one as God's watchman's right (bartered compensation for labors). This led to the now Gaborone (GoB) bureaucracy ruling—being pressured--to officially evict the Bushman from the CKGR in 1986 or 20 years on in GoB's post-UK rule. This international legal battle over the Bushman's land rights in their Brit created CKGR has gone on since.

That's with some misguided wildlife conservationists siding against the wildlife protecting Bushman (their cattle). Bushman plus their African wildlife did not destroy the fragile Kalahari ecosystem over centuries but introducing domestic cattle was doing it very rapidly in months or a very few years where tried (circa 1986). Meanwhile international endangered people's none government organizations (NGOs) like the UK's Survival International, Cultural Survival and Kenya HQed Ecoterra et al have taken up for the Bushman vs. the GoB bureaucracy et al to give the San (Bushman) legal support and assistance but to little avail to date in stopping `death-by-dispossession' policies against Bushman and their British intended homeland (fragile Kalahari ecosystem). The next misguided faux pas was the European Community (EC) offering GoB an unsolicited beef subsidy as a reward for their 'better-than-most' African-nation's-economic-progress-since independence. This ill-conceived EC beef subsidy encouraged ruling GoB cattle people to expand their beef industry W to introduce cattle into the Bushman's Kalahari (W Botswana) not fit for domestic cattle or only for hardier African wildlife species like eland, gemsbok and wildebeest et al or wildlife that could survive without waterholes. Then the EC (further faux pas) encouraged drilling wells for beef cattle in the Kalahari. That's with herded cattle congregated around the well to destroy the adjoining fragile vegetation by being herded in one spot overgrazing it in a matter of months. It could be called European-subsidized-misguided-African-environmental destruction. Then the next misguided horror was the European Community (EC's) Veterinary Department got into the act.

 This EC bureaucracy `feared' Kalahari beef cattle would get hoof-and-mouth disease from wildlife. That's by beef mixing with Okavango Delta wild Cape buffalo to thus taint Europe's beef supply. The EC's Vets demanded Kalahari cordon fences be built protecting Kalahari beef from mixing with Okavango Delta wildlife. Botswana did so to now maintain their unsolicited EC beef subsidy to build wildlife cordon fences between wrongly-introduced-into-the-Kalahari-beef cattle and rightfully there Okavango wildlife to solve the EC's tainted-African-beef conundrum. Botswana was thus made to destroy endangered African wildlife to maintain Botswana's misguided EC beef subsidized high price gift. Next there was a seasonal drought. Wildebeest migrating to water died in the thousands up against the hoof-and-mouth-protection cordon fences keeping wildebeest from water! This out-of-sight-out-of-mind wildebeest tragedy was then reported in passing by the young USA (Georgia) Owens couple. They were studying the brown hyena in the CKGR. That's as reported in their international best-selling book CRY OF THE KALAHARI (1992). The Owens then returned to America to complete their doctoral studies. They were then refused reentry into Botswana as persona non grata by GoB embarrassed worldwide by GoM's wildebeest-hoof-and-mouth-disease-fence saga exposure. The Owens then went to the wildlife Luangwa Valley NPs in Zambia to continue their wildlife protecting careers. This is an example of GoB's reaction of outsider `intrusion'. 1st naïve Euro outsiders (EC) wrongly encouraged GoB's introduction of cattle into the too-arid-for-domestic-cattle-thorn-thirst Kalahari vs. protecting it (developing it for tourism) as a larger-endangered-wildlife-reserve-international-wildlife-watching-tourist destination (GoB cash cow) per its Mother Nature's architect's 'green' design.

Botswana's Kalahari with scattered wildlife NPs needs them further protected,properly outfitted (via an international-regional-master-feasibility-development plan) to attract more international wildlife-watching tourists. vs. wildlife killing cordon fences being added, why? Because naïve EC bureaucrats gave away Euro tax money to subsidize expansion of GoB cattle into a fragile-arid ecosystem, beef cattle wells for water for anti-ecosystem- ie vs. waterholes (a-la-Etosha NP) for belonged-there wildlife while there were no requested wells for thirsty Bushman or their God given wildlife as in Etosha. Wildlife travel long distances for water. Herded beef cattle stay close to a well, quickly overgraze that region. That's Bushman as traditional occupants of their now-invaded-by-domestic-beef cattle Kalahari Desert (Bushman-land). That's in the Kalahari where more hardy wildlife have survived for `forever'. That's wildlife survived off limited moisture on scant foliage finding moisture from tasama melons or tubers that grow in there while historically belongs-there wildlife never despoiled the fragile ecosystem. That's as introducing beef did in a short time. The known too few Kalahari tasama melons etc. are also a main source of moisture hardy nobody-else-can-survive-there Bushman! My Bushman green cause book was published in 1992. Books arrived with no book distributors deals. I hired a FL PR outfit. They sent me on a year's book tour resulting in 332 media events of published news articles, radio and TV appearances, speaking appearances at libraries, etc and other venues USA coast-to-coast. Like at a book fair in Frankfort, a booth at the Rio 1992 Earth Summit in the NGO designated area all to slim my IRA by some $400,000 for no apparent help for Kalahari wildlife-cum-Bushman.

.

That's plus an appearance (1993) on CNN's International Hour with Frank Sesno for the Bushman cause dilemma-cum-travesty. I am still trying (see below) in a `Nick-Nobody-From-Nowhere' ongoing unfunded `help' Kalahari Bushman effort. Then I later got off on another 1995-6 bleeding heart saga (the Mozambique Elephant Coast CPD-NP) to create a MZB NP development effort then eventual not for profit internet site www.savemec.org. This was for-a GoM-land-use feasibility study conceptually created in partnership with the land owing Government of MZB (GoM). It evolved into a huge wildlife CPD-NP plan plus a proposed option of translocating some Botswana Kalahari Bushman to our MZB's NP to be appreciated while encouraged to roam free as protectors of endangered NP wildlife. The Bushman's unique presence would add to it as an international-tourist-attraction-wildlife-watching destination draw. They once not so long ago survived in MZB too leaving their haunting Bushman rock wall paintings to record they're living there beyond question pre southern African Bushman massacre `ethnic cleansing' epoch. That 'next' bleeding-heart-wildlife affair after our 1988 Bushman visit or Bushman cause effort was in 1995 to create a wildlife-botanical CPD-NP in MZB of 914 Sq Mi up from a 63 Sq Mi originally offered Indian Ocean Machangulo Peninsula site by GoM's P:resident Chissano.

In MZB I became 1st hand aware of, plus gained real world experience in game management. That's wildlife translocation (big business in South Africa), wildlife refuge creation, tourist-wildlife management to create a MZB world class wildlife-watching-tourist destination via a create-operate-protected-MZB-CPD-cum-NP. That's plus dealing with international wildlife watching markets plus politics in creating a Mother-Nature's-ecosystem-international-tourist draw as the development project approved by GoM in 1996 as their ECNP (Elephant Coast Indian Ocean 914 Sq Mi wildlife-botanical NP) via a 99-year-lease to create-then operate (turnkey) a new world class-high-profile-international-wildlife-watching destination. Not a glitzy destination like Dubai with billions in investments required to create a tourist draw but rather one harnessing Mother Nature's fare (already there) of native and unspoiled endangered African restocked wildlife in a fragile UN designated CPD ecosystems with tribal bush people as active partners. That's to safeguard native and unspoiled for future generations an already existing Mother Nature's ecosystem with wildlife gift cash cow as a MZB international destination CPD-NP. Now based on this more than arm chair MZB experience is my outside the box GoB proposal. That's to resolve the Bushman's dilemma plus a win-win-economic-environmental-alternate-best-land use for GoB in-partnership-with-ecosystem-gift-donor Mother Nature. That's a best GoB plan to save their Bushman (DNA) asset `problem' solved.

That's while conserving their fragile Kalahari ecosystem (Bushman land) with endangered African wildlife augmented via restocking. That's to best safeguard it all unspoiled for future generations of world humanity in a win-win for everybody solution as GoB (economically and environmentally). That's plus the now dispossessed Bushman and their God given wildlife via international ecotourism (new wildlife watching destination) et al and ultimately world ecology in creating, protecting a huge `green cause' ecosystem for future generations vs. a world trend toward less 'green', more over developed `asphalt jungles'. Botswana is a relatively rich African country with diamonds, beef, with an already established international wildlife tourism contribution (already 38% of Botswana's land mass) contributing to their annual GDP with the Okavango Delta, Chobe National Park plus several other already operating wildlife watching destinations (thanks to Britain for creating NPs before independence), now GoB `maybe' since.  My off the wall proposal is to help GoB toward including the rest of the total Kalahari (32% more of far W Botswana's total land mass) of the now isolated W Kalahari added to the already `necklace' on the map of NPs and wildlife sanctuaries largely defining the E border of the Kalahari SANDS with four Brit `not-yet' filled hiatuses in a W Kalahari NPs circa 700 mile (from Werda or E) then N wildlife electric fence and E boundary of all the Kalahari sands to be enlarged whole Kalahari NP. Botswana has a low population density concentrated almost entirely in its more fertile non-Kalahari far E or its N to S border corridor good for raising beef.

Currently GoB is or was EC promoted to despoil their fragile Kalahari asset by being conned by EC et al into introducing domestic cattle while dispossessing the Kalahari Bushman plus their endangered African wildlife vs. GoB with international advice and help (feasibility study) guarding and developing their total W Kalahari ecosystem for wildlife watching tourism for now and future generations, their best competitive land use option. GoB's poorer choice has been short term Kalahari ecosystem destruction. That's vs. a long-term-future-generations-cash-cow-wildlife-watching-ecotourism-land-use-option development. GoB is naively, unknowingly destroying an existing international tourist draw destination while earning bad marks from the kibitzing international environmental community be they wildlife or Bushman bleeding hearts or both. Botswana has a potential diamond-in-the-rough land development (far underdevelopment to date) opportunity to cash in on. That's in a today's changing world's more `green' cause epoch of African wildlife-watching. That's now via a growing international wildlife-watching-tourism-industry-market craze where African hunting was enjoyed by a few (Teddy Roosevelt and Hemingway's days) but now by millions as cameras have replaced hunting rifles. Botswana could become more of a top-tier-international-wildlife-watching-tourism destination to compete with East Africa's Serengeti with its adjacent Ngorongoro Crater, Lake Manyara et al. In Botswana the Creator and his earthly curator Mother Nature (plus Brits) have already done the ground work of creating (protecting in NPs) wildlife rich ecosystems as the Okavango Delta, Chobe NP, CKGR, Gemsbok NP, Nxai NP, Makgadikgadi Pans Game Reserve in Botswana.

They could couple that with more in between these already 'stepping stone' wildlife refuges via a regional-master-planned-more-Kalahari land on W dedicated to wildlife watching tourist development in the 'Serengeti Shall Not Die' (Kenya 1960s) type paradigm. Or the Kalahari semi desert `thirst and thorn' acreage surrounding the jewel Okavango Delta (not fully developed for `now' wildlife tourism). Plus a bit more Kalahari sands territory (yes) E of Okavango Delta's Maun in filling in the Brits' four hiatuses in the proposed E enlarged-consolidated NP's E fence and essentially E edge of the Kalahari sands proposed NP. Instead Botswana has been conned more toward ignoring, degrading, despoiling their fragile Kalahari wildlife-Bushman ecosystems via introduction of mollycoddled domestic cattle for which the arid Kalahari Desert regions is completely unfit for as too arid with too sparse and thorny vegetation. International tourists worldwide will come for endangered wildlife watching, but they won't cross a street to see a fragile Kalahari-ecosystem-destroying-domestic-beef cattle! But they will happily eat Botswana beef steaks while photographing Kalahari wildlife. Then international tourist will be more encouraged if endangered-human-species-God-Must-Be-Crazy-Bushman people are there living free as they wish by protecting, managing their God given endangered African wildlife in a huge NP as frosting-on-a-unique-international-tourist-destination draw (cake). Create a wildlife-watching-Bushman-involved visit site rather than destroy it! Botswana doesn't have to spend billions making a silk-purse-out-of-a-sows-ear-top-draw international-tourist destination like UAE's Dubai is trying to do of camel pasture and Arabian Sea (Persian Gulf) frontage and dredged up offshore islands. Good on them, but GoB has Mother Nature's gifts more on their side.

Properly master planned GoB wildlife watching tourism with Bushman involvement is surely Botswana's very best alternate land use for the 70% of their total territory which is now considered thirst-and-thorn-Kalahari Desert W of the already existing CKGR, Okavango Delta, Chobe NP et al. or the W Kalahari to be added NP territory in the four Brit left out hiatuses to create a 'wildlife NP fence' of a whole-then-W-of-Botswana's wildlife-Bushman enlarged NP development as a GoM cash cow wildlife watching destination. That's four times the size of the now largest world GLTP joining of three nations NPs, South Africa, Zimbabwe and Mozambique. International tourists have to eat. They will fall in love with their Tswana beef menus and tasama melon desert. That's a not-so-off-the-wall master plan after my key man planning a similar major 914 Sq Mi 1995-96 wildlife NP development for MZB's Elephant Coast CPD-cum-NP (1995). That's as an upgraded version of an original GoM offered target development of only 63 Sq Mi Indian Ocean Coastal Machangulo Peninsula. That's which enlarged version led to GoM's 1996 then 99-year-develop-operate-land-lease-914-Sq-Mi concession award my 2007 book revisited to resurrect to 4000 Sq Mi. That's which included resurrecting the Maputo Elephant Reserve shot out from Cuban military helicopters (target practice) post-independence from white Portugal in 1975 on in then-raging-Cold-War-days of that epoch.

That's then to expand UN CPD protection of the 4000 Sq Mi CPD-Elephant Coast NP to now connect N with the post 2002 new 38,500 Sq Mi three country NPs GLTP while UN (CPD) mandated as a fallout of the new CPD paradigm of the World's Leaders International Biodiversity Accord voted in at the Rio 1992 EARTH SUMMIT. A similar Botswana proposed enlarged all W Botswana Kalahari Desert NP development plan is to get known, respected entities like South African Peace Parks, World Bank, et al to guide GoB in how starting via a regional GoB economic feasibility study to thus alert GoB of their `diamond-in-the-rough' land use opportunity. To influence Botswana to create a W Kalahari region-master-planned-wildlife-watching region expanded NP in their W Kalahari Desert. That's W of the outline of smaller, scattered NPs Brits left that defines a herein proposed enlarged essentially E border of an all W Kalahari NP to complete an enlarged-consolidated W Kalahari NP. Botswana isn't an overcrowded India or Japan where wildlife loses to humanity in land availability.

The Kalahari W region is almost devoid of human habitation but fit for wildlife that's been there with its Bushman `owners' forever while for little else. A master-plan is to develop it to share it with international wildlife watching tourists as a destination coming from over populated countries with no surviving wildlife for a `green' Mother Nature tourist break destination. The `thirst and thorn' Kalahari is all traditionally, historically Bushman country where they (their wildlife) survived but now both face extinction as endangered (human-wildlife) species, or the despoiling of the fragile Kalahari semi- desert ecosystem. Why South African Peace Parks (PP) involvement? By recent track record this is their unique specialty or their reason for being via increasing the numbers and size of NPs or TFPs. It was Peace Parks who influenced South Africa and Botswana (year 2002) to take down their international border fence between their then separate W and E Gemsbok NPs to create the combined (now Kalagadi TransFrontier Park in SW Botswana and in bordering South Africa to the W (I visited it in SA in 1984). The Kalagadi TFP has 15,000 Sq MI, about ¾ in Botswana and ¼ in South Africa with the international border fence removed. This TransFrontier Park (TFP) paradigm was to increase the range of wildlife against seasonal drought.

That's to allow migration and breeding was a simple but big improvement. Then next world class Peace Parks after their two countries Gemsbok NPs conversion to one TransFrontier Park stature success pulled off their biggie. That's when they influenced the creating of the 38,500 Sq MI Grand Limpopo TransFrontier Park (GLTP). That's the handiwork of South African breweries billionaire Dr Anton Rupert with South Africa's Nelson Mandela as one of their three cofounders. PP persuaded South Africa, Zimbabwe, MZB to create (2002-3) a combined three country wildlife reserve international internal border fences to be removed to create our world's current largest wildlife sanctuary. The herein proposed enlarged Botswana all Kalahari wildlife-Bushman NP would be four times as large. The GLTP concept includes South Africa's Kruger NP SW, Zimbabwe's Gonarezhou NP NW to be physically connected to Kruger, then both adding newly created E `mirror-image' Limpopo NP in MZB in 2003. That's for new resulting largest (38,500 Sq MI) no-internal-fences-wildlife reserve in this world. For GoB we tell Peace Parks let's create a bigger one (over four times as large) in Botswana by tying together several existing wildlife refuges in W Botswana's Kalahari Desert territory.

That's as Peace Parks's already Kgalagadi Trans Frontier Parks in SW Botswana and filling in with NP territory between several other existing 'stepping stone' E border wildlife reserves as CKGR, Kalahari Desert territory E of the Okavango Delta, to existing Chobe NP on Botswana's N border then creating NP territory with all Kalahari sands to the W of this continuous S to N fence or NPs E border of the enlarged all Kalahari NP in Botswana. Or add more W Botswana NP territory as mortar between these now existing bricks (Brit created before 1966 independence isolated NPs and wildlife reserves). Finish the Kalahari job they (Brits) started. Via feasibility-study-cum-master-plan fill in between the E border wildlife sanctuaries and then add the whole 'Kalahari sands' W of these already existing chain of stepping stone (border fence) wildlife refuges-NPs. That's to create an all Kalahari W of that fence as one all consolidated Kalahari-Bushman-wildlife NP.

See the schematic sketch map (pg 16) of where the enlarged NP's E border could be (best option) via Botswana's S to N border or via filling in to better start at Botswana's S border near Werda village (or E) S of CKGR on South Africa's border on the Molopo River (border). Then CKGR E border on to Nxai Pan NP E border, to Makgadikgadi Game Reserve on to Chobe NP's E border to Botswana's border with Zambia. This wildlife fence would be W of Orapa (town) but include Banes Baobab, possibly further E for Makgadikgadi Pans or further E than shown on the 1ˢᵗ cut sketch map (pg 16). See the book *KALAHARI, Life's Variety in Dune and Delta* (1987) by Michael Main for the extent of Kalahari 'red sands' E in Botswana essentially the roughly enlarged NP border established by the pre Botswana Independence by E borders of British created scattered NPs or wildlife reserves. Main's book shows the ragged E boundaries of the Kalahari sands. Keep the proposed enlarged Kalahari NP essentially W of the wildlife domain Kalahari 'sands' limits per Main's map's ragged E border of the Kalahari Desert `sands' E extent map.

Our 1995 and on MZB 'create-an-Elephant-Coast NP' effort (as a key man) we tried but were unsuccessful in getting interest or communication response from Peace Parks on a then post 2007 effort to resurrect, expand the MZB Elephant Coast's 1996 GoM approved 914 Sq MI plan resurrected to 4000 Sq MI to connect to the by then now known GLTP. That's to resurrect our 914 Sq MI MZB awarded version, then connect up with the already (by then) Grand Limpopo TransFrontier Park (38,500 Sq MI) our 914 Sq MI plan enlarged to 4000 Sq MI Elephant Coast Wildlife Botanical CPD-NP in S MZB expanded W to Swaziland and N to connect up with (to enlarge) Peace

Park's brokered 2002 GLTP (Grand Limpopo TransFrontier Park) wildlife reserve handiwork (International wildlife Park). It would have simultaneously protected *native-unspoiled* as UN mandated the Maputaland Center of Plant Diversity (CPD) all within a 4000 Sq Mi Elephant Coast S addition to the GLTP to its N and given gigantic GLTP Indian Ocean frontage that is nonexistent in major African wildlife NPs. All the existing NPs of East and Southern Africa are `landlocked' without Indian Ocean frontage (except shot out MER-273,000 Sq Mi)-in MZB (see in Cpt 3)

So again what's a (MZB) CPD? We learned about Centers of Plant Diversity (CPDs) in 1995 during our MZB Elephant Coast NP saga. The CPD concept was created at the 1992 UN Rio Earth Summit via the International Biodiversity Agreement signed by the then attending world's Heads of State. It was to identify and protect 250 richest endangered exotic botanical regions worldwide "native and unspoiled for future generations." My 2007 SMEC book proposed our GoM approved 914 Sq Mi Elephant Coast CPD-NP be expanded to a 4000 Sq Mi bigger Elephant Coast MZB CPD-NP. If it was so created it would have linked up via 100 % UN designated CPD territory saved with the then already 2002 three nation GLTP to its N. The 4000 Sq Mi increased Elephant Coast in MZB could also have saved 5000 Kruger Park elephants then scheduled to be culled (killed) for `overgrazing' Kruger. See our Elephant Coast green cause's net site www.savemec.org re the proposed 914 Sq Mi-cum-4000 Sq Mi MZB Elephant Coast CPD-NP to expand the already 2002 International Grand Limpopo TransFrontier Park (GLTP) wildlife preserve already at 38,500 Sq Mi. USA's Yellowstone NP for comparison is 3468 Sq Mi.

In 2007 Peace Parks may have taken a breather. That's after the death of their fireball founder Anton Rupert in 2006? A now proposed development strategy to save Botswana's-African-wildlife-fragile-Kalahari ecosystem plus dispossessed Kalahari Bushman is in more detail herein above. Like engage Peace Parks (PP) et al (or equal) to do what PPs past plus ongoing present track record is in being a leading catalyst in creating-enlarging southern African Trans Frontier wildlife parks. That's this time in historically Kalahari Bushman territory in Botswana's W or S (Werda) to N border (in Botswana's 70% Kalahari Desert sands W). This can be achieved by (1) simply tying together major already existing wildlife reserve NPs in W Botswana S to N to create a continuous E enlarged amalgamated-NP-wildlife-fence border. Then incorporating the rest of Kalahari to the W regionally master planned for consistency, logistics as tourists in and out, overnight beds lodging etc. The total Kalahari Desert region is suitable only for wildlife which has survived there for eons. If it is not broke don't fix or change it! Protect and safeguard it, rather develop and outfit it as a (master planned) world-wildlife-watching-tourism-DESTINATION NP. The fragile ecosystem (W Kalahari region) is suitable for ONLY the Bushman's hardy God given wildlife which have survived there forever now already a somewhat international-tourist-attracting-endangered-African-wildlife destination. But that to date is minor compared to what could or should be with creating GoB's enlarged W NP.

Below are Brit hiatuses to tie together the already existing W Kalahari wildlife preserve regions. That is expand on them to establish a S-N wildlife fenced E boundary of an enlarged-all-Kalahari NP to protect the total Botswana Kalahari semi-desert region for wildlife-Bushman W of a proposed electric wildlife fence vertical length of Botswana outlining the largest W portion of Botswana's 70% surface area which is classified as (is) Kalahari semi-desert `sands' as compared to the likes of the N African Sahara, Saudi Arabia or Dubai. Keep the otherwise 'human useless' (but not to wildlife) Kalahari as an international cash cow for Botswana's international-wildlife-watching-tourist destination development for now and future (forever) generations. Start the proposed E-of-here-(E border fence) of enlarged Kalahari NP with Brit left hiatuses filled in is-for-wildlife-Bushman only protected 'E boundary line (electrified wildlife fence). That's from Botswana's S border in the Werda (or E) village region on the Molopo River on SA's N border with Botswana near where the Kalahari sands E border continue S into South Africa.

This proposed development plan boundary is conceptional, the exact E border-fence details to be sorted out with GoB by a provider of professional feasibility study with exact details as to then development costs, projected tourist destination revenues. The `provisional feasibility E border with a final fence to be sorted out with GoBThat's when or after GoB buy the overall feasibility study of an enlarged Kalahari W one NP plan. The border `order of magnitude' is essentially the E extent of the Kalahari sands, or Botswana's Mother Nature decided now Kalahari sands NP to be. From Botswana's S to N international borders from E Kalahari `sands' extent the S end of the wildlife fence would be somewhere near Botswana's S border with South Africa on the Molopo River is best to start near Werda village (or E). Then N to the SE corner of tacked onto the S CKGR's Mabuasehube Game Reserve.

Then around Mabuaschube's E border to the CKGR's most easterly bulge. Then from the CKGR's E Border bulge N to SE Makadikgadi Game Reserve (MGR). Then it's MGR's E border. Thet next hiatus is to Nxai Pan NP's SE corner, then Nxai Pan's E border. There's a hiatus to Chobe NP's SE corner. It's E Chobe NP border to Botswana's N border with Zambia. Rough scaling that's four gaps (or hiatuses) between Werda (or E) then existing NPs E borders some (355 MI) of not yet filed in `NP hiatuses' starting from near Werda (ot E) 700 MI from near Werda N to the Zambian border. That's a now NP E border total line (wildlife fence) from the South Africa's border to N most Chobe NP (Zambian border) is in the order of (scales 700 MI from Werda (or E) is a starting point as it's near the E edge of the Kalahari sands as the `sands' continue near S into South Africa on the Mololo River as Botswana's S border with South Africa. That's a continuous 700 MI S to N wildlife-NP-border fence to keep lions in and domestic livestock beef out.

This proposed `Brit NP border gaps' to be filled in Botswana's S near Werda (or E) to N (Zambian border) enlarged Kalahari W NP's E `would surely be wildlife fenced between wildlife designated W, then cattle et al E of the resulting W NP's E boundary fence. Many reasons for a fence, like US border with Mexico. One reason keep the W of the border lions from poaching on E of the border cattle. Cattle are easier prey for old lions. A fence defines the proposed West-of-line (enlarged composite NP border) as NP and E private or other land to be designated the all West Kalahari NP for wildlife tourism all in what is now Botswana Kalahari Desert sands territory. This is to schematically know how-much fill-in-is-necessary and NP designated territory to the W order of magnitude. This would still leave ragged edges of diminishing Kalahari sands tailings E of the line (NP wildlife fence). The line could be adjusted further E between the CKGR and Chobe NP by a line more E just W of Orapa town or further E in the case of the Makgadikgadi Pans (with wet season tourist attracting wildlife). I visited Magadikgadi Pans Game Reserve to camp out with Peter after our 1988 main Bushman visit.

We then saw poachers (white faces) running zebra herds in vehicles for their striped skins. The wildlife was thus very skittish with no Bushman or other GoB game guards. In creating an enlarged W Kalahari NP as proposed ties all these new now W Botswana game reserves (Brit 1960s hiatuses) together. Then includes all the arid country in between (W of this established fence line) to enhance Botswana as an international wildlife-watching-tourist destination. Once the border is established any development W could be all at once or for such a large area with regions stretched out over longer time or a few other such regions. Ghanzi has farms (M. Main's book's-map pg 238) which are or might be fenced off, bought out or whatever, early or later on. GoB et al would decide such details. The developing entity should be for NP fencing off more vs. less before civilization invades areas around the edge. Main's book has many maps with greater details. It is best to clean up such `islandbprder' situations up front or as necessary to protect it for later or gradual development. That's to achieve the enlarged NP goal, or find it's not too late for such minor problems to be solved. What's important is an international feasibility study for GoB to make a now before it's too late decision if they want a bigger W NP feasibility study.

This enlarged W Botswana NP would be world news as a very positive aid to endangered African wildlife especially against current increased elephant-ivory and rhino-nose-horn poaching because of the enlarged NP's huge size and enhanced GoB's GNP money to supply wildlife protection with plenty of armed wildlife guards helicopters (and or drones), 4x4 vehicles all coordinated via radios vs. poachers. Any such enlarged Kalahari development plan should offer a young new generation of Bushman education in international English and wildlife-tourism management. That is as a perpetual Botswana's cash cow international tourist destination draw with Bushman now as GoB assets vs. `dying out' Stone Age embarrassments. That's better than irreversibly despoiling it as is (or was) currently happening by trying to introduce beef cattle in a too arid thorn Kalahari ecosystem. That is designate all W of this established S to N Botswana E NP border line (fence) of now designated NP game refuges (with Brits four NP E border hiatuses filled) all now an African wildlife reserve-enlarged NP for wildlife (no cattle) except the Herrero tribe's tiny-one-well herd at Xai Xai as long time since tourist attraction thus exception.

There is international precedent for such a development paradigm. Australia gave Aborigines back long established Kakadu NP, much more as world famous Ayers Rock under their Land Reform Act of 1976 a stark change from prior 'death by dispossession' of Aborigines as what Bushman have faced, more so since Botswana's 1966 independence. In Botswana there is sparse to no human habitation in the W. Except there's the small-one-well contingent of pre-World War I Herreros from German persecution in way-back-then South West African (now

Namibia).   Urban developments are Maun which is already a 100% tourism supporting town. That's its airport as the portal to the Okavango Delta tourism. Ghanzi is one other town out W. Ghanzi could be fenced off or included-as a logistical asset to increased tourism. Already tourist draws would include Gcwichaba Cavern S near Xai Xai (we visited in 1988), one well Xai Xai and small contingent of Xai Xai Herrero tribe tourist on (photo opportunity). It would include the internationally significant Bushman Louvre or Africa's best collection of Bushman rock art painting at Tsodilo Hills far N.   Maun with population of 56,000 is already essentially an Okavango Delta wildlife tourism town. Ghanzi with a population of 12,000 with very few others W of the proposed NPs E wildlife fence line add infrastructure for more tourism or could be wildlife fenced off 'islands' in the otherwise NPs with residents therein given first priority to be hired in huge tourist developed openings.

Or that's bought out via varied possible avenues of action. Let such smaller details not block GoB's cash cow GDP enhancing `forever more' development opportunity by going NP-cum-international tourism. That is all this in place opportunity with current surging African international-wildlife-watching destination enthusiasm. Its tourist draw is already all created-by-Mother-Nature-for-low-added development cost to create water holes, restock with wildlife, add wildlife management facilities, provide access plus overnight lodging by GoB's developer or 3rd third party entrepreneurs as big international hotel chain or S African wildlife lodge standouts like Mala Mala et la. That's all to be a high-return-cash-cow-international-tourist-wildlife-watching destination with added water holes for more in numbers and diversity of wildlife species possible while not over grazing the fairly-open-Kalahari-good-wildlife-viewing-near-flat-terrain-with-fair existing bush, tree, and grass-ground-cover-wildlife terrains.   Such a development needs a total regional feasibility-study-cum-master plan with game management facilities, a way to get tourist there, providing unobtrusive (like one story thatch roof) overnight tourist lodges by 3rd party entrepreneurs like a la Mala Mala et al wildlife watching lodge builders and operators (the new wildlife watching way) in South Africa via bid long term leases of defined regions around their wildlife viewing lodges.

International wildlife watchers are not looking for glitzy overnight Dubai (UAE) skyscraper accommodations but rather South Africa's model, one story thatched roofs. That's successful models like Mala Mala, Singida, Londolosi et al W of Kruger or Phinda in KwaZulu Natal (et al).   That's which Kalahari NP lodge concessions would be auctioned to be built, operated by a big international hotel chains interested in the growing international wildlife-watching tourism demand, evolving industry for a new African wildlife watching destination. That'd train and employ Bushman. That's in the game park wildlife management for added international applause a worldwide tourist draw to feed off the Bushman's asset international 'The Gods Must Be Crazy' fame for a win-win for Botswana producing beef to feed hordes of visiting wildlife-watching international tourist after finding out where Botswana is from world news stories. That's simultaneously for land hungry endangered African wildlife thus protecting the fragile Kalahari ecosystem for humanity for a forever legacy of conserving it all naturally (native and unspoiled for future generations) vs any ecosystem alternate asphalt jungle development plans.

Am I against beef cattle? No, hardly as I grew up on a northern California 4th generation since 1865 cattle ranch . Just keep beef in green pasture, not semi-desert. B eef are great in Notswana's E , Argentine pampas, America's W, but not in the far too arid and thorny Botswana Kalahari semi-desert. Or beef cattle have their placebut it's not in such as the camel's only bare of a blade of grass huge Sahara desert. That's semi-arid fragilr Kalahari Desert of western Botswana should be for wildlife only while safeguarding not destroying such a potential Mothe- Nature's provided-omternational-tourist draw for an endangered Africn wildlife-watching destination. I have also lived too many years in REAL world deserts. That's in North Africa's Sahara and Saudi Arabia. Those regions do not have sucha greener choice as is offered Botswana by our Creator, his earthly caretaker Mother Nature as semi-arid wildlife supporting (especially by adding a la Etosha windmill water holes) on top of the already tourist developed portion of world famous Okavango Delta. This would stop the since 1966 misdirected side show (or horror show) effort of ejecting the Bushman from what the British created (1961) now CKGR as their Bushman reserve.

That's erroneously renamed (1980s) the now CKGR. There are rumors there are diamods in the CKGR? If so compromise to mine diamonds inside a greater wildlife NP, a small acreage, a short term distraction but then still a wildlife NP forever more. Thus have a game reserve restocking of that vast CKGR area with African wildlife looked after by also endangered human species Lalahari Bushman. Treat endangered human species Bushman as the treasures they are to mankinds logacy, evolution, roots or DNA for archeologists et al. Yes, too big a dream?

No it's only choosing a very best land use, good common ECONOMIC and ENVIRONMENTAL sense for GoB to get a feasibility study factual objective chance to choose after seeing such an international top feasibility study. Give cloistered GoB politicians a break and the whole real world world wildlife-watching craze facts. Where else is there such a competing wildlife NP development opportunity? A huge generally considered worthless region with a Noah's Arc (when restocked) of endangered African wildlife. Adopt a can do approach. GoB is now updaed to the facts that their scruffy Bushman are world famous tourist draws via their GODS movie and their scientifically discovered-unique-to-the-rest-of-our -world-outside-of-Africa-matchig OOA DNA vs. formerly regarded as just Stone Age embarassments, as PROBLEMS, now ASSETS in any pro international wildlife-watching enlarged Kalahari NP (via international development feasibility study) of GoB's generally considered worthless Kalahari sands region. After the success of the Gods Movie, the dNS discovery, total Kalahari NP Bushman would be considered (1) as international tourist draw assets, (2) game management protectors, guides in an international wildlife-watching tourism wildlife NP (3) a GoB asset in its cash cow GDP enhancing W Kalahari development.

 How could GoB subjectively be against such? Like sell now to a younger GoB generation bringing thousands of wildlife-watching tourist to eat Botswana beef.   Arrange for likr our MZB Elephant Coast 1995 feasibility study costing our NO developer only $ one million dollars for GoM to expand its 1st loffered 63 Sq Mi development upgraded to a 914 Sq Mi GoM NP 99-year-lease- concession award (1996); per my 2007 book SAVE MOZAMBIQES ELEPHANT COAST. With a study report in process, get Peace Parks, Botswana's Commonwealth cousins Canada and Australia et al, our world's not for profit wildlife bleeding hearts, NGOs for endangered wild life and natives to lobby GoB with news of what Commonwealth Countries in recent years finally did for their native peoples, the Canadian Inuit and Australian Aborigine precedents. That is make a W Kalahari NP (enlarged) development an opportunity for world news in our otherwise `going to hell in a handbasket' world with African wildlife poaching, a threatened Bushman extinction. That's for GoB to enhance their generally favorable world (African) image more via (1) protecting their fragile Kalahari Desert ecosystem, (2) endangered wildlife protection (haven for black rhinos and elephants et al vs. poaching (3) GoB humanitarianism toward ndangered Bushman's DNA.

GoB (4) to use Bushman as assets vs. a `problem'. The (5) (perpetual cash flow in via creating an wildlife-Bushman NP international tourism destination win-win is the big sell with positive international green cause kudos. That's with a then new GoB's world's largest wildlife NP internationally applauded as saved for our world's t unborn generations, more so in 50, 100, 1000 years by whatever humanity becomes in the future as probably a continued back to nature or increasing the value of very few sites having been guarded `native and unspoiled' for future generations. GoB has a unique international GDP enhancing opportunity. That's with a low population of only less than two million, GoB doesn't have China, India, Japan or Indonesia's over populations or has no problem of such a thirst-and-thorn Kalahari NP (otherwise useless territory) to dedicate to wildlife-watching being the fast growing future element in international tourism, where only Africa has its Noah's Ark of African wildlife to qualify. How to get this ball rolling? Peace Parks (or equal) helps GoB become informed, interested, involved, to accept a study. Hire a top international feasibility planner such as Bechtel-WATG-Horwath out of London (or equal) who did our feasibility study to upgraded MZB's Elephant Coast NP plan for GoM from an offered only 63 Sq Mi to an awarded 914 Sq Mi in less than 10 months at a NO developer's cost of one million (1996) dollars only!

Get an international billionaire or two involved as the initial charitable Developers for GoB, plenty are into wildlife and ecosystems to offer as their charitable living legacies. Those professionals did know of the opportunity of involvement in what could have (should have) been a resurrected at 4000 Sq Mi MZB NP (2007) connected to the adjacent by then 2002 creation of the world's largest GLTP to the MZB Elephant Coast's then N which was a world-class opportunity that the NO developer's NOL sabotaged and destroyed in by Bechel London's teas for MZB's Elephant Coast GoM winning feasibility study. MZB's development was then upgraded to an exotic cash cow 914-Sq-Mi-99-year-develop-operate lease CPD-NP. -GoM's award was from a Peninsula only offered 63 Sq Mi without WILDLIFE. That's by converting it to a huge wildlife watching destination NP. GoB has another bigger candidate for feasibility study, lacking only MZB's UN CPD botanical status replaced by GoB's BUSHMAN`s DNA saga. The 914 Sq Mi MZB Elephant Coast NP version provided economy of scale, critical mass while a new world class endangered African WILDLIFE watching destination with world green-tourism-parties salivating. Wildlife refuges should not be postage-stamp-size-mom-and-pop affairs, rather big for wildlife seasonal movements.

Plus the major wildlife-watching market is international not local-regional. African wildlife needs large areas for seasonal movement. See www.savemec.org or the book *SAVE MOZAMBIQUE'S ELEPHANT COAST* (2007) including detailed proposal with costs, economics to complete MZB's 1996 then original 914 Sq Mi plan as an example. Then expand it to 4000 Sq Mi to tie into the GLTP to its N. That's while safeguarding 4000 Sq Mi of UN mandated Maputaland CPD as a NP. Saved *"native and unspoiled for future generations"* as a UN mandated CPD-NP. Plus it could have saved 5000 Kruger elephants from being euthanized for lack of terrain euphemistically guilty of overgrazing Kruger NP. This now proposed western-Kalahari-Desert-wildlife-NP-enlargement-feasibility study would provide a factual basis for GoB to decide an exact S and mostly E boundary fence of the W Botswana combined, enlarged world's four times largest WILDLIFE NP. The Botswana E boundary of the area W of which line is to be 100 % dedicated to wildlife tourism development which would be master planned thus developed in professionally managed critical path stages as GoM approved. But it is essential up front to have a feasibility-study-cum-master plan to organize then install the how-tourist-get-there, overnight logistics and all. With the boundary set the development pros plan what wildlife to restock with.

That's with drilled well windmill water holes (like Etosha NP) thus where to locate GoB to lease out each overnight tourist facility with its assigned exclusive surrounding wildlife viewing area. That's after wildlife biologists have determined what wildlife species (numbers) are to be restocked in each different wildlife region. That's of the greater development region without internal fences. There's only the external enlarged Kalahari NP E fence. The one E NP boundary line wildlife fence between W or Kalahari sands wildlife-Bushman and E raise-beef-for-tourist meals beef raising regions. That's let wildlife roam at will with seasons, droughts, whatever. In also fairly arid Etosha NP of N Namibia wells were drilled with windmill pumps creating water-hole ponds for wildlife to allow a more diverse semi-arid wildlife adding like zebras, giraffes, springbok et al to be stocked like black rhinos now being poached for their nose horns! That's all wildlife to now be protected by Bushman. That's others with helicopters, radios, 4X4 vehicles in all of a S-to-N with E border fence in a huge W Kalahari Botswana NP producing an upgraded wildlife tourist destination where poachers dare not enter. Some overnight tourist lodges could be near Gitchwa Caverns, Tsodilo Hills, the Herrero's well at Xai Xai or the upper Okavango River (both banks) with access to Okavango Delta from its Nw border, W, S sidesxnow tourist undeveloped. The wildlife-tourism pros would master plan waterhole locations, tourist lodge locations vis-a-vis water holes, viewing areas for each lodge. The development plan would define all transportation means to get tourist in and out, garbage out by a combination of by air, land (roads) even a tourist rail as approved in 1996 in MZB's created Elephant-Coast-NP development plan. Our MZB NP rail (1996) was to be a first wildlife NP internally accessed by railroad.

 Rail (trains) would be a boon for `livestock car' restocking wildlife (elephant, Cape buffalo et al). MZB 1996 failed to materialize only as our NO developer was a troubled-bait-then-switch character (next chapter) . A similar train system (loop) on the flat Kalahari region would be investigated as a now world's 1st as a unique tourist draw. Maun would be a good rail head to W into that wildlife viewing region. Have a rail link to Gabarone, on into the now South African rail system for rail-wildlife buffs. Get experienced wildlife translocation PhD gurus out of SA   They'd plan wildlife handling facilities needed, then numbers by species for restocking via translocated wildlife from SA wildlife reserves (as Kruger's 5000 elephants et al). Wildlife are culled annually from NPs due to oversupply via annual auctioning off of overstocked wildlife a big industry in SA, neighboring countries. Get sovereign country funds like Saudi Arabia, Kuwait, Abu Dhabi, Qatar, UAE (Dubai), Singapore et al to aid GoB as copartners (financial risk partners) if Gob so desired in up-front financing initial development stages. Get the EU to kick in feasibility study funding vs. their misconceived GoB beef price `subsidy', hoof-and-mouth disease barrier fence faux pas. With wildlife windmill water holes a-la Etosha a larger variety of hardy wildlife could adapt to the arid W Botswana Kalahari wildlife development. If the water table precludes windmill pumped wells in some regions then pipe water from the Okavango River and Delta for wildlife water holes. Once development breaks ground at an appropriate stage as 18 months of restocking, transportation infrastructure, lease out wildlife viewing lodge building.

Then Botswana's international engineer-architectural-manager pros would organize for GoB an international auction to long term lease out the individual wildlife watching tourist overnight lodge facilities concessions. To be built by them or project others. That's with adjacent viewing regions leasing at well published international auctions. London pros (or equal) would keep tourist numbers at overnight lodge sites controlled. That's by a limited overnight beds numbers to keep the wildlife viewing vehicles per lodge to a controlled-vehicle-density-high-quality-photographing experience as per South Africa's top lodges vs. Kenya Masai Mara's too many uncontrolled vehicles bad example. But to keep those beds fully booked a year ahead. This is a proven paradigm to follow as such top drawer sites in SA as Mala Mala, Singida, and Londolozi W of Kruger, or Phinda in Kwa Zulu Natal that draw booked-up-for-a-year-ahead-international-wildlife-viewing tourist at cash cow daily lodge room rates. This is where Dr Jack's 1988 Bushman visit could lead us or to still hunter-gatherer Bushman's 1988 "don't just come and gawk at us" revival. That's a do something long term positive for them, their wildlife for their precious fragile Kalahari haven ecosystem. That is for Bushman (via DNA) our oldest now none African international populations' blood relatives! Here's a parting thought on this all Botswana's expanded W Kalahari one NP proposed wildlife-watching destination. Before independence the UK created what is now called (renamed) the CKGR as a Bushman homeland and other wildlife NPs. But Bushman have since been run out of that their CKGR homelands or other Kalahari havens. There were several other Bushman tribes given nothing as to protected homelands. For GoB to follow the proposal herein, to make all W Kalahari an enlarged one composite Kalahari W NP with Bushman brought up belatedly to the 1970s level of Australian Aborigines, and Canada Inuit as their appreciated Commonwealth (by DNA) cousins late, but better than never and not extinct.

It would be GoB to expand everything not already designated NP or game reserve (rest of W Kalahari) into an expanded now combination wildlife-Bushman homeland one NP to replace the smaller pre-independence Bushman Reserve-cum-CKGR taken away. What about letting Bushman hunt in a wildlife game reserve? Re Chap 4 herein was originally Cpt 8 of my 2015 book (the Impala Paradigm) most wildlife males (85% or more) are redundant. It takes about as few as one male to cover 30 females (be it wildlife or domestic livestock). Let the few Bushman who still want to hunt (hunter-gatherers) do so but restrict their minor hunting to none endangered species, redundant males only per the Impala paradigm saga. That's an interesting tale of African wildlife vis-à-vis on our ranch what my dad did, see the `impala paradigm' herein Cpt 5 pg 99. That's like in USA, only Native American's are allowed to net salmon on the Colombia River. White faces et al (others) are allowed to hunt only limited male deer, elk, and moose. Having some still bow and arrow hunting Bushman would be a rare international tourist draw while an asset in anti-poaching-cum-NP wildlife management. According to recent DNA discoveries, the Bushman are the world's oldest surviving humans, they are DNA special. Give them recognition like Australia did belatedly for their Aborigines and Canada did for their Inuit in the 1970s better late than never. That's which the Brits did for some Bushman in the early pre independence (1966) or created the now CKGR but which has since been GoB withdrawn. The western Kalahari Botswana region should be first class international tourist developed to be just for wildlife (and Bushman) tourist watching, no domestic cattle for lions to prey on. Thus no EC hoof-and-mouth disease concerns, no-wildlife-drought-killing inside the NP due to internal fences.

In Livingston's time the quagga and Bushman were everywhere in SE South Africa. The quagga are now long gone (extinct circa 1878). Killed by we `others' not by the endangered human species Bushman who are now on the edge of an extinction cliff. It was NOT the Bushman who killed off the quagga but rather 'we others'with our firearms. But we others have the gall to condemn the Bushman (for hunting as hunter-gatherers) and to throw them out of their officially designated now CKGR homeland in the mid 1980s! Bah humbug! From our 1988 Bushman visit "I had a recurring dream." This enlarged total Kalahari NP plan evolved especially after my 1995-96 MZB Elephant Coast NP creating experience in MZB as the development's key man who got Bechtel's London's feasibility study and development team hired. This resulted in the plan that resulted in GoM happily awarding a 99-year-develop-operate land lease in 1996. I have six wishes (1) that such further development of the Kalahari is not too late already. That (2) via an international feasibility study GoM can be objectively advised that a larger total Kalahari sands NP is by far their best alternate land use choice (approve it). Then (3) it will be an endangered African wildlife and endangered Bushman (DNA) homeland NP. That's (4) a forever more GoB cash cow GDP enhancer, while making Bushman a GoB asset vs. a now `created' problem. Thus (5) create a largest wildlife NP sanctuary where rhinos, elephant and lions et al are safe from poachers and land gobbling `civilization'. That's (6) save this unique Kalahari wildlife, Bushman ecosystem "native and unspoiled for future generations" as a world class wildlife-watching destination. That's God to be willing before we humans have put it off until it is far too late. God help us to see the light, finance a feasibility study that so convinces GoB of the extreme merits of one larger W Botswana Kalahari NP, Amen.

3

Mozambique Elephant Coast 4000 Sq Mi Wildlife National Park Saga

Why would a career pipeliner be a key man creating an Indian Ocean Coast Government of Mozambique (GoM) wildlife-botanical National Park (NP)? First GoM awarded a development project at 914 Sq Mi upgraded from the GoM President's originally offered only 63 Sq Mi? Then who (NOJim) after GoM awarded it's 914 Sq Mi MZB NP world class development would let it fall in a crack. For me (etal) later to try to resurrect it expanded to 4000 Sq Mi? That's to safeguard "native-and-unspoiled for future generations" the heart of the MZB Maputaland Center of Plant Diversity (CPD) as UN mandated. That 1992 Rio Earth Summit created CPD region concept is one of the 250 richest surviving botanical regions worldwide, 84 located in Africa with plants mostly found nowhere else worldwide. A CPD is comparable to a botanical version of the endangered species list of mammals, birds, serpents and fish. But CPDs are whole regions vs. individual plant botanical species. In 1994 UN CPDs were gazetted by publication of *Centres of Plant Diversity* (1994) in three volumes covering the globe per Rio's 1992 International Biodiversity Accord signed by our World's Heads of State at Rio's 92 Earth Summit creating a new CPD paradigm.

Saving MZB's Elephant Coast CPD cum-NP development is this pipeliner's-tree-hugger-green-cause-post-1995 primary ongoing interest, environmental 'green' cause, activity over the years since 1996 via my second bleeding-heart-green-cause book *SAVE MOZAMBIQUE'S ELEPHANT COAST* (SMEC) in 2007 via a try to resurrect our 1995-96 GoM awarded MZB Elephant Coast NP creating project HOPED now to be expanded to 4000 Sq Mi from our 914 Sq Mi development version awarded by GoM in 1996. That's a project its developer NOJim (my boss) failed to produce on in a huge bait-then-switch human character failure. It's a revised cause for which I created an IRS 501 (c) (3) net site www.savemec.org of an ongoing saga to create this world class Mother Nature's gift MZB wildlife-botanical CPD-NP but being unable to seal the deal WHEN my `invest-when-there-is-still-blood in-the-streets' New Orleans (NO) developer entrepreneur's `human frailties' plus his Machiavellian lawyer's "I'm in charge" greed, project sabotage queering this WORLD class possibility. That's this actually happened saga 1995-96 and on, a dream project-cum-nightmare detailed herewith. A CPD saving larger 4000 Sq Mi project is still there now. But it is all now much thornier. The native-unspoiled region's 1995 nature is now being GoM et al challenged.

That's by GoM itself with less noble none GDP worthy land uses being involved. What a saga was this missed opportunity to create the MZB Elephant Coast Botanical Wildlife CPD-NP at 914 Sq Mi to or then resurrect it at 4000 Sq Mi. It's acronym is MZBECNP (Mozambique's Elephant Coast National Park). It's right time was 1986. My 2007 SMEC book provides the history up until then. I update this tale herewith as a saga that needs telling or as is told in more detail in my book SAVE MOZAMBIQUES ELEPHANT COAST, Recreating Mother Nature's Wildlife Wonderland Africa (2007). See the 501 (c) (3) net site above. It's a really happened nonfiction story about creating a large world class unique keep-it-native-and-unspoiled-wildlife-ecotourism-NP-international-tourism destination with Indian Ocean beach connection (E border). The development plan was approved by GoM in 1996 at 914 Sq Mi upgraded from what GoM's President Chissano offered (shanghaied) NOJim to develop of only a 63 Sq Mi Machangulo Peninsula only which the Bechtel London professionals deemed was not economically feasible.

CENTRES OF PLANT DIVERSITY

VOLUME 1
EUROPE, AFRICA, SOUTH WEST ASIA
AND THE MIDDLE EAST

UN CENTRES OF PLANT DIVERSITY (1994) book Volume 1 of 3 covering the Globe established locations, details as the UN bible for 250 CPDs worldwide, 84 in Africa. The Maputaland CPD was centered in S MZB. All were as created under the International Biodiversity Accord as signed by the World's Heads of State at the Rio 1992 Earth Summit UN mandated to be protected "native and unspoiled for future generations." In 1995 this concept (book) was unknown in MZB or to our London Bechtel feasibility study office(s). Pretoria U's Professor van Wyk wrote to GoM's President Chissano alerting him of GoM's CPD, a missed message. This Maputaland CPD was a project `divine intervention' to GoM in awarding us our 99 year project lease to develop our 914 Sq Mi Elephant Coast Botanical CPD-Wildlife NP.

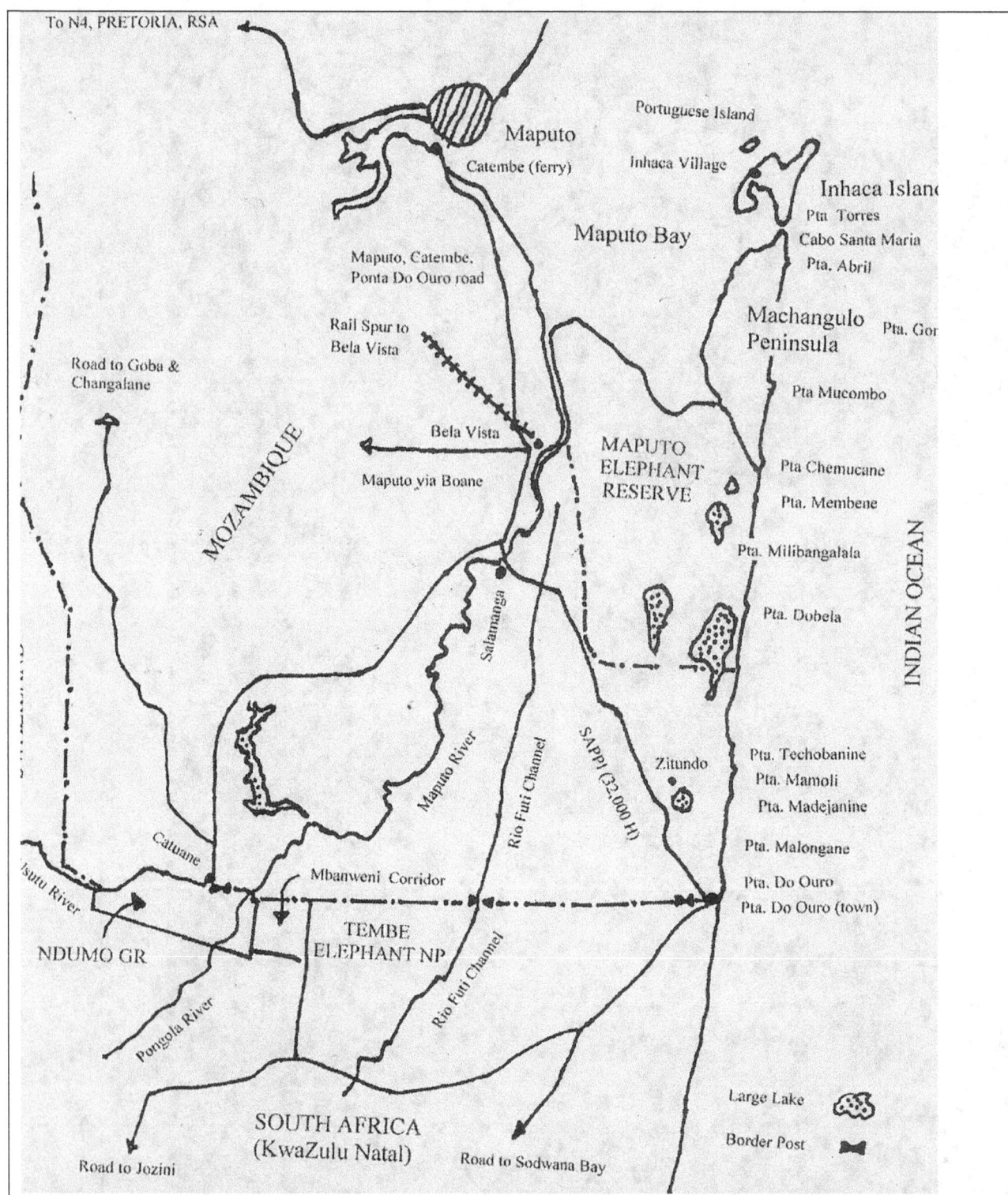

1995 sketch map of our 914 Sq MI version of Elephant Coast CPD-NP GoM gave NOJim a 99 year develop-operate lease on in fall of 1996 vs. only 63 Sq MI Machangulo Peninsula version. The Peninsula was a jewel but with expensive access. The 914 Sq MI version included a deep water port on W Inhaca Island plus to renovate the 273 Sq MI Maputo Elephant Reserve S of the Peninsula. Then due to its CPD status of territory S of MER to the KwaZulu Natal border. That's to rescind a years earlier GoM development to SAPPI for a eucalyptus plantation when it was belatedly discovered the whole region was a UN CPD mandated to be kept "native and unspoiled for future generations." The 914 Sq MI version of the Peninsula S had access across Inhaca S to SA's border, Indian Ocean Coast W to E bank of the Maputo River. A later 4000 Sq MI version was to resurrect ECNP then N to connect to the GLTP.

I've no wildlife images from MZB in 1995. They were most all shot out in the pre and post 1975 Independence era. Wildlife images in this Chapter are from earlier in other African NPs to show what we are trying to resurrect in the 4000 Sq Mi MZB Elephant Coast CPD-NP. Here's Ahmed (1973) in Kenya's Marsabit NP. He's now a full body mount in Nairobi. He died of natural old age causes in 1974. He had four armed men around him 24 hours to prevent ivory poachers. He survived to his 50s in Marsabit NP.

1966 Machangulo Peninsula (63 Sq Mi) looking S tip of Inhaca Island R foreground. Peninsula alone had 40 lakes, a beautiful untouched 20 miles of Indian Ocean Coast, a few starving traditional land dwellers men fishermen, wives tended bare survival gardens.

1995 looking NE, Peninsula R. S tip of Inhaca Island L. Shallow inner bay, could dredge up airstrip W of Peninsula plus rail route going S from deep W of Inhaca shore S for steam train to deliver tourist to wildlife lodges to the south.

1995 typical Peninsula fisherman's wife's gardens small 'home', bed at night, shade in day, minor protection from hippos, wild pigs, monkeys who raid wife's garden at night, natives at high level of poverty, need food, water supply, medical, schools.

1995 Marco collecting 'people information' for development feasibility study. Woman is typical with baby on her back, head loaded, poverty. NP development would cure ills of GoM's forgotten native class of inhabitants of Peninsula and S.

Civil war pre and post 1975 independence left most all inhabited areas as our NP development site heavily mined with EC too slowly removing mines, while warning humans with these RED mine signs.

1995 we fight SAPPI eucalyptus plantation for GoM award of 99 year development lease over land S of Maputo Elephant Reserve. Our T-shirts tell public of CPD saving GoM NP cash cow.

1995 back of our Elephant Coast NP vs. SAPPI gum trees. BME was Blanchard MZB Enterprises, name changed as we transitioned to 914 Sq Mi MZB wildlife-botanical NP phase of our proposed 914 Sq Mi GoM National Park (CPD) development.

1996 S of Maputo Elephant Reserve Marco displays ire at SAPPI eucalyptus plantation GoM has rescinded in favor of our 914 Sq Mi botanical-wildlife NP in this region now known to be UN mandated to be protected native and unspoiled for future generations as our CPD-NP.-

From here on in our `information presentation' we will present the Elephant Coast 914 Sq MI MZB Botanical (CPD)-Wildlife NP evolution (99 year lease awarded by GoM in late 1996) with a 2 ½ year build out allowed as numbered Bullet Paragraphs of where the project got to in 1996, where it is now 20 years later (NOWHERE). Can it be resurrected now at 4000 Sq MI all in UN CPD territory, connected up to the since evolved (2002) GLTP to the N for a much better wildlife watching destination economic outlook? But (more details below) NOL (NOJim's New Orleans Lawyer) got into NOJim's head that we (Bechtel, I et al) were trying to steal NOJim's project. NOL got us run off to sabotage (steal-kill) the project which he (NOL) despised as he being against NOJim's `wild' African adventure. NOL rewrote NOJim's will in 1994, made himself NOL sole Trustee of NOJim's estate, was out to protect NOJIM, Bechtel and I didn't lose NOJim's estate's wealth on a MZB Elephant Coast NP development opportunity, a projected GoM cash cow endeavor. Talking with NOJim without NOL's knowledge, I told NOJim our (Bechtel et al) next move was to get international funding partners to buy in to NOJim's development, to fund the development that was beyond NOJim's order of magnitude $30 million net worth. But NOL got into NOJim's sick head, destroyed or sabotaged NOJim's opportunity which Bechtel and I (et al) had won for NOJim, an international travesty.

Below we start numbered BULLET PARAGRAPHS to call out the main significant history, Pros and Cons of our 1995 on MZB Elephant Coast CPD-NP GoM 1996 awarded 914 Sq MI development. That's why it wasn't built out in 1996 on or how it wasn't later resurrected at 4000 Sq MI. It's still a UN Rio Earth Summit 1992 CPD thus mandated to be protected "native and unspoiled for future generations." Thus it's still now better as a GoM CPD-NP resurrected, enlarged to 4000 Sq MI to connect up with since 2002 GLTP of 38,500 Sq MI in W MZB's Limpopo NP, NE South Africa's Kruger NP, plus Zimbabwe's SE Gonarezhou GR with all internal border fences removed.

(1) The whole region of MZB Indian Ocean Coast W to Swaziland, N to the latitude of S Kruger NP came late in our 914 Sq MI feasibility study era discovered to all be well inside Rio's 1992 Earth Summit Maputaland CPD as UN mandated to be safeguarded as a CPD "native and unspoiled for future generations." The CPD status was only discovered just before the London Bechtel 914 Sq MI feasibility study went out London's door to GoM's President Chissano in mid to late-1995. But its CPD status made GoM cancel a several year's earlier development lease to SAPPI for a destructive eucalyptus plantation S of the shoot out by Cubans Maputo Elephant Reserve (MER) of-1932. But this our diamond-in-the-rough development opportunity fell in a crack when its developer NOJim became a white-knight-savior-then-after he was awarded the development by GoM his NOL got NOJim to change into a bait-then-switch nonperformer in an extremely sad saga. NOL got NOJim to run Bechtel and I (et al) off, NOJim threw craps on the MZB NP development then died in 1999 at 54 failing to ever break ground thus jilting MZB and Mother Nature and the World's future generations of what was to be a challenge to East Africa's Serengeti as a world's primer worldwide-wildlife-watching-tourist destination with solid cash cow GDP projections for GoM et al. That's with residents inside the development 'native black partners' positively involved, their situation thus now greatly improved. It would have upgraded downtrodden-remote-bush-resident people who were without work, housing, schools, food, water or any medical facilities to get all these improvements due to NP development (developer's budget not GoM financed) as promised GoM in our feasibility study award. Yes at our project development cost, not via any GoM such commitments or their Marxist not caring for our local residents.

(2) The local bush folks (`traditional land dwellers') inside our 914 Sq MI GoM awarded Elephant Coast NP development were starving, ignored or forgotten by GoM's governing bureaucracy. How were we to protect it as a `discovered' CPD? Make it a NP with cash cow projections. It was a double barreled charitable plus green-cause-ecosystem-ecotourism development project. I was by divine intervention the key man who organized hiring a Bechtel London team (my prior six continents 30+ year employer) feasibility study which led to the 1996-GoM-99-year-GoM develop-operate-land-lease concession for the 914-Sq-MI-Elephant-Coast-wildlife-CPD-NP ecotourism development. Then NOJim (influenced or sabotaged by his lawyer NOL) got NOJim to throw craps-as the developer. NOJim and I 1st became closely acquainted on a serendipitous-1988-stranger-than-fiction-North-Pole visit. To our surprise the same day as a several month's Canadian-Russian ski team was there on a 1000 mile Siberia to Canadian Elsmere Island ski trip. Dr Wheeler's 1988 North Pole visit then hitch hiked the last 18 miles from a Russian floating iceberg weather station to the North Pole. On this exciting adventure travel trip NOJim came to know of my international Bechtel engineering-construction resume which had taken me to live, work on every continent but Antarctic then already 16 years in Africa. We were both African wildlife plus tribal people aficionados. He was an occasional African holiday visitor while I was more a long term African resident.

(3) NOJim seven years later hired me to do his GoM required feasibility study originally targeting only a 40,000 acre (63 Sq Mi) Indian Ocean Machangulo peninsular concession personally offered (or shanghaied) by GoM's then President Chissano. After project near death episodes we (divine intervention) increased its proposed size of development to 914 Sq Mi. That's to make our larger NP economically feasible and consistent with its late UN CPD nature, via a huge needed economy of scale and critical mass revision. That's with an African wildlife watching international tourist destination type via increased size to 914 Sq Mi that SA's 'green' press dubbed "Mother Nature's Wildlife Disneyland Africa" including revitalizing the 173,000 acre (270 Sq Mi) Cuban military decimated Maputo Elephant Reserve (MER) in Cold War days after MZB's 1975 independence from Portugal. The Portuguese created MER (1932). It was shot out from Cuban military helicopters in post-1975 MZB independence from Portugal. At 1975's independence 600 strong resident elephants were reduced to 100 gun shy survivors via Castro's military by when we developers arrived (1995). A last black rhino was Cuban killed in 1981. The Cubans left only a few hippo and Nile crocodile at a few of 45 development (914 Sq Mi) lakes. Otherwise post two wars pre-and-post independence the MER offered us only bleached skull and bones, a graveyard silence begging to be saved "native and unspoiled for future generations" all in UN CPD designated exotic territory. My second book **SAVE MOZAMBIQUE'S ELEPHANT COAST (2007)** threats this all in greater detail, or see its net site of www.savemec.org, book published by IUniverse available from Amazon for a more in depth treatment.

(4) But it was belatedly discovered all 914 Sq Mi to be part of a UN Rio 1992 Earth Summit created Maputaland CPD with exotic botanical virtues—and much more surrounding CPD designated territory. The Indian Ocean Coast region was of breath taking botanical quality via an untouched 50 miles of MZB coastline to SA's Natal-Zulu border. Our GoM approved concession plan would keep it so, restock it all with endangered African wildlife to create a new worldwide MZB CPD-NP with an international wildlife watching tourist destination desirability in this 914 Sq Mi sleeper project development sandwiched between the pristine Indian Ocean coast on its E, W to MZB's major Maputo River's E bank. The NP's Indian Ocean coastline was a starkly beautiful uninhabited, undeveloped high forested dune structure with its significant Maputo River W boundary with over 43 lakes sandwiched in between all with CPD per UN quality botanical ground cover throughout. An initial threat was GoM had several years earlier given a 99 year development lease concession to a South African timber company South African Paper Pulp Inc (SAPPI). That's which development would destroy a major part of Mother Nature's UN CPD jewel.

(5) That's with SAPPI's despoiling eucalyptus plantation which our NP better plan got GoM to cancel. A brief of our MZB-Elephant-Coast's-rise-and-fall-'green'-cause saga follows. My 11" by 8 1/2" 365 page 2007 SMEC book provides a more detailed history, evolution detailing a then eventual human character failure of NOJim `developer' plus his lawyer-saboteur NOL not to follow thru on the development then NOJim's death in 1999 with my 2007 book's why, how the Elephant Coast development should be resurrected, expanded then completed ASAP at 4000 Sq Mi enlarged size all still in UN CPD saving land. This green cause opportunity all started by my meeting Dr Jack Wheeler in Lhasa, Tibet's capital in 1986, then Jack's later North Pole trip in 1988 of my third book HUGEUNOT ROOTS-cum-SIX CONTINENT ODYSSEY (2015) wih NOJim in the context of this then later-to-be MZB 1995 project. Cpt 35 of my 2015 book revisits this SMEC story. At the Pole NOJim learned of my Bechtel-engineering-construction resume that later fit for his `desperate' need for doing a GoM required project development feasibility study. That's NOJim post-North Pole seven years called me professionally for his desperately required GoM feasibility report help. He was then about to lose his development opportunity for failure to provide GoM (President Chissano) the required feasibility study in a timely manner. It was old hat for this Bechtel veteran.

(6) That's as a career-Bechtel-mega-development Project Manager (PM) to be Jim's MZB development's at site in MZB key man. NOJim was an investment-news-letter guru, gold, numismatic coin dealer who puts on a high profile annual-fall-investment-gold conference in New Orleans. At Nixon's inaugural NOJim is credited with having a small plane fly over trailing a banner "Don't go off the gold backed dollar" which Nixon did do in 1971. France's Charles de Gaulle requested Fort Knox US gold bullion for his USA paper green backs which Nixon refused. There after US dollars were no longer redeemable or fully backed by gold. Jim was known in investment circles for his mantra "invest when there is still blood in the streets" which is an apt description of our MZB venture following closely on 28 years of civil wars in MZB from a Portuguese colony thru 1975 to independence then an anti-Marxist Cold War battle up to MZB's war torn UN peace in 1992. NOJim had a thing for Africa as a wildlife-watching tourists. He was also an aficionado of African tribal people, endangered African wildlife and their ecosystems.

1969 Seronera River Serengeti NP Tanzania. Night shift leopard takes a midday snooze in his safe tree to wait his night's hunting work shift. With my camera in hand I only saw leopards up a tree several times in Serengeti. Endangered African wildlife needs large NPs as Serengeti away from poachers, guns, snares, for survival of endangered African wildlife "native and unspoiled for future generations" especially like lions, leopards, ivoried elephants, nose horned rhino all need to be guarded by armed NP staff with helicopters, vehicles and radios.

1968 Serengeti NP Ma black rhino and young. Note tick birds (2) on her back, one on L rear leg. In the current
day, Ma's large two horns would get her killed by rhino horn poachers. I visited Serengeti often in the
60s and 70s. Bach then I never saw armed guards or helicopters needed in Serengeti. With today's rhino horn
poaching for a resurrected 4000 Sq Mi MZB Elephant Coast resurrected UN CPD-NP I would plan for plenty of
armed wildlife guards with 4x4 vehicles, helicopters and radios necessary to protect the wildlife.
Big NPs with funds to so protect the wildlife are a needed trend to win the fight for endangerd wildlife survival.

1968 Lake Manyara NP bull Cape buffalo smells intruders, shows white teeth a warning sign. If you were to get
out of your vehicle you'd risk his charge. Hunting in 1973 I faced a Cape charge at 14 paces afoot, it was at
daylight, we faced off. I waited, he then charged, died at 7 paces. Elapsed time of charge, ½ of one second.
I was the object of the bull's attack, but we three `whites' were close his wide horns would have got we three.

1971 Masai Steppe TNZ outside a NP in a remote hunting area rare of vehicles this lioness was alone without a male lion pride, unused to NPs many vehicles? Is she puzzled over if we're a hippo, rhino, elephant, Cape buffalo or other African beast she has yet to meet? Vehicle's exhaust kills human smell for her curious, lack of fear. Lions know man have firearms and fire, RE wary. Do they know hunters bag only males as trophies. This is a very rare none NP photo of a `curious lioness' in a remote region situation which leaves me curious why she's alone not accompanied by a lion pride male or other lionesses and as to her unusually curious unafraid seeming calmness.

(7) NOJim was an *"Out of Africa"* or a Teddy Roosevelt-Hemingway enthusiast of that 1985 movie plus an evolutionist. NOJim was a since-18-years-old-wheel-chair-bound paraplegic due to an auto accident. He was reported as the only paraplegic ever to visit the North Pole! But Jim had his fatal flaws. He was a Doctor Jekyll and Mr Hyde split personality character as per Robert Louis Stevenson's 1886 book. His problem was manifested in substance abuse or as his lawyer divulged to me "Jim had a monkey on his back." I came to appreciate what this all meant in the rise-and-fall of his (or our) world class MZB Elephant Coast CPD+NP wildlife development to rival East Africa's Serengeti as a world's number one wildlife watching tourism destination but with ocean connection. After our 1988 North Pole trip I was in Jim's rolodex as the 30 year Bechtel construction PM who'd run mega projects on every continent but Antarctica already then 16 years in Africa. That's as a guy known by CEO Steve Bechtel Jr, Bechtel's number two George Schultz. Or that's as a guy who killed a man-eating lion in Kenya (1965).

(8) That's who spoke Swahili, had hunted in Africa for months without a pro hunter, who would be a good PM candidate if Jim decided to do some kind of Indian Ocean coastal wildlife development in Africa his eventual dream. On our North Pole trip I told Jim "If you ever need an African gun bearer just call me." Our 1988 North Pole meeting became a before-the-fact divine intervention meeting for Jim when he was later shanghaied by MZB's President Chissano with an exotic big-little development opportunity on MZB's Indian Ocean Coast in 1995 but had to produce something called a `feasibility study'. That's seven years after our North Pole visit meeting. Thereafter we rehashed our North Pole adventure over beers at Jim's annual fall New Orleans gold bug conference which I attended most years. In April 1995 I returned to TX from a consulting key man job bidding a major gas pipeline over the Andes taking Argentine gas to Chile. The Chile Andes pipeline was routed in the wrong places.

(9) That's an Andes box canyon river vs. hog back ridges by its Canadian owner's degrees-PhD's-route-selection-naïve novices. The few extant trans-Andes pipelines are the world's highest as there are none over the higher Asian Himalayas (Everest) or Karakorum's (K2). On my return to Texas (95) I'd a phone message from Jim seven years after our North Pole gig. MZB's President from 1988 to 2008 Joaquin Chissano offered Jim a cushy Indian Ocean coastal land development (or shanghaied Jim) with a 99-year-develop-operate-land-lease opportunity on the 63 Sq Mi Indian Ocean Machangulo Peninsula just E of MZB Capital of Maputo. After the Portuguese left in 1975 MZB's Marxist infiltrated black revolutionaries took over. There was no longer any private land ownership in MZB or only 99-year-GoM-development-concession leases. President Chissano offered NOJim such a development lease target on the Indian Ocean horizon 18 MI E of MZB's capital Maputo or formerly Portuguese Lorenzo Marques. Jim had a deadline to present GoM with a feasibility study that they accepted. Jim didn't have a clue. He needed help from his 1988-North-Pole-lead-husky-sled dog. Was this Dubai's African Oceanside competition?

(10) The offered Peninsula was like three times the distance from Maputo looking E across the Indian Ocean bay as being in Oakland California or Berkeley where I got my engineering degree looking W across SF Bay to the similar SF Peninsula which is 47 SQ MI SF city limits or only 75 % the size of Jim's original MZB offered development target. Jim was stalled on producing his feasibility study for the President and GoM bureaucracy to seal his deal or land development of Machangulo Peninsula 63 Sq Mi only Indian Coast 99-year-lease-develop-operate concession. Jim was about to lose his deal to delay. His outfit's gold sales people were putting out shiny promotional pie-in-the-sky crap. Jim's April 1995 phone message was inquiring "Was I ready to go be Jim's PM on his MZB feasibility study?" To me a trip to Africa's MZB was hell yes. But was this a for real development site or an Alice-in-Wonderland-mom-and-pop pipe dream? What of MZB? In early history Arabs were the first northern colonizers of Africa's southern hemisphere Indian Ocean coast comings S from Muslim Middle East by Arab dhows.

(11) Then in about 1500 Portuguese rounded the Cape via the Atlantic to the Indian Ocean to be a presence on Africa's S Indian Ocean coastal region in bigger sailing ships. They'd soon trading posts, forts to largely displace Arabs in now MZB and TNZ. Then 460 years later was African black native vs. white Portuguese, MZB's war of independence from 1964 until Lisbon's newly elected Socialist came into revolutionary power in 1975. Lisbon-European socialists abandoned MZB to independence in 1975. Angola, Portuguese Guinea also got independence all to which were to anti-colonial-Marxist-infiltrated guerrillas who took over as to-the-victors-go-the-spoils new rulers. Ian Smith then ruler of Southern Rhodesia (now Zimbabwe) plus South Africa, CIA et al, other W free market powers didn't want a Cold War era Marxist Communist country imbedded in southern Africa. Post 1975 MZB independent of Portugal was a pro-west-free-market instigated vs. Marxist-run MZB new civil war.

(12) That's up to a UN negotiated Nairobi peace in 1992. NOJim was in on that UN sponsored peace, caught Chissanno's eye. By 1994 it's five years after the Berlin Wall came down. The Russians, their Cuban henchmen had all left MZB. In 1994 NOJim visited MZB looking for his "blood-still-in-the-streets" investment development opportunity, in Jim's case an Australian Barrier Reef like island on the MZB far N coast. In 1994 MZB had a first two party election won by prior-appointed-by-Marxist President Chissano. GoM was thus majority controlled by the had-been-Marxist left vs. western leaning right when Jim came looking for his still-blood-in-the-streets investment in 1994. Then NOJim returned to MZB in early 1995 to look into a GoM development lease on his chosen MZB barrier reef island he'd visited in 1994. MZB's President Chissano was waiting for him. Jim was ushered in to a private meeting with Chissano who essentially shanghaied capitalist Jim with the Machangulo Peninsula 63 Sq Mi target as a GoM-develop-operate-land-concession 99 year lease. There was no more private land in MZB as a result of independence from Portugal vs. now all land was owned by more Marxist GoM rulers.

13) When Jim called me in 1995 he was already in trouble not knowing how to go about the MZB required feasibility study. This was clear to me when I returned his call coming back from bidding my South-American-trans-Andes pipeline Argentina to Chile. "Could I do Jim's feasibility for him?" he asked. Yes, but I had two off the top queries, as (1) was it for real, if so (2) I'd want to have a Bechtel (or equal) pro outfit involved so the study was a bankable quality study not so much for GoM as for worldwide other investors et al. Should I join Jim in MZB? I was initially dubious of what sounded like it might be a too-good-to-be-true fantasy. I was ready to go, but needed to see it, test my gut feel to bless it, before committing. In May 1995 Jim and I flew to MZB to see it all. In route thru London coming, going we visited my former employer Bechtel, plus competitor Bovis both previously unknown to Jim. Both were top-feasibility-study producing engineers for major international touristic development projects.

(14) Then in 1995 my experience was to have such major, known, respected professional big outfits perform our feasibility study so it would be accepted or held water with big international boys be they bankers, investors, rich oil billionaires or whoever. But only if the offered MZB site stood up as international class not a mom-and-pop fling or whim. A Bechtel London or equal would not do a feasibility study just for the study money as the 2nd step would be for them to manage any sizeable development. It had to measure up to difficult strict international criterions. Though originally not an issue but soon to figure in NOJim's MZB activities was the 173,000 acre or 270 Sq Mi Maputo Elephant Reserve (MER) just S of NOJim's offered by GoM 63 Sq Mi Machangulo Peninsula. The MER's E boundary was the Indian Ocean Coast with the Maputo River its W limit all joining Jim's offered Peninsula to its S. The Portuguese created the MER in 1932. But it was shot out mostly from helicopters by Cuba post-1975 as Cold War babysitters for the post-independence from Portugal Marxist GoM in still then Cold War days.

(15) MER had 600 elephants at MZB's 1975 independence plus a *Noah's Arc* of other African wildlife. In Cold War days Russia was busy in Afghanistan. They delegated Cuba's Castro the chore to protect Marxist's Cold War gains in MZB despite the west's instigated second pro-west civil war up to MZB's 1992 final UN peace. In military helicopters Cubans flew over MER for machine gun target practice, desire for ivory to reduced 600 elephants to 100 gun shy survivors by our mid 1990s era. MER elephants hated lead spitting helicopters. After 1992 MZB peace the Cubans left. HIV-AIDS, malaria were regionally rampant. The world's epicenter of HIV-AIDS was nearby Swaziland on MZB's SW border reducing their life expectancy to 40 years. I agreed to be Jim's PM after visiting his MZB site to kick the tires. I expected it to be a wild goose chase until I saw it. Our MZB visit was in May 1995. MZB was in war torn human misery of 60% unemployment! But MZB had Mother Nature's blessing with an Indian Ocean coastline stretching from South Africa N to Tanzania or that's a MZB coastline equivalent to the USA Pacific Ocean's San Diego to Seattle. There had been a 28 year two phase civil war first against the European Portuguese colonialist. When we visited in 1995 the country was mined and swarming with firearms.

(16) That is then (post 1975) it was the West against the Cold-War-take-over Marxist MZB second civil war phase then a final 1992 UN brokered Nairobi peace by which time MZB was an economic basket case having regressed from more free market capitalist Portuguese pre-1975 days. When the Portuguese bailed out in 1975 then Lorenzo Marques (LM) was an international tourist hot spot but by 1994 long since no more. It had digressed to a renamed dog eared capital of Maputo after 1975 independence. It was like MZB had suffered 28 years of hibernation or 1992 was Rip Van Winkle emerging from a long sleep while the world had passed MZB by. MZB fit Jim's mantra of "looking for investments when there was still blood in the streets." That is MZB had been

Inoculated with the Marxist-Socialist-Communist virus a negative to consider. Was land cost a bargain? An unusual positive was all the land was now GoM owned. In MZB developers took in the GoM as a 10% of their developer's issued corp stock partner. There was thus no development-budget-cash-flow land cost per se just the cost of improvements. This could lead to a cash cow development if everything else was in order. But for me LM meant 'lingering memories' of white European former happy rule as MZB was now a Socialist basket case.

(17) To my surprise on visiting it the 63 Sq Mi Machangulo Peninsula turned out to be a later discovered UN CPD-dream site botanical treasure with forty lakes with hippos in several along with pink flamingos. It included 20 miles of starkly beautiful Indian Ocean coastline E plus a sheltered inner Maputo Bay (Indian Ocean) W. It was all breath taking beautiful UN CPD class native-and-unspoiled or what a developer, his architects and planners would die for in virgin green `native-and-unspoiled' real estate. There (the Machangulo Peninsula) it was as if the wheel had yet to be invented. It was completely undeveloped or civil wars reduced to such. It was in post war ruins where one "couldn't buy a candle or a match to light it with" on Jim's offered remote Peninsula where a few mud-hut-thatched-roofed-dirt-floor residences were found for its barefoot near starving fishermen residents. The fishermen's wives had small gardens they tended days but which hippo, monkeys and wild boar then raided and destroyed at night. In Jim's offered development region there thus was war between the starving natives and meager surviving wildlife. There were no schools, medical facilities or much of anything civilized. We had visited London's Bechtel office on the way down, alerted them of a maybe project. Returning thru London it was "We need your feasibility study proposal ASAP" as I had seen the potential MZB opportunity, then hired on with NOJim.

(18) That's not to "create a silk purse out of a sows ear" but which was a potential 'diamond in the rough' Mother Nature's treasure development. There were some real hurdles ahead that might need divine interventions. I advised Jim to hire livewire Bechtel London over London competitor Bovis to get his best international bankable quality feasibility study for GoM. The London Bechtel-WATG-Horwath feasibility team and I traveled to MZB at the end of June 1995 for their feasibility study site visit. The Bechtel study team was in love with the Mother Nature's unspoiled quality of the MZB offered Machangulo Peninsula and Indian Ocean coast site but what about the economics? That's the feasibility question? There was nothing to bring international tourists to this remote site. It was a near day's long circuitous drive from Maputo but only 10 minutes across Maputo Bay E by helicopter. After their site visit Bechtel's team was barely started on the study when Bechtel et al raised the white flag. Their counsel was "Forget it as it is not economical. It was too remote an area with no infrastructure so it is too costly to develop with high hotel room rents with nothing for international tourists to come for which wouldn't fit."

(19) There was no-ace-in-the-hole-African-wildlife-watching-tourist-destination draw nearby. Bechtel advised Jim to throw in the towel vs. wasting money to complete his quarter million dollar feasibility study. But as NOJim's PM in MZB this was my time for outside-the-box action! Marco Basto was my white Portuguese MZB chief assistant. He was MZB knowledgeable, sagacious. He'd been the Minister of Forests-Wildlife just after 1975 independence. Marco's white Portuguese consulting partner Jao was post-1975 independence in charge of the Ports-Railroads in the MZB early independence epoch. That's until GoM could in early times convert to all black faces in top GoM ministries. Marco got me a meeting with his black replacement as the Minister of Forests and Wildlife. I queried when GoM was going to fix up the Cuban-shot-out Maputo Elephant Reserve (MER) to save his President's pet Peninsula project. African wildlife watching brought international tourist to Africa. A renovated and wildlife restocked MER would make an adjacent Peninsula tourist development realistic and economical. The black Minister's Marxist tainted reply was "why don't you Capitalist with all your money fix it up."

(20) It was a short and sweet meeting. I was out the door with a smile for our needed critical divine intervention. The Minister had unknowingly (divine intervention) opened the door to saving NOJim's and President Chissano's project providing what the Bechtel team said was missing. That's a cash cow for GoM wildlife-watching destination goal. I told Marco "We can get the international wildlife watching `destination' the Bechtel team say's the Peninsula needs by fixing up the Cuban shot our Maputo Elephant Reserve immediately S which GoM doesn't have the money or plans to do." Marco fixed us up with a South African architecture outfit who fielded a team of PhD-wildlife-tourism gurus to make a quickie mini-feasibility study of a MER wildlife revamping. But during their study the PhDs expanded their study scope S to KwaZulu Natal (South African border) W to the Maputo River the eventual 914 Sq Mi size (S, W) was) further divine intervention. The wildlife-tourism PhD gurus were in love with

the whole region with its now smashing 50 miles of `native and unspoiled' Indian Ocean coast terrain, lakes, botanical treasures, wildlife to be restocked then with its UN CPD status yet unknown to the (PhDs) or GOM including us (Bechtel feasibility team). Our South African architect then did a next level up quickie mini-study to expand our GoM offered Bechtel London dinged 63 Sq Mi Peninsula only development target S to 914 Sq Mi or 14.5 times larger now for 50 miles of `it-will-take-your-breath-away'-pristine-untouched-Indian-Ocean-coastline.

(21) It was now (UN CPD gift not yet known) a potential world class development as a botanical (CPD) and endangered wildlife region to compete with East Africa's Serengeti et al as an Indian Ocean fronted top international botanical-wildlife watching tourism destination. That is all to be outfitted and operated on a 99 year GoM land development lease concession. There was no land budget cost per se just partnering with GoM as 10% common shareholders, land leased for 99 years at no land rent cost. That was to keep it native and unspoiled wildlife watching with over nights in rustic one story thatched roof lodges, concessions auctioned off at an international auction to lodge-tourist-wildlife-viewing operators including such as Mala Mala, Londelosi, Singida and Phinda South African `new deal' wildlife watching paradigm. Operators to build-operated lodges to create an international tourists draw with transport means of getting them there from by air or water direct from Maputo, a bells and whistle option of an antique steam train delivering tourist S to their reservations in lodges with bed numbers controlled to relatively low numbers per lodge to guarantee good uncrowded photography commanding high per bed charges and fully booked up to a year ahead to get in like in top lodges W of Kruger or Phinds in Natal. We could outdraw Dubai with African endangered wildlife protecting CPD botany a GoM cash cow, economy saver, MZB NP to protect it "native and unspoiled for future generations." That's as UN mandated for CPDs.

(22) At the overnight lodges (South African Mala Mala Lodge paradigm) guests viewed wildlife in AM and PM game drives with mid-day lunch and pool swim. When the whole 914 Sq Mi ECNP region was only later discovered to be a UN CPD, it was logical to upgrade the development to a MZB NP status rather than just a competing animal watching commercial status a further one up on any wildlife watching destination competition. I was a week in South Africa to ramrod and hammer out our new September-'95-stop-gap-expand-to-914-Sq-Mi-version report around the wildlife-tourism guru's glowing positive report. Our report to the Minister (sly copy to MZB President Chissano) hit war torn MZB like a California 1848 Sutter's Mill gold rush mine discovery. It was a manna-from-Heaven revelation to-post-war(s)-poverty-stricken GoM or their version of divine intervention with MZB and the big-South-African-environmental-green-development press being more than supportive. The world press got wind of it and visited (WSJ, NYT, *The Economist all visited then* published positive articles) with a dozen South African newspapers invited and visiting with ongoing articles that kept the Indian Ocean coast Elephant Coast NP development alive as regional front page `environmental' and MZB-positive news. Many tree huggers, green cause NGOs, environmentalists, animal lovers joined in supporting our well received wildlife-NP development.

(23) NOJim's London feasibility study was resurrected by Bechtel on a now 914 Sq Mi scope as a top-drawer-five-star wildlife-watching destination project. A major South African newspaper dubbed it "Mother Nature's Wildlife Disneyland Africa." The project was drastically revised as a 15 times larger 914 Sq Mi vs. GoM's originally offered or London dinged uneconomical 63 Sq Mi Machangulo Peninsula only version without any type of wildlife watching destination The now development project went from a dog to a potential international high profile wildlife tourist destination. It was now potentially an economic self sufficient cash cow or a post war boom to MZB's struggling tepid post two civil wars economy. It now provided the Bechtel team's desired economy of scale and critical mass with many interesting bells and whistles as an antique steam train for access S with world-class-international-wildlife-watching destination feasibility. It had sand-sea-sun activities in the bay to the Peninsula's W as scuba, Indian Ocean sports fishing at the Peninsula's N end. There was only high quality wildlife watching for its majority of acreage in the renovated, restocked MER then on S. It evolved from a mom-and-pop target to a world-class-international wildlife tourism destination eventually MZB 914 Sq Mi CPD-NP development.

(24) Marco said "The 63 Sq Mi Peninsula was only the dog's tail. Extending S to 914 Sq Mi with the project is reborn as the entire now show class dog." I went to New Orleans in Oct 1995 to man NOJim's MZB Elephant Coast booth for Jim's annual fall-gold-show-investment conference MZB PR booth at his NO investment show. I'd in MZB produced a project PR video. It was first shown in New Orleans (NO) then later to the GoM Council of Ministers et al. GoM Ministers had to vote yea or nay on MZB President's now immensely bigger improved pet tourist

development. Returning to MZB from NO I was two weeks in London at Bechtel team's WATG's (architect) office hammering out the now expanded to 914 Sq Mi bankable feasibility land development report addressed to President Chissano (and ministers) from NOJim. NOJim's study was looking to be a smash hit in southern Africa. WATG (WimNO berly Allison Tong and Goo) was a world leading tourism development architect. In NO Jim's lawyer had queried "did I know Jim had a monkey on his back?" Was this veiled word a warning of bad things to come? A big yes, as NOJim and I were all for his MZB project, but `laying in the weeds' NOL hated (sabotoged) it.

(25) WATG of Bechtel's feasibility report team produced a brown-hard-cover-bound-11x17"-181 page eye-opener feasibility study known in MZB as "the Brown Bible." NOJim, I chose Bechtel for his feasibility report. Bechtel chose WATG to publish the report in London as Bechtel's study PM was in Egypt building hotels, sending Bechtel's input from there. The London report upgraded quality vs. our SA `quickie' including the PhD's report that got our Elephant Coast NP's scope upgraded to 914 Sq Mi.  London's report stole-the-show-over our teaser-SA edition.  The London study polished my `quicky' SA mini-report that got the scope upgraded from 63 to 914 Sq Mi the critical path lifesaver. The London report was with one startling last minute discovery added, a seal the deal item or further divine intervention. I was at the world's first UN 1992 Rio Earth Summit in the adjacent NGO Park with a poached booth then promoting my Kalahari Bushman green cause (book). At that Earth Summit the World's Heads of State voted in the International Biodiversity Accord which created the Centers of Plant Diversity (CPD) concept or new international paradigm of protecting 250 large endangered botanical ecosystems regions worldwide. Earth's botanists submitted candidate sites, reduced to a 250 best worldwide CPDs selected, published in three Volume CENTRES OF PLANT DIVERSITY (1994) gazetted books, with odd French spelling of title's CENTERS?

(26) The UN CPD paradigm named the 250-most-unique-surviving exotic-endemic-botanical ecosystems worldwide per Rio 92's International Biodiversity Accord new botanical protection UN statute. The UN sponsors ruled any country blessed with having a CPD site insigning the international accord was thus committed to protect their CPD "native and unspoiled for future generations." The three volumes or bible(s) of CPDs was issued two years after the Rio Earth Summit in 1994 after sorting out selection of 250 CPDs worldwide with full details of those global CPDs. That's Volume one of three covered Africa plus Europe and South West Asia. There were 84 CPD's in Africa. Ours was the huge Maputaland CPD (Vol I pgs 227-233) that extended from N of Maputo (S of Kruger NP's latitude) S into KwaZula Natal South Africa, W into Swaziland. No one in MZB had heard of the CPD concept. A contributor to identifying our CPD was Pretoria U's SA Professor van Wyk who'd written to MZB's President Chissano to advise him of his CPD treasure (no response), thrown out by Chissano's staff not understanding its importance?

(27) Van Wyk then wrote to advise WATG, me in London of the UN CPD story of MZB's huge Maputaland CPD which our MZB 914 Sq Mi NP project proposal all fell well within. Our project's Elephant Coast NP development would protect the heart of MZB's CPD as UN mandated. When our SA PhDs (wildlife-restocking report) of our mini-report to expand to 914 Sq Mi did not know of the UN CPD status. But they had unknowingly agreed with what the UN had mandated as that the 914 Sq Mi should be guarded native and unspoiled by being dedicated to its botany, African wildlife, as a NP. This eventually evolved into our MZB botanical-wildlife-UN-CPD-NP concept. The wildlife-tourism gurus didn't know about the recently published 1994 CPD story nor did GoM or anybody in the region yet. So we republished van Wyk's letter to President Chissano in NOJim's to Chissano London feasibility study. He'd read every page of NOJim's study to discover about his MZB's CPD UN gift for a pleasant serendipitous GoM surprise. We now gave stacks of UN's CPD Vol 1 bibles or Centres of Plant Diversity (1994) to GoM's President, his Ministers plus regional media. The CPD-manna-from-heaven (divine intervention) surprise of van Wyk's letter was added just as our London's MZB Chissano feasibility report went out the door in London to MZB.

(28) Sappi's eucalyptus plantation was S of MER. Killing it was further divine intervention. Our now clamored for Elephant Coast feasibility study to GoM made NOJim who had been earlier featured in the press by some as an American land grabber to now be a CPD green savior creator of a MZB wildlife-botanical CPD-cum-NP development! Especially in the now battle over who was to get the region's development rights S of MER in our now proposed 914 Sq Mi NP version. GoM had years previously given SAPPI this 99 year land development lease to install a eucalyptus plantation there delayed for the then ongoing MZB civil wars. That's now to maybe permit SAPPI to destroy the belatedly discovered UN CPD ecosystem despite our recently discovered CPD native and

unspoiled quality had to be safeguarded as UN mandated as an International CPD site. I returned to MZB from NO via London in early Oct 1995. I had the Bechtel London's NOJim's feasibility study to President Chissano as a bound hard cover 11 x 17" masterpiece of our development plan plus the CPD bibles to MZB President, ministers to make the Dubai developers die of envy by comparison. What was the 914 Sq MI Plan with 50 MI coastline?

(29) The 63 Sq MI Machangulo Peninsula was to be an exquisite housing development around the 40 lakes for a separate `big five' African wildlife private wildlife sanctuary. There was a hotel at the N end, plus bell and whistle activities mainly in the W sheltered bay between the Peninsula and Maputo. That's scuba diving, international trophy fishing, a dredged up airstrip W of the N end of the Peninsula plus rail connection to Inhaca Island tourist ferries ex Maputo. GoM gave us an easement across Inhaca Island from its deep water W coast. There were to be hover craft type transport from Maputo to Inhaca for tourist across to the private housing and rest of the 914 Sq MI GoM NP developments S. The NP started S or the Peninsula's 63 Sq MI. On the 63 Sq MI Peninsula were to be private homes, in its private game reserve with the Big Five of African endangered wildlife running free, electric wildlife fences around individual homes. The rail track would go from Inhaca, parallel to the airstrip, take wildlife tourists hovercraft crossing to Inhaca S by rail to wildlife watching lodges via antique steam engine rail. There was an existing rail to a rock quarry on the W bank of the Maputo River. With a rail bridge there, Inhaca S rail would have an international connection. Lodge dwellers would do wildlife drives AM and PM (and night) from lodges by lodge guide driven 4x4 vehicles. There could be other international tourists that had day trips through the NP wildlife watching from trains only. It was an exquisite CPD-NP development plan.

(30) Rolling SAPPI, or it was now a battle of whom, our 914 Sq MI Elephant Coast NP or SAPPI's eucalyptus plantations got the portion of the Maputaland CPD S of the renovated-restocked MER (Maputo Elephant Reserve). SAPPI's was a losing battle with us having Mother Nature's or UN CPD blessing on our side. Their eucalyptus plantation would destroy the CPD world class quality botany. I was back in Maputo with President Chissano's report just in time for the first of SAPPI's to be six-months-of-public hearings for GoM to give a yea or nay to SAPPI's destructive to GOM's Maputaland CPD via SAPPI's-ecosystem-despoiling-water-sucking-eucalyptus-plantation scheme or us. With what we now knew it was actually SAPPI's UN-CPD-environmental-destruction plan! We got Pretoria University's Professor van Wyk to attend SAPPI's eucalyptus plantation public first then ongoing hearings in Maputo. SAPPI had not divulged to GoM the intervening UN CPD quality of SAPPI's many years earlier 99 year land lease concession. But van Wyk did in no uncertain terms to bring the roof down on SAPPI. He told all that had transpired at the UN Rio 1992 Earth Summit creating sites called CPDs. It was now out in print on the street in NOJim's GoM's London feasibility study to create daily negative news reports opposed to SAPPI as a CPD-ecosystem destroyer in MZB, JNB and world press. Especially in South Africa where the active-press-tree-hugger-environmentalists already hated SAPPI. This evolved to a year's end (1995) GoM ejection of SAPPI.

(31) GoM rescinded their several years' earlier SAPPI development concession for our much superior now MZB land use Elephant Coast UN-CPD-NP project which development was now GoM's much bigger bird in the hand. This made NOJim and his plan more of an environmental hero. Our 914 Sq MI Elephant Coast project fit to a T the UN mandated "native-and-unspoiled' Maputaland CPD criterion. Jim had promised to give MZB's president a gold surfaced copy of Jim's to GoM feasibility report in Oct 1995. But Jim was seriously ill. His 'monkey' or substance abuse was active. Jim had to dry out in London before his next, by then 6 month's overdue meeting with President Chissano put off to March 1996. NOJim had last been in MZB when I visited it with him in May of 1995 near a year earlier before a transition from GoM's 63 Sq MI to our now 914 Sq MI NP development project! But there was a sinister plot developing. That is a threat to the 914 Sq MI GoM ECNP development. NOJim's lawyer (NOL) had rewritten Jim's will in 1994 after Jim married Ukranian born Leisa his secretary on our North Pole trip in 1988. In the process scallywag NOL had made himself sole executor of Jim's estate. More importantly upon Jim's demise everything Jim owned went into a Trust with NOL as sole trustee. NOL it evolved was taking advantage of Jim's illness to sabotage Jim's Elephant Coast project. Why? He feared the MZB project would eat up Jim's estate. That NOL would be trustee of `nothing', robbed of NOL's otherwise life access to his montly trustee payment as NOJim's estate's trustee. So I allege NOL destroyed what was a world class GoM-UN-CPD-NP for his own self-serving Machiavellian greed. That's for NOL's distain for African wildlife, ignorance of a huge wildlife-botanical-CPD-NP. International humanititarian projnect. MZB and all the world suffered at the chicanery of NOL.

1973 Lake Manyara NP TNZ five `tall ones' that live there. That's along with three of 'Africa's Big five', lions, nice elephant herd, another of Cape buffalo. Get there at 6 AM (daylight) when the gate opens as by 8 AM when the `tourist' in zebra stripped VW buses show up after a leisurely breakfast Mother Nature's show is most over except for a squirrelly band of baboons absent in most NPs. Manyara is well worth one's camera in hand visit, bring plenty of film. In the dim background is Lake Manyara NP's west wall of the Great Rift Valley. Mother Nature's great gift, Lake Manyara, Ngorongoro Crater, Serengeti, Masai Mara all adjacent.

1968 Ngorongoro's Crater NP's 100 Sq Mi bottom, zebra-wildebeest drink, members of the well over a million that make the annual migration to Kenya's Masai Mara NP Kenya and back, losing significant members when they cross the Mara River Kenya border to lying in wait Nile crocodile twice, both going into and returning from Kenya, which is popular on wildlife TV as herbivores plunge into the Mara River, crocodile take their yearly share which is something to see. Crocks annually kill more native Africans than the big African five.

1973 Ngorongoro Crater NP up close to this lion, vehicle window open for picture. I was too close, he smelled human, and snarled. It was obviously time to move on or be charged with a lion claw in he open window.

1973 Serengeti NP TNZ. This cub it perched in a thorn bush tree limb. As a NP lion he does not show any fear of we gawking tourist. Wildlife in NPs are calmer. It's said that the vehicle exhaust kills human odor.

1973 Ngorongoro Crater NP this pair of lions is watching a tourist who's out of his vehicle ¼ mile away while ignoring us only yards away. The message is stay in your vehicle especially when near king of beasts lions

1973 Lake Manyara NP female lions climb acacia trees to midday nap to avoid flies. Males are too heavy. The gals get away from their bossy pride male who always eats his share first while the gals are the food hunters.

1968 Ngorongoro Crater NP a usually nocturnal hyena stirs out of its burrow. Wildebeest in the background across the water pond which hyena harass at night.

1968 a crested eagle on a snag on track to Wimbe hunt camp around W end of Ruaha River headwaters wetland and our S shore Cape buffalo herds haven.

1967 Mikumi NP TNZ this is the only wild African hunting dog I ever saw in Africa in years. They are carnivores that hunt in packs, run their prey down.

1965-1973 these thorn caused tire punctures galore. We saw no such thorn bush in MZB in the CPD terrain for one up for our Elephant Coast over East Africa.

1967 Masal Amboselli NP Kenya male in black and white, female ostrich in dull brown anxious for five chicks. Kilimanjaro is in close view S behind camera.

1973 Ngorongoro Crater NP (bottom 100 Sq Mi) a male waterbuck peaks from behind thorn bush. NP has a Noah's Arc of species, rhinos, lions, elephant, the lot.

1973 Lake Manyara NP Ma elephant nurses. How many folks know elephant nurse from up front (like humans) vs. most mammals nurse from their back loins. The little one can care less, says "just give me my milk."

1973 Lake Manyara NP where behind the `tall one' is the W wall of the Great Rift Valley. Behind the camera is the lake, the NP is the narrow N-S in between. NP is a cul-de-sac the way in is the only gateway back out.

(32) That was simply for narcissistic NOL's unfounded fear Jim with Bechtel and I et al would piss away NOJim's fortune on Jim's to NOL's point-of-view wild African dream. NOL could thus end up to be Trustee of an empty Jim's Trust, NOL's fear. This was an egregious self-serving NOL conflict of interest. NOL was now acting simultaneously as Jim's now know-nothing-absentee MZB project PM (hating the African development) while simultaneously as Jim's project saboteur to draw a big fee for his chicanery. NOJim was so out of it in late 95, early 96 that NOL cooked up that we (Bechtel and I) were trying to steal Jim's now 914 Sq Mi created-GoM-MZB-CPD-NP project we'd procured for Jim. So team Bechtel plus Marco and I et al the positive pro-project people were dispensed with essentially by NOL plus now mentally out of it Jim, by NOL bamboozling Jim. That's Bechtel and I (et al) unceremoniously run off in March 1996. That's after GoM's ejection of SAPPI's CPD destroying eucalyptus plantation assured Jim would get his UN CPD safeguarding 914 Sq Mi MZB creating wildlife-botanical CPD-NP concession. But NOJim only got his official 99 year create-operate lease concession from GoM's bureaucracy in Oct 1996. GoM didn't have a clue as to NOL's extreme chicanery that killed their world class project, left the UN CPD to be unprotected thus despoiled. The CPD-NP 4000 Sq Mi should still be created via new for GoM study.

(33) Things took that long in MZB for the Council of Ministers to vote etc. Jim groused he'd spent $1 million (only) to get his concession thru Bechtel and my March 1996 exit from MZB after 10 months to get Jim's order of magnitude now $800 million budget CPD-NP 914 Sq Mi GoM development concession upgraded from his 63 Sq Mi original Peninsula only GoM offer. NOJim's 99 year development, operate lease award decree allowed him 2 ½ years to perform. Jim's `NoGo' NOL took over as absentee PM of NOJim's-hated-by NOL Africa project to fake it. The development now became a bait-then-switch-rip-off of GoM by NOL doing nothing as promised in NOJim's winning London feasibility study to President Chissano. Scoundrel NOL had completely changed the Developer's 'terms and conditions' of the development from what was featured in our feasibility study the basis of GoM's concession approval or NOJim's lawyer NOL's Machiavellian development sabotage of our world class project.

(34) Jim died on 20 Mar 1999 at age 55 just at the end of NOJim's contractual `complete development' in 2 ½-year-concession allowance as NOL faked it while doing nothing of what was promised to GoM and the supportive international greens. Naïve to such a project rip off GoM failed to blow the whistle on NO's or NOL's project nonperformance for months on months. That's Developer not adhering to the London `Brown Bible' development plan at all. That is obviously it was now a NOL bait-and-switch-rip-off of GoM by NOL in NOJim's 'mental' monkey-on-his-back absence, then demise. Then eventually GoM was so embarrassed at NO's failure to perform on their President's pet-MZB-economic-life-saver project that rather than immediately rescinding Jim's 99 year lease at two and half years (April 1999) with Jim dead GoM stalled to only rescinded now NOL's (Jim's estate's) concession later in the fall of 1999. That is until after MZB's national elections in which Chissano won reelection.

(35) This was so President Chissano avoided the project failure's embarrassment to thus win reelection first without bad press. But the awarded 99 year land development lease concession was now severely flawed. NOL took over in the fall of 1995 when we had been working in the field (Africa) on the MZB land concession terms and conditions. Jim had agreed with me to make the bush residents within his concession preferred stock holders. This was unheard of in Africa bush residents to have their preferred stock income divvies to be out of NOJim's development funds budget not GOM's 10 % common share interest and ownership. That is not cash from the GoM's divvy as 10% shareholder partners as if landowners. Jim thus took the barefoot bush people in as friends of the project, the former wildlife's enemies by giving them first crack at employment. The NP development was to give them water, sanitation, schools, medical facilities against high infant mortality, malaria, HIV-AIDS as if they were land owners-cum-now-preferred shareholders. With the post 1975 independence from Portugal Marxism there was no more private land ownership in MZB. But Jim's resident natives would be the first to get preferred shareholder dividends, even if they were very small in early years but greater than 1ˢᵗ common share dividends.

(36) GoM's euphemism we had to use in our (their) feasibility study was to refer to the region's starving, unattended resident bush people as *"traditional land dwellers."* This was our preferred share holder scheme agreed by NOJim in the concession's London published version of 'terms and conditions' signed by Jim. NOL ran us off (Bechtel et al) having completely changed the legal terms and condition from or as stated in the concession for GoM feasibility document. After NOJim's death, before GoM cancelling his 99 year lease development concession, NOL tried to sell NOJim's concession before it was belatedly rescinded but the 99 year concession was a "bait then

switched" travesty version of our Brown-Bible feasibility study. It was manna from heaven for the 'traditional land dwellers' but now no more or NOL would essentially have evicted them vs. taking them in as employed partners. Their traditional enemy, wildlife was now to be their savior in a cash-cow-wildlife-CPD-NP scheme where they got their fair share divvy guaranteed by Jim or upgraded from Stone-Age starvation to for them well off MBZ citizens. NOL unilaterally changed the terms and conditions via his conflict of interest sabotage for his self-interest, chicanery, took all these benefits away from the bush folks, made them unwelcome in their own homelands vs. what the official London feasibility had established, NOJim agreed to, what was approved by the GoM Ministers.

(37) In 1975 at MZB's independence from Portugal most white Portuguese left with only the clothes on their backs with their property nationalized. One of them was a Portuguese MZB bush family doctor. His daughter born in 1938 in Lorenzo Marques was by 1975 (MZB's independence) out of country where she had earlier met then married (Feb 1966) American billionaire Pennsylvania US Senator H John Heinz III of Heinz (catsup) company. Heinz was killed in an air crash (1991). Heinz's wife Maria Teresa Simoes Ferreira Heinz later then married Democratic US Senator John Kerry in May 1995 four years on but kept as her legal sir name Heinz as her three son's sir names. She's a known philanthropist who was in the mix of those active in a possible resurrected MZB Elephant Coast NP, 914 Sq MI concession with others as Ted Turner, Peace Parks creator (along with his cofounder Nelson Mandela) billionaire Anton Rupert et al. But NOL had intentionally cocked up MZB's 99 year land lease concession legal terms and conditions so for anyone else to step in to resurrect the NP creating project our London feasibility study's development plan was A-Okay but NOL's lousy abridged terms and condition had departed drastically from what was planned in the London feasibility study document thus approved by GoM.

(38) The land concession terms and conditions would have to be completely renegotiated or the now left out traditional land dwellers would have to be evicted or would revolt with plenty of guns. NOJim's 99 year GoM concession award was based on Jim's Brown Bible London feasibility study but was being ignored, the books cooked by NOL or the 914 Sq MI concession terms and conditions so self-serving Machiavellian NOL's greed destroyed a near billion dollar MZB NP development opportunity, MZB, the world having a NP of the Maputaland CPD as UN mandated for CDPs. There's the old adage "It takes one to call one." The saboteur or stealer of the project was malicious conflict-of-interest NOL, not Bechtel or I et al. He killed our fits-like-a-glove development plans to protect the Maputaland CPD-NP as UN mandated. That's via a cash cow GNP augmenting development-operate MZB 914 Sq MI CPD-NP. After Jim died NOL then tried for months to sell GoM's concession before GoM's delayed for fall election rescinding it for NOL's failure to perform. GoM should have rescinded NOJim's concession when NOL did nothing in the early few months of late 1996 or early 1997. That is vs. three years later in 1999 well after Jim's death. NOL then claimed New Orleans's project cost to date (1999) was now $5 million. How was this?

(39) That's 80% of NOJim's cash flow out accrued since the Bechtel team, Marco and I had been dispensed of in the spring of 1996. That is 80% of the New Orleans project cost (1999) was to cover NOL's smoke screening daily bait-then-switch chicanery plus his dip into Jim's Trust to pay himself a conflict-of-interest-monthly sabotage fee as Trustee or managing NOJim's estate. There was plenty of interest to resurrect-the-project money as above based on the project feasibility study but not on NOL's evil criminally abridged terms and conditions. There was a second fly in the ointment. Besides project saboteur Jim's NOL's chicanery there was Canadian Maurice Strong who had been the UN Secretary General of the 1992 Rio Earth summit over strong objections of US President Bush the elder. Strong was then high up in the UN's hierarchy. But he was a one-world-government type, Marxist leaning socialistic running mate of billionaire Hungarian born George Soros. Strong was not prepared to put in any money but was pushy. He scared interested money away as did NOL with his cooked MZB concession terms and conditions. Strong plus NOL contributed greatly to scaring off real investor's money. So via NOL or direct with GoM all failed to resurrect the 914 Sq MI development. But eventually GoM refused to meet with I'm-in-charge M. Strong, parceled out spoils of the 914 Sq MI CPD-NP project to MZB's self-serving politicians if anybody.

(40) Our project's story I knew, now followed in hope to assist any new 'real' developer with our 914 Sq MI plan and terms and conditions. "It takes one to call one" describes Machiavellian NOL's project theft accusations activities vs. Bechtel, et al of what he was doing to sabotage our world class project. If was self-serving NOL who stole, destroyed the 914 Sq MI MZB Elephant Coast CPD-NP project being built per the GoM approved 1995 London plan. Bechtel et al could have found investors for NOJim but they were run off by NOL in early 1996. If Bechtel and I et al

would have still been on board when NOJim got his concession in Oct 1996 we would have recruited sovereign country wealth funds or Disney that would have put up most of the first phase development money for equity positions. Jim would have been reduced to less than a majority interest but on an as built 914 Sq Mi cash cow near billion-dollar-order-of-magnitude MZBECNP development that would have materially increased his net worth, international legacy vs. losing all he had invested in MZB and any legacy family name bragging rights.

(41) Thanks to NOL Jim lost his established positive 99 year GoM lease on the CDP-NP development to an eventual failed negative legacy. We others would then have had a phase two international auction to sublease the individual wildlife watching concession to a wildlife watching tourist industry with the antique steam rail in , the region restocked with African wildlife to preserve the heart of MZB's Maputaland CPD "native and unspoiled" as UN mandated. But hell is now `repaved' with all our good intentions. Unfortunately America has an oversupply of self-serving Machiavellian characters like NOJim's NOL. NOL's greed driven chicanery lost it all, NOJim's concession, NOL's now Jim's trust's MZB $5 million mostly spent on NOL's mismanaging, sabotaging Jim's CPD-NP development. Later there were other positive regional developments. Peace Parks (Anton Rupert with Nelson Mandela et al) in 2002 got South Africa, Zimbabwe to agree with MZB to create the GLTP to create a mirror image NP in MZB of South Africa's Kruger NP, Zimbabwe's Gonarezhou NP both already long existing to MZB's W.

(42) This was to then eventually take down international border fences to have the world's largest no-internal-fence wildlife refuge of 38,500 Sq Mi in three countries. That's NE corner of South Africa, SE corner of Zimbabwe, mirror imaged E in MZB's adjacent SW border area to create the Grand Limpopo TransFrontier Park (GLTP) three nation's international Wildlife Park (IWP) a new world paradigm with all internal (national border) fences removed to let wildlife go where the seasons, mating took them like in the huge annual Serengeti migrations in TNZ and Kenya. In 1995 when we first enlarged our Elephant Coast to 914 Sq Mi no one involved (nor GoM) knew the whole region was a UN CPD. Marco and I were chastised by Professor van Wyk for not making it bigger. That's both sides of the major Maputo River. That's the river as the limiting W border of our 914 Sq Mi GoM awarded 1996 concession. Everything W of the Maputo River to Swaziland border was also UN CPD designated so why wasn't van Wyk correct? He certainly was. But of the 914 Sq Mi version back then (1996) we also didn't know the three nations Grand Limpopo TransFrontier Park was coming down the pike in 2002 (then six years later).

(43) Or that in 2005 in South Africa wildlife tourism would replace gold bullion as their top GDP earner. That a resurrected 914 Sq Mi EC NP to a 4000 Sq Mi NP (all UN CPD) could save 5000 to-be-killed Kruger NP elephants (cows and calves). The global wildlife watching craze was now on as a major GNP contributor in African countries with idle land (or CPD) to dedicate to being an international wildlife-watching destination as times changed. This is sad history of an `almost' CPD NP expanding N to connect to the later (2002-3) GLTP. Our 914 Sq Mi would have been built out by then (about when it was taken from NOJim's estate) after he died in 1999. The GLTP was coming in 2002. Increasing our NP (CPD) to 4000 Sq Mi to connect up to the GLTP would be a natural next step with wildlife watching industry's boom, GoM option. That's a by then even better proven GoM choice. It still could (should) be so dedicated as a UN CPD plus the international wildlife watching paradigm is now more economically apparent and it's anti-poaching stops haven needed. That's to save that much of the Maputaland CPD still intact.

(44) That's the TIME is still now to make a resurrected wildlife watching EC-CPD NP even more meritorious in saving the Maputaland CPD, African endangered wildlife and finally uplifting the "traditional land dwellers" therein. Real estate's mantra is the three important property virtues are "location, location *and location."* Our MZB Elephant Coast's NP location is the UN designated Indian Ocean Coast CPD and more! The southern African region via JNB was by 2000 on now replacing Nairobi as the No 1 world-wildlife-watching-tourist destination. Looking at the map the light comes on. Expand our 914 Sq Mi awarded GoM 1996 concession to W of the Maputo River to the Swaziland border, N to link up with the GLTP to the N as it was all in UN CPD mandated to be guarded "native and unspoiled for future generations" territory to be protected as UN mandated via the Rio 1992 Earth Summit created CPD paradigm. Thus resurrect our Elephant Coast 914 Sq Mi scope enlarged to a circa 4000 Sq Mi CPD-NP development to join up with the huge GLTP to the N. Where in this world is there a better such opportunity. The only one with like merits is the all Kalahari W in Botswana (Cpt 2) but both should be developed for a laundry list of world class reasons, like to add these two large regions vs. the current elephant and rhino POACNING. Only wit development as a CPD-NP will there be 24 hour anti-poaching money and (guns) protection. .

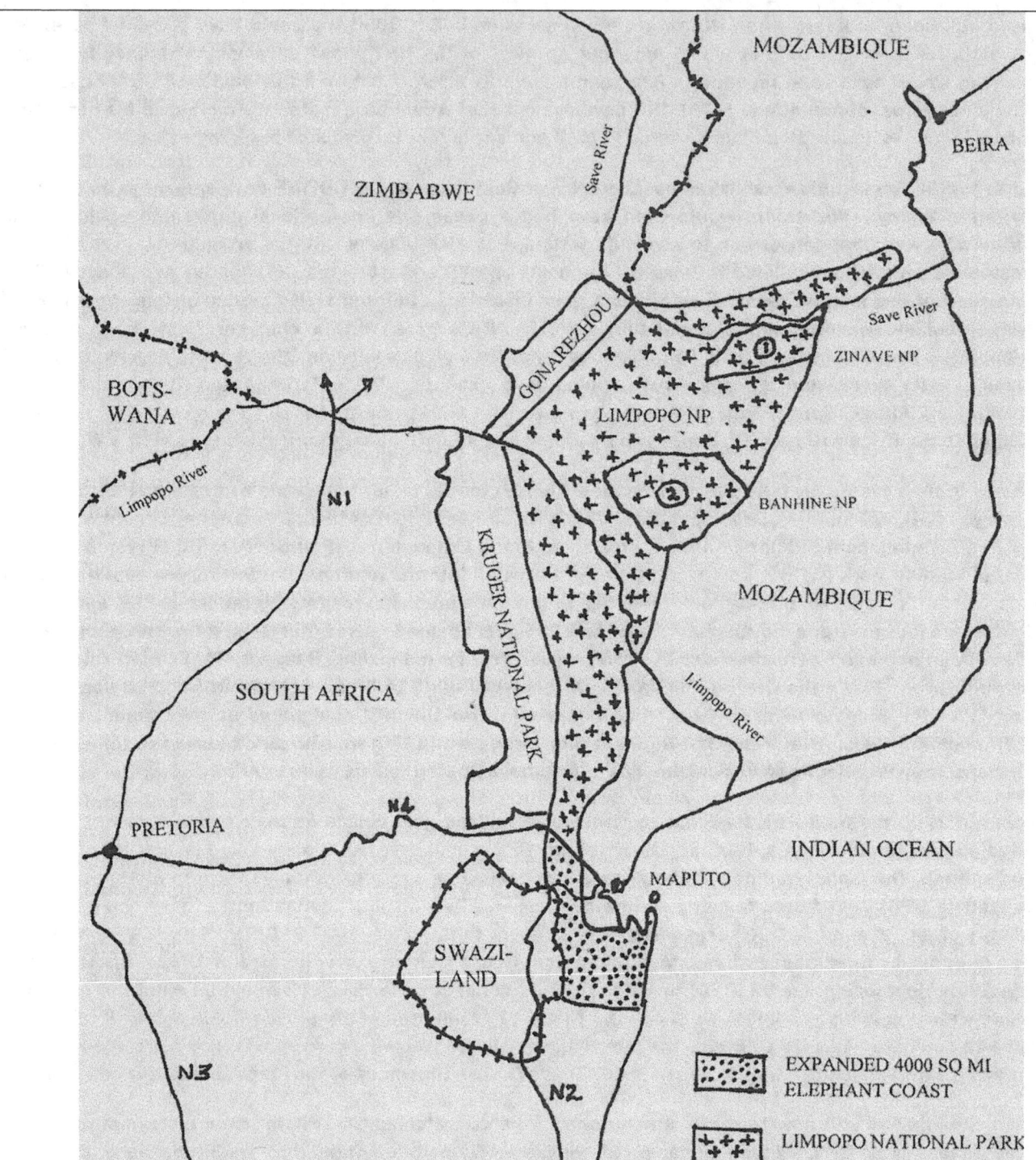

2007 this map was after NOJim had lost his 914 Sq MI project, but the huge Grand Limpopo TransFrontier Park (GLTP) three country wildlife `international' sanctuary of 38,500 Sq MI (world's largest such wildlife sanctuary) had evolved to the N in circa 2002-3. It was the handiwork of Peace Parks of SA, proposed by breweries billionaire Dr Anton Rupert and his founding co partners Nelson Mandela and the Netherlands Crown Prince. My pitch was then to resurrect our 914 Sq MI version expanded to 4000 Sq MI to link up with the now GLTP at 38,500 Sq MI and find a new `for real' developer to replace defunct now dead NOJim. But unfortunately anti-Africa NOL had sabatoged the terms and conditions for our 914 Sq MI version so though that version had a feasibility study accepted by GoM it didn't have the real developer to step in to do a feasibility study for the four times larger 4000 Sq MI to be resurrected CPD-NP `now'. There were interested parties with the money heft but they were put off by the combination of mess, confusion, local GoM politics so nothing positive ever evolved to do it.

(45) My now advice to MZB is don't look a UN CPD gift horse in the mouth. Resurrect your CPD-NP to 4000 Sq Mi, connecting up with the GLTP to the N. Our 1995 Bechtel London feasibility study is still valid with minor alterations. That is all the now 4000 Sq Mi ECNP expanded as UN CPD saving of wildlife, botanical MZB Elephant Coast CPD-NP! That is that much more (4000 Sq Mi) of the UN Maputaland CPD saved, protected "native and unspoiled for future generations" as UN mandated. That seemed the right (divine intervention) Mother Nature's common sensible thing to do plus made real world economic sense with the established, rapidly expanding southern Africa international-wildlife-watching-tourist-boom or craze. That's as a MZB cash cow GDP enhancer. nt Coast development. In 2006 I started to write my Nick-Nobody-From-Nowhere's how to save MZB's Elephant Coast (SMEC) 2007 book. I created an accompanying 501 (c) (3) net site www.savemec.org as a real effort to right my wrongs of being too timid in not doing more back in 1995 W of the Maputo River per Prof van Wyk's gripe or critique. My 2007 book's theme was MZB (entire world) was in love with our 914 Sq Mi MZB Wildlife-Botanical CPD-NP plan. Now with seven years of enhanced regional merit in improved wildlife-watching destination boom, a chance to marry up with the three country GLTP N, save UN-CPD-NP all the 4000 Sq Mi way.

(46) This was MZB's by far best economic, environmental land use choice option, LOCATION wise to create a new international-wildlife-watching destination. Do it right now belatedly by incorporating current positive regional, political, economic changes since the 914 Sq Mi version fell in a 1996-99 New Orleans crack. Enlarge our GoM original 63 Sq Mi development to its now-makes-more-sense-4000-Sq-Mi NP to connect up with the world class Grand Limpopo TransFrontier Park (GLTP) to the N. In between it was all UN CPD territory in need of safeguarding. Meanwhile in SA they were then about to kill 5000 Kruger NP elephants accused of over grazing. That's BS see Cpt 5 herein. Those sentenced to death elephants could find a home (live) in a resurrected, enlarged 4000 Sq Mi MZB Elephant Coast NP development. That's also to replace the 500 Cuban Army target practice elephants killed from helicopter post 1975 MZB independence. I tried to get billionaire boss Steve Bechtel Jr interested or Bill Gates-Warren Buffett as then two top billionaires in the world between them with the world's biggest combined charity. I applied to the Gates's Foundation for just seed money to find other heavy hitter investors. That's as the oil rich Middle East sovereign wealth country funds. But being Nick Nobody From Nowhere (NNFN) with limited funding I've failed to date. The time was right in 1996 on to develop it when it was still `native and unspoiled".

(47) When NOL lost the 914 Sq Mi concession in late 1999 then GoB which has its share of crony corruption led to GoM giving out private bureaucratic concessions in the CPD S on the Indian Ocean Coast (914 Sq Mi). That is to individuals to build remote private homes on the previously pristine CPD designated 50 Mi Indian Ocean coast as a first step in despoiling the "native and unspoiled for future generations" previously sleeper CPD region. When we (NOJim) first step persevered, created the 914 Sq Mi concept as GoM approved for a CPD-NP development in 1996 with no original knowledge of its being a UN CPD , then my spending 10 months on the MZB site (1995-6) plus ensuing developments I strongly believe in the top drawer international merit of our project economically, environmentally to save the now known UN Maputaland CPD from despoliation, righting MZB's then war torn economy-cum-improved GDP. That's to save the Maputaland CPD, endangered African wildlife-wise, and uplifting-the `traditional land dwellers' lives. A wildlife-botanical CPD-NP was the best land use for this UN CPD location for economically struggling post 28 years of civil wars MZB. I dreamed, I prayed that someone would want to take advantage of this world class `charitable' investment development `green' cause special UN CPD opportunity.

(48) That's our creator's earthly foreman Mother Nature offered opportunity to assure tsome developer's name, living legacy into future generations via their being financial risk `charitable' seed money investors for a critical path updated feasibility study construction plan for a resurrected 1996 (914 Sq Mi CPD-NP) prected to a now 4000 Sq Mi MZB Elephant Coast CPD-NP that challenges East Africa's Serengeti with our `triple threat' (a) Indian Ocean coast, (b) CPD botanical pedigree and (c) being linked to the `world's biggest' GLTP @ 38,500 Sq Mi yet. That's Serengeti-Masai Mara NPs to the N hosting its annual wildebeest-zebra migration into and back out of Kenya N of crocodile trap Mara River with crocks taking their annual crossing toll in migrating wildlife, a Serengeti with Lake Manyara NP, Ngorongoro Crater NP on its SE flank. What's chances of resurrecting the 4000 Sq Mi Elephant Coast connection to the NOW GLTP? In save it "native and unspoiled for feature generations" mantra re our sound reasons. But with the human values (African politics) the hurdles are significant. Let's all add our voices, votes for a resurrected 4000 Sq Mi UN CPD-NP in MZB as concrete aid vs Africa's current ivory, rhino horn poaching.

1971 S Wimbe TNZ common black vulture swoop in, maribou storks prance about (background) to await there better mannered turn as nature's morticians.

1968 Ngorongoro Crater NP a night shift hyena has a look about. Wildebeest in the background. Hyena in large numbers will drive carnivores off their kills.

1973 Lake Manyara NP this Ma cow elephant is testing the wind with her trunk up as a warning sign she could charge if she gets that human smell (usually killed by vehicle exhaust). Wind is everything with wildlife. My experience cows are a lot more apt to charge all the way vs. bulls who shriek, flap their ears, but usually then back off and leave. Calf protecting cows are more dangerous than most bulls. With elephants the females are the `protect-their-young' fighters. Stay in your vehicle. Only very rarely do big elephants attack vehicles.

1973 Lake Manyara NP a little guy is well protected. In Chobe NP in Botswana there are large herds of elephant. There some lion prides live off small elephant, but this is unusual. Big sized elephants are more than most lions will tackle. Lion sometimes live off a Cape buffalo herd, but have to pick their targets, the very young, the very old or the wounded. So it is thus that lions are now called Africa's `king of beast' which only rarely kill elephant.

1983 Kruger NP South Africa, two male greater kudu which are not seen in East African NPs, some few outside parks in TNZ only, unknown in Kenya. Sable and roan antelope have the same East Africa poor distribution, but all three, that's greater kudu, sable and roan antelope are plentiful further south as in Kruger NP. These three larger antelope are the choice three trophy animals (photography targets). The fact that they are plentiful in southern Africa, non existent in East African parks is another 'one up' for a resurrected 4000 Sq Mi connected to GLTP for the S vs. the Serengeti et al N in East Africa. In hunting days I collected three in TNZ but not seen in their NPs.

1968 Wimbe hunting camp TNZ we were here for a month. Seven maribou stork installed themselves with us night and day for scraps vs. competing with bad mannered aggressive black vultures for bush carcasses.

1983 Kruger NP South Africa. This spectacular starling pitched up to kibitz our camp out barbecue meal from its tree perch a welcome friendly visitor for us to chat with.   Kruger's overnight camps are protected by locked wildlife fences vs. carnivores (as lions-hyenas).

1971 S Wimbe TNZ the common black vulture cover a carcass squabbling for their share. One maribou stork (or vulture) prances (L) avoiding the feeding frenzy.

1968 S Wimbe TNZ a feeding frenzy of black vultures while the maribou storks (vultures) distain from joining the black vultures undisciplined unruly main mob.

1965 Serengeti NP TNZ a cheetah has run down a Thompson gazelle meal, awaits her cubs to all dine together. In an enlarged W Kalahari Sands NP, an electric fence (solar generators) is advisable to protect large expanses, and keep such as the African wild hunting dog packs and lions from attacking cattle outside the NP regions or beef entering wildlife's zone.

1973 Serengeti NP 's seronara River in my several visits there 1965 thru 1973 I was always able to get a daylight photo of a leopard up a tree. That was true no where else. To see leopords elsewhere didn't happen for me. A golden spotted leopard in sun light is a memorable sight that I missed until I toppled to this Serengeti NP's Seronera River leopard's haven.

1971 S Wimbe TNZ a nine egg ostrich nest in a surprisingly wide open exposed area with carnivores.

1968 Masal Steppe a `too old' elephant sign to track but indicates that we are yes in elephant habitat.

(49) As maybe mentioned elsewhere NOJim's (plus me et al) cost of the 10 months to London feasibility study era to procure the GoB 99-year-develop-operate-lease concession for our proposed 914 Sq MI CPD-NP (with discovery that it was a CPD) was ONLY one million dollars to produce a near $800 million construction-outfit budget cash cow development option!   That's for example two billionaires (USA Bill Gates, Saudi's Al Waleed) already in the tourist or hotel business a big part of wildlife watching developments. Saudi Arabia's Al Waleed had also already bought into South Africa's Sun City the South African Las Vegas. He reportedly was looking for addition regional wildlife tourism investments with Indian Ocean frontage. Like if this had been known would he have been in for a new feasibility study to resurrect the 914 Sq MI version to 4000 Sq MI of the Elephant Coast CPD-NP? He would only have taken one such investor. The problem an opportunity like MZB is so unexpected how do you get the word out to such as Gates or Al Waleed? I did my 2007 Elephant Coast book to alert the world of this then unbelievable world-class opportunity. (see book SAVE MOZAMBIQUE'S ELEPHANT COAST (2007) and project details net site at www.savemec.org an IRS 501 (c) (3) site not for profit book green (Amazon)cause internet site.

(50) That's a good green-cause-cash-cow-UN-CPD-saving development, a book dealing with "does it not make sense?" That is with the nitty-gritty of "how to do it?" My Elephant Coast book updated the 914 Sq MI-cum-4000 Sq MI financial projections. NOJim had the Elephant Coast 99 year lease concession in hand or awarded for about $1 million only. NOL then pissed away another $4 million smoke screening, bait-then-switching while not performing contractually to keep NOJim's concession. NOL was three years doing nothing until NOJim's concession was rescinded by GoM well after NOJim's death. I estimate for well inside $10 million seed money from say Bill Gates GoM could be persuaded to resurrect (our) MZBECNP 1996 build out plan. Get the likes of an updated Bechtel-WATG Elephant Coast (EC) feasibility study enlarged to 4000 Sq MI to connect N to the GLTP (2002). That's to resurrect the 914 Sq MI plan enlarged to 4000 Sq MI to connect up N to the GLTP.

(51) Those Bechtel pros run off in early 1996 (by NOL), their international clout (like George Schultz) would find investors like sovereign wealth funds or Middle East oil countries like Saudi, Kuwait, UAE's Abu Dhabi, Dubai, Oman and Qatar, et al or Disney or equal to fund a new feasibility study, the game opener. There were others like private investor Saudi Prince Al Waleed or Bill Gates together with Al Waleed. Those two business associates together bought into 95% of Four Seasons hotels to take it private for $3.8 billion in 2007. The MZB-ECNP project was a much more exciting total "with Indian Ocean frontage" land development. What could be better than the 4000 Sq MI MZBECNP to protect the UN Maputaland CPD? Al Waleed was a big investor in Disneyland France. The cash-cow-charitable SMEC development at 4000 Sq MI fits most all required criterions. That is for like $200 million Phase One development of across the water from Maputo, then antique steam train rail to get to the S lodges. Plus wildlife management facilities and staffing, restocking with endangered African wildlife etc.

(52) Then London pros or equal would organize, proceed with a well-publicized international auctions after 18 months with restocked wildlife in place, transport infrastructure to get the tourist in plus garbage out functional. Each wildlife watching tourist lodge's auction would be won by a highest-qualified bidder. That's for individual-tourist-wildlife-watching-GoM-sub-lease-wildlife-watching concessions. That is a la Phinda in KwaZulu Natal or W of Kruger operations like Singida, Mala Mala, Londlozi et al who in 1995 already charged $600 per night per person or S1200 per night double occupancy while being fully booked up to a year ahead. The projections indicated hefty cash cow returns for the MZB Elephant Coast NP land owner's GoM, their sovereign wealth funds investor shareholders or whoever. That's also to the individual-tourist-concession-entrepreneur-investor operators for a win-win for everybody including the suffering *traditional land dwellers* now with jobs, food, water, housing, schools, medical facilities, the whole lot, call it a decent survival. That's including the land owning GoM bureaucracy as a significant GDP contributor as MZB comes back from its independence days `two' civil wars.

(53) While also their previously forgotten MZB `traditional land dwellers' or our project preferred shareholders while also the whole world for a saved "native-and-unspoiled UN-CPD-NP for future generations." But not to forget a new home for dispossessed endangered African Wildlife like 5000 otherwise sentenced-to-death-too-many-Kruger-NP elephants. Or say it another way. There is Dubai (UAE) where billions are being spent on dredging to create offshore real estate. Then they add glitzy steel, glass, concrete, plastic improvements for their tourist draw skyscrapers to create their idea of the world's number one tourist destination out of camel pasture and Persian Gulf sea frontage. By comparison Mother Nature who created the CPDs, has an African Noah's Ark of endangered

African wildlife to be restocked thus enjoyed as an international tourist destination. There are different strokes or interests for different folks. But in a competitive sell situation the MZB Elephant Coast NP at 914 Sq Mi or more so now at its 4000 Sq Mi resurrected, enlarged version beats Dubai as infinitely better Mother Nature's quality tourist draw all for unbelievably less investment to produce a real self-sustaining GoM et al cash cow enhanced GDP multi wins world class international CPD-NP-wildlife-botanical destination to draw international folks.

(54) A win for (1) poor traditional land dwellers, (2) win for war torn MZB's GDP, (3) win by safeguarding the UN Maputaland CPD for future generations, (4) win by saving endangered African wildlife, (5) win by saving a choice Mother Nature's site good for mankind. I can't help but think that somewhere there is a billionaire trying to find a unique, worthy, charitable someplace for his billions to create a living long term legacy in a charitable giving-cum-green creating undertaking. If this isn't it in MZB what is? I'd love to help bring it to fruition in the Program Manager or key advisor capacity. That is having worked key man on our winning MZB Elephant Coast feasibility study, just a pipeliner I now have a fair knowledge of African wildlife, international tourism, the latest in Mala Mala et al lodge wildlife-watching paradigms. But my heart is in the Elephant Coast NP concept to be adopted, then completed. I would like to see Peace Parks (or equal et al) take this MZB Elephant Coast jewel on to increase their winning record of improved wildlife sanctuaries left "native and unspoiled for future generations" God willing. What are great differences of this now 4000 Sq Mi enlarged vs. awarded 914 Sq Mi 1996 heart of the project NP?

(55) Like (a) it already has a Bechtel London (1995) feasibility study award for its heart, (914 Sq Mi) across Inhaca easement (deep water access) S via Machangulo Peninsula, it then resurrects 273 Sq Mi (1932) Cuban shot out MER. Then (b) that expanded to 4000 Sq Mi to connect up to the 38,500 Sq Mi Grand Limpopo TransFrontier Park of Kruger NP in NE South Africa, Gonarezhou NP in SE Zimbabwe, and their mirror images W in MZB is all UN mandated to be guarded "native and unspoiled for future generations." As Maputaland CPD. (c) LOCATION a CPD-cum-NP in the international wildlife watching center in South Africa via Johannesburg (JNB) international airport as East Africa (Nairobi) gives up the top wildlife-watching destination to southern Africa. (d) South Africa has in recent years created new NPs and has the where with all of moving wildlife to restock new wildlife watching NPs like 200 Sq Mi Pilansberg NP N of South Africa's Sun City (Africa's Las Vegas) a wildlife watching destination was created virtually overnight pre our 1995 MZB study, (e) South Africa is the place where the paradigm of wildlife watching lodges like Mala Mala, Singida, Londilozi, and Phinda was born, their new ideas to be used in MZB developments, and (f) those Lodges owners prospective bidders and operators of all important wildlife watching lodges of wildlife watching DESTINATIONS. (g) The 4000 Sq Mi Elephant Coast NP would be the first major African NP with Indian Ocean frontage except shot out MER, a positive unique distinction.

(56) In Portuguese days before MZB independence from a European state (Portugal) now MZB capital Maputo (then Lorenzo Marques) was the `place to go on vacation' in southern Africa. It is now coming back from its double-barreled-before- and- fter-independence civil wars. That's 1st for independence from Portugal, then post-independence Cold War Marxist vs. the Free World West. Those old LM days are now but a `lingering memory'. But Maputo could have a glorious rebirth as an international wildlife watching DESTINATION with a 4000 Sq. Mi Elephant Coast CPD-Wildlife NP at its W door. With the GLTP nearby plus the 4000 Sq Mi Elephant Coast surrounding Maputo to the N, S, E and W. It has evolved in the recent past decades that Johannesburg (international airport) has replaced Nairobi (East Africa) as the wildlife watching destination. Or to say Maputo in MZB is in a good wildlife watching regional LOCATION. What are the chances of resurrecting the 4000 Sq Mi version of MZB's Elephant Coast CPD NP? It is now a matter of black MZB politics their having been once jilted by NOJim (or actually by Machiavellian NOL) being baited then switched to no development on the original 914 Sq Mi Elephant Coast NP development. To resurrect it to 4000 Sq Mi connected to the GLTP GoM would need a new feasibility study (Bechtel London or equal) , a believable (real) developer to assure build out, no more NOL chicanery, thanks. The fact the 4000 Sq Mi Maputaland CPD is UN mandated to be kept "native and unspoiled for future generations" means a lot. Someone should help MZB reconsider and do it now or NEVER. The pyramids and the Great Chinese Wall are forever. That's MZB's EC's `green' cause development opportunity should be also.

(57) NPs are forever, protecting their limits. Somebody has to have foresight to see such as the Elephant Coast CPD is converted to a 4000 Sq Mi CPD-NP now (if not already too late) before it is in fact too late. It was discovered in 1995 to be a UN 1992 Earth Summit's Maputaland CPD, including the shot out Maputo Elephant

Reserve (MER). With such qualifications, a new generation in MZB, efforts to resurrect it at 4000 Sq MI should be tried, probably some outsider selling the idea via an international bankable feasibility study to prove this is the very best competitive land use to protect it as a cash cow-cum-GoM GDP economical enhancer as a wildlife watching CPD-NP destination. It's hello Peace Parks. That's anybody with idea   s, somebody who will `invest'  in  a charitable `living legacy' into the far FUTURE (forever) if there is such a thing (like back to the age of the dinosaurs).

58) So for me envision a billionaire who wants to leave an enduring long term living legacy. He or she who can buy shares in Dubai but who is already a billionaires or can invest in the resurrection of MZBs 4000 Sq MI version of the MZB Elephant Coast NP creation and development which NOJim once had but NOL and he blew it. Look down the road, 100 or 1000 years, what would be better as a living legacy than the development in MZB or shares in Dubai? Or in a 'what's each worth' competitive sell situation the MZB Elephant Coast NP at 914 Sq MI or more so at 4000 Sq MI would beat Dubai as infinitely better Mother Nature's quality living-legacy-charitable fare for unbelievably less investment to produce a real self-sustaining cash cow for GoM while saving endangered African wildlife and CPD, the starving MZB 'traditional land dwellers'. Give them a life, drinking water, food, schools, medical assistance, work, homes, a life. Or wildlife-watching destination option would support higher overnight bed tariffs plus higher occupancies, thus higher return on investment for GoM, their international development partners in the mix, the much improved lives of GoM's 'traditional land dwellers' (that is real world charity).

(59) But that's the test as a living legacy 100 or more years out? National Parks (NPs) live on especially ones with endangered African wildlife like Serengeti or Kruger. Has a world NP once dedicated, in operation been closed and converted back into an asphalt jungle? It can happen in war, otherwise never happens. Look at it (funding CPD-NP) as charitable giving but for the MZB 99 year lease period it would be a developer's cash cow returning investment then charitable NP gift into decades-cum-century's future in a MZB created CPD saving NP guarded "native and unspoiled for future generations." This resurrected NP creating project needs a tree hugging billionaire. That's who wants to leave a real LIVING LEGACY into a forever future. I throw my hat into the ring as a Program Manager (or key man) candidate to see it built out, then to be buried in the shade of an African baobab tree therein. A (my)final project built, "a-ead of schedule and under budget." That would be my lowly claim. That's my since some 20 years ago MZB Elephant-Coast-NP saga dream. This Elephant Coast saga's history can all be found in greater detail at my IRS 501 (c) (3) internet site www.savemec.org or in my book SAVE MOZAMBIQUE'S ELEPHANT COAST, Recreating Mother Nature's Wildlife Wonderland Africa (2007) available from book sellers Amazon or Barnes and Noble et al. Let's still try to resurrect it to save the huge Mother Nature's Maputaland CPD for future generations as UN mandated via the Rio 1992 Earth Summit, God willing.

(60) Here's a PS of what could have happened to the Elephant Coast NP development project hurdle to resurrect the 914 Sq MI version to a more total CPD saving 4000 Sq MI version with all its international, continental, and national merits. What if Bill Gates, Peace Parks Anton Rupert or individuals of that ilk had come and we alerted them and GoM's Chissano of NOL's Machiavellian story. GoM could have rescinded NOJims estate or better three years earlier when it was apparent NOL was guilty of planned nonperformance. My published book was then already too late in 2007 was that warning, but after GLTP came on the scene in 2002 or wildlife tourism in South Africa passed up gold mining as the ever before SA's top GDP earner in 2005. But GoM was asleep at the switch not having project progress meetings to catch NOL's nonperformance in a matter of months, not several years on. I should have hired out as Chissano's advisor but who I was never allowed to meet via MZB flunkies NOJim had hired who were eventually NOL's sabotage partners. Our 1996 approved GoM version should have been built, as things developed it would have been unthinkable not to increase it to 4000 Sq MI size to connect N to the GLTP to save much more UN mandated Maputaland CPD plus 5000 then threatened of death Kruger elephants.

(61) Bechtel and I could have simply reinstated our feasibility study terms and conditions with GoM that were in our feasibility study as approved by GoM's Council of Ministers or reinstated our terms and conditions to fit. That's back to what MZB thought they were getting. It was too much of a world class project to let die. Bechtel with their worldwide reputation would have found GoM REAL investors to replace NOJim (NOL) to build out our Bechtel London feasibility plan.   But Chissano was naïve to it all, snowed by NOJim and his NO saboteur NOL. NOJim meant well, but was monkey-backed, NOL's takeover should never have happened.

SAVE MOZAMBIQUE'S ELEPHANT COAST

RECREATING MOTHER NATURE'S WILDLIFE WONDERLAND AFRICA

John Perrott

2007 was the publication date of my *SAVE MOZAMBIQUE'S ELEPHANT COAST, Recreating Mother Nature's* Wildlife *Wonderland Africa* book. Working for NOJim the Bechtel feasibility team and I (et al) essentially got GoM's 99 year develop-operate-land lease for the 914 Sq Mi Elephant Coast NP in less than a year. Jim was ill (drugs-booze), his Machiavellian NOL (lawyer) fired Bechtel, me et al. NOL failed to perform, then NOJim died in early 1999. GoM took his 99 year lease back from his estate in late 1999. I followed the action, should some billionaire take the project over. Bechtel and I could assist. But it was too messy, NOL had fouled up the terms and conditions to not as promised GoM (our feasibility study). Our 914 Sq Mi NP project fell in a crack. But in 2002 the GLTP was born, in 2005 wildlife tourism passed gold mining in South Africa. I wrote this book to resurrect the ECNP project at 4000 Sq Mi connected to the GLTP, to save a NP 4000 Sq Mi CPD win, win, for future generations as UN mandated.

A basic problem GoM or Chissano were naïve to development or construction contract administration. They didn't have to wait 2 ½ years to know that Machiavellian saboteur NOL had no intention of performing. It was obvious to the Bechtel team and me that NOL was sabotaging the project. What happened in MZB when they belatedly discovered NOL was on a bait-then-switch path? They had our feasibility study plan. Because of its UN CPD nature and MZB cash cow nature it was to be for GoM they should have taken it away from NOL, kept it going, but instead, they did nothing, except later then let a lot of MZB politicians build houses along the coast to detract from the "native and unspoiled" nature of the world class international destination CPD. That's what GoM did or didn't do positive for their starving resident natives. What's more to expect from African politicians. Marxist leaning with African hyena like reactions, just kill the project and then eat or destroy the evidence.

(62) I visited MZB in 2007 with my by then too late `tell all' SMEC book published when other `international vultures' were still trying to get hold of our 914 Sq MI CPD-NP project like 'world government's' UN minister Maurice Strong. That's long after NOJim's demise, his (our) project being taken back from his estate after project saboteur NOL not being able to sell it. NOJim's estate was out $5 million. In MZB I flew the 914 Sq MI project, saw ministers remote housing being built on what we had known as 50 miles of "native and unspoiled" Indian Ocean coast line Peninsula S to KwaZulu Natal border. Sometime later back in TX I got a call from an American guy in Washington state who had read my 2007 SMEC book. Our plan was to have private homes on the 63 Sq MI Machangulo Peninsula but surrounded by an African big five private wildlife sanctuary. That's with electric wildlife fences around building sites. This Washington guy had bought a Machanguolo Peninsula building site. GoM had given it to some `swindler' according to him. That `developer' had sold quite a few sites, then did nothing as to his developers responsibilities to provide water, ways of getting to the Peninsula, etc. Then I heard a story that one of the maybe ripped off lot buyers was the then Prince in waiting, son of the Queen Beatrix of Holland. The Prince was getting political heat for getting involved in the questionable MZB Machangulo Peninsula development.

(63) Now in 2015, I searched the net to see if I could find out anything, having last visited MZB in 2007. I was surprised to find a "Machangulo Affair". Who would be on about that remote, off the beaten track place. This had been picked up off European Netherlands news. From that's back at the time of the news story, the Prince of the Netherlands (Holland) had bought into (2007) a housing development there (our original 63 Sq MI) of NOJim's eventual 1996 GoM 99 year lease develop-operate 914 Sq MI Elephant Coast CPD-NP project. This became a hot story in Holland vs. the Prince getting involved in this development, purchasing a lot, building a holiday bungalow, which was largely opposed back in Holland. That's such that the Prince sold his finished house in 2009 to put his political fire out in Holland. In that era, hearing of the story, I emailed the Prince my knowledge of our 1996 project, sent him a copy of our 11 x 17" Bechtel London (1995) `brown bible' feasibility-development plan for the 914 Sq MI including the Machangulo Peninsula (63 Sq MI), which he acknowledged receiving with thanks. I submit this tale so any readers will have some idea of possible lost `native and unspoiled' nature of the project I herein discuss resurrecting. The Dutch Prince was Willem Alexander. His mother Queen Beatrix stepped down as the Dutch ruler in favor of her son on 30 April 2012 to be crowned King. Beatrix had ruled for 33 previous years.

(64) So what does this say as to resurrecting the 4000 Sq MI all CPD NP hooked up N with the 38,500 Sq MI GLTP? The whole area including the Peninsula is the UN blessed Maputaland CPD. Our awarded 914 Sq MI plan was Peninsula (63 Sq MI) a private housing development-cum-wildlife reserve. MER was 273 Sq MI, rest on S 578 Sq MI. In a serious move to resurrect a 4000 Sq MI version of CPD-NP would need a new Bechtel London (or equal) feasibility study, development plan with a bought out 63 Sq MI Machagulo Peninsula back or the `where-it-all started' or Peninsula omitted of a resurrected 4000 Sq MI to connect up with the GLTP to the N, the now big picture. If the Peninsula was out, rail access would be by building a bridge at the rock quarry on the W bank (existing rail ending there) or the mouth of the Maputo River, both sides of river, E side for coastal and MER access S, W side river bank on W for access overland from Maputo city N to the GLTP. Our 1995 feasibility study development plan is now 2016 (21 years later) despite the Peninsula now in or out. The big picture is that the whole 4000 Sq MI NP version is all IN the UN Maputaland CPD. That's what but making it a CPD-NP would protect it "native and unspoiled for future generations?" Make it all pure MZB NP and forget the Machangulo Peninsula private big five game park with individual housing. In 2002 GLTP became a previously unknown positive development. In 2005 in SA tourism (to wildlife watching) replaced gold as South Africa's largest GDP contributor.

Summary: I would be optimistic that despite changes in MZB any big picture feasibility study result would be as or more optimistic than or Bechtel London in 1995 for the 4000 Sq Mi version with or without the Machangulo Peninsula included. World `civilized encroachments' are such that a 4000 Sq Mi CPD-botanical-wildlife NP is a NOW OR NEVER proposition to save this opportunity to guard the UN CPD "native and unspoiled for future generations." GoM should be approached with the offer of a new 4000 Sq Mi feasibility study, knowing now from day one that it is to save "native and unspoiled for future generations" the Maputaland CPD, that will renovate the since 1932 MER shot out by Cubans in the post 1975 independence plus it would connect up N with the since 2002-3 GLTP. It is still a candidate for a world class CPD-NP. Where in the world is a better one. That might be completing what the Brits left half done in making all of the Botswana Kalahari an enlarged and amalgamated GoB NP. Or do both, get a friendly competition going between GoM and GoB NPs toward save "native and unspoiled for future generations" both. The one liner for MZB is create a CPD-NP to SAVE endangered wildlife plus a UN CPD. For GoB it is to expand a wildlife Kalahari NP and save from extinction the DNA famous Gods Must Be Crazy Kalahari Bushman giving them a survival haven. Both are super five star double-barreled-world class developments. They should both be done. A basic difference is GoB has light Kalahari population to benefit from, but no UN CPD. But thriving NPs will create a lot of employment in both cases. Honest feasibility studies would favor both being done NOW as GDP enhancers. That's `now' like in NOW or NEVER, the opportunities can fade like in MZB's lose since 1996 (20 years ago). But let the chips fall where they may re an international feasibility study.,

but GoM and GoB should both have at least the feasibility stage done to know what special unique `diamonds in the rough' they each have, international class NPs as cash cows for real GDP enhancers, and a blessing to our more `green' world, a huge positive answer to the slaughter of elephants for their tusks and rhinos for their nose horns, all the accompanying Noah's Arc of endangered African wildlife to be saved "native and unspoiled for future generations." That's good on Dubai for what they are doing but vis-à-vis different strokes for different folks, Mother Nature's African editions would be winners. The world is now going more for Mother Nature `green' vs `asphalt jungle glitz'. Needed feasibility studies have a good chance of getting GoM and GoB headed in the right green direction, toward saving "native and unspoiled" two regions with great international wildlife-watching destinations. Both of these NP developments would enthrall the international news, billions of people would be highly interested, and in their youth these two NP would be meccas they would set their sails to visit in their lifetimes. Let this not be the end of this story (opportunity) to increase this world's African endangered wildlife NPs, saving the heart of a gigantic UN CPD in MZB, wildlife-homeland for Bushman (DNA) in Botswana, God willing.

Save the endangered Gods Must Be Crazy Botswana Bushman (DNA) in their enlarged Kalahari NP homeland as their last on our earth homeland ecosystem with their accompanying few left (but always been there) endangered African wildlife. Then in MZB's Elephant Coast resurrect the 4000 Sq Mi Elephant Coast NP development project to connect up N with the world's now largest wildlife refuge the huge three nation 38,500 Sq Mi GLTP. Rescue the therein MZB's impoverished `traditional land dwellers' while both needed NP developments efforts are doing something world class win-win positive vs. Africa's current elephant ivory and rhino nose horn poaching and endangered African wildlife extinction NOW before it is too late. Step one is to present GoB and GoM with international class bankable NP feasibility studies to stop the idle `stop African wildlife poaching' discussions and get down to brass tacks and create these two NP additions to protect them "native and unspoiled for future generations. But do it NOW or NEVER.

4

Arctic National Wildlife Reserve Tourist in Oil out Win-Win Plan

Many with strong opinions against ANWR 'oil out' (OO) have never been there inside the Arctic Circle to know the unique tundra permafrost-summer-surface-thaw-wetlands region that attracts annual caribou calving, huge international nesting waterfowl, a 24-hour-summer-sunlight-blooming-botanical-breath-taking extravaganza! But on 21 December it's bitter cold frozen 24 hours of darkness. As Bechtel's key man on Alaska's mid 1970s 800 mile 48" crude oil pipeline build out I was there thru all seasons. Earlier I was an African hunter who joined my Kenya pro hunter in killing a man-eating Kenya lion in 1965 that was eating on its Wakambe tribe native victim. Then in 1973 on my last E Afrocan hmt a Cape buffalo charged at first light from 14 paces. LESS than one second later he was dead at seven paces. Since Alaska 1974 I'm a non-hunting-wildlife-photo guy, more into developing while safeguarding wildlife ecosystems like ANWR when not on an international mega pipeline or African wildlife sanctuary creating saga. That's such as my National Park (NP) development for African wildlife tourism feasibility study for 914 Sq MI NP in Mozambique in 1995-6. I authored *SAVE MOZAMBIQUE'S ELEPHANT COAST (2007), my second `green' cause* book proposing to resurrect our GoM awarded 914 Sq MI UN Center of Plant Diversity (CPD) NP to save the botanical-wildlife Elephant Coast GoM approved CPD-NP development. But my New Orleans developer went bait-then-switch, then `threw craps' and did not perform. Then he died in 1999. No one has resurrected it as a 4000 Sq MI MZB wildlife-botanical NP to connect up to the since created (2002) three country or South Africa, Zimbabwe, Mozambique three country Grand Limpopo TransFrontier Park (GLTP) of 38,500 Sq MI the world's largest TransFrontier or international wildlife-sanctuary Park. For ANWR I now propose herewith an approach to get international tourist (IT) into ANWR thanks to oil-out (OO) by encouraging no-oil-out (NOO) folks, (OO) people to discuss a simple frozen winter built roads plan as proposed in my memo to Alaska's Sarah Palin (below) re an ongoing ANWR stalemate to get international tourists (IT) finally into ANWR summers.
###333333333

Governor Sarah Palin
1140 W Parks Highway
Walla, AK 99654

Subject: ANWR TOURIST IN WHILE OIL OUT WIN-WIN PLAN

Dear Alaska Governor Palin

This memo offers a possible sound, simple quid pro quo solution to our ongoing national ANWR impasse conundrum. I see four front line players involved in ANWR as (1) the strategic Oil-Out (OO) folks of Prudhoe Bay ilk, (2) objecting No Oil Out (NOO) conservationist et al who for a laundry list of reasons are against oil recovery, (3) the ignored, forgotten International Tourists (IT) robbed of seeing ANWR's annual-Serengeti-like Alaska caribou migration for the lack of access roads, overnight facilities and wildlife watching destination developed NP developments, (4) the caribou, nesting waterfowl et al that could care less as proven at Prudhoe Bay oil installations in recent years. Secondarily there is the State of Alaska, the Feds, Inuit et al interested and involved entities. A maybe simple solution is (OO) is allowed to get the crude out in the 24 hour dark frozen winter months but offers to (while there) build gravel roads and lodge pads in frozen winter beyond their limited (OO) needs for (IT) (touristic developers) to finally have summer access to ANWR via a quid-pro-quo so all people or (IT) international wildlife-watchers of a booming new industry mainly in E and Southern Africa to also see ANWR's wildlife migrations, waterfowl nesting, blooming botany in the 24-hour-daylight-summer-thawed-tundra-permafronst time of year surface wetlands. That's for (IT) to have (OO) to WINTER build (IT) summer access for (OO's) oil out.

I'm an "I-lived-in-Alaska guy" two years in the mid 1970s kick off of crude pipeland construction I later signed an internet petition to John McCain to choose Alaska Governor Sarah P as a young Margaret Thatcher like common semse conservative as his VP running mate well before he did in 2008. I'm still a conservative Sarah P supporter. I did military US Navy flight training in Pensacola FL a year ahead of Senator McCain. With a U of Cal Berkeley engineering degree I joined giant SF Bechtel International in 1958 to 16 years later be Bechtel's for Alyeska early days site manager on Alaska's oil pipeline in a 35 year Bechtel career of living and working on every continent but Antarctica with 17 years in Africa on mega construction projects. I resided in Fairbanks in 1974-75 as Bechtel's key man in Alaska on the break ground front end years of the road N of the Yukon River with construction camp building or 19,000 add-on remote area beds to post-1969's project North of the Yukon (NoY) false start number of camp beds to a total of 25,000 beds for the full pipeline's length, then transitioning into the 800 mile 48" diameter crude oil pipeline's kickoff, half above ground in thaw unstable permafrost. In eight months in 1974 we built the gravel access road's 380 miles Yukon River N to Arctic Ocean Prudhoe Bay.

That's moving 32 million CY of gravel for a then construction world volume record in that short time. I drove Bechtel's second ever vehicle Yukon River to Prudhoe Bay in November 1974 in the ceremonial opening of the North-of-the-Yukon-pipeline road a few yards behind friend Nate Bauer, owner Alyeska's then senior guy in Alaska. ANWR is near enough E of, fronting the Arctic Ocean as our pipeline at Prudhoe Bay. Working in the ANWR region we learned Mother Nature's, plus BLM's rules of inside the Arctic Circle survival and construction. As it's frozen dark 24 hours on 21 December, transitions to 24 hours of daylight on 21 June with the up to 1000' deep permafrost there's a short summer melted ONLY to a tundra surface depth of five to eight feet to create a vast short summer wetlands. Bureau of Land Management (BLM) lets no one on the shallow spring thawed tundra post spring breakup. Gravel roads are built primarily in more frozen darkness winter to thereafter provide summer tundra thawed season access roads despite BLM's spring thru early fall thawed-no-vehicle-et al `tundra' access. That is taking construction's advantage of Mother Nature's winter freeze for gravel road and camp pad construction which we dod from 11 BLM allowed gravel pit road construction camp sites.

Currently the world's wildlife-watching international tourists (IT) are kept from enjoying Mother Nature's ANWR summer show of caribou calving, water fowl nesting, the explosion of colorful botanical blooming in the 24 hour summer sun daylight season. Such annual wildlife migrations are rare worldwide except for the African Tanzania-Kenya Serengeti which the ANWR international tourist (IT) unseen edition challenges for a world's top wildlife-watching destination. I've seen both. ANWR is more colorfully impressive in its three summer months vs. Serengeti's averaging out its whole year's near equatorial climate competition. A break-in-the-ANWR-access-impasse plan is to have (OO) propose they be let in ANWR to get oil out with their well drilling, pipeline construction ONLY in frozen winter, but beside building their limited needed roads, well, camp gravel pads (OO)'s quid pro quo is to build added winter gravel roads, pads to permit (IT) access for summer wildlife-watching to FINALLY let our world's (IT) have seasonal access despite the surface thawed summer tundra to enjoy caribou migration, nesting water fowl, 24 hour sun blooming extravaganza which is world class to witness. That's with seeing caribou kibitzing wolves, wolverine, grizzly and polar bears, musk ox et al other wildlife.

That would be that (OO) had frozen winter ANWR access but when spring thaw came they would abandon ANWR to wildlife-watching (IT) et al. In the early interim stages until IT's own road and overnight facilities were built out, turn (OO) camps over to (IT) for its summer-thawed-tundra visit. (OO) in winter would thus build additional roads and pads for (IT) wildlife-watching access along with what relatively little roads and pads (OO) needs for oil extraction. (OO) would have their well heads congregated on small acreage sized pads reaching out with horizontal oil drilling. ANWR oil would flow to Prudhoe Bay then S. ANWR to the 48" pipeline S flow would be via buried pipelines installed in winter, buried by summer (IT) visit time. Transfer pipelines would be buried, unseen vs. above ground. The pipelines would be buried with insulation if needed for hot oil or buried in gravel roads or thaw stable terrain. In the startup, transition (OO) would turn their camp, facilities to the summer overnight tourists while pads, roads were being winter built for the erection of more permanent summer (IT) overnight facilities for (IT) permanent summer access to ANWR. (OO) would have ANWR on the night (frozen winter shift; (IT) et al would have exclusive access during the summer-thaw-daylight-migration-annual shift. (OO) or Alaska Gov to get this plan launched might offer to hire an engineering third party like Bechtel (or equal) to do a feasibility study of the whole. That's to include interfaces with (OO), (IT) like (NOO), Alaska, Feds, Inuits, et al.

Or this could lead to an auction to let ANWR-tourist-destination entrepreneurs bid competitively on tourist sub concessions for individual lodges with adjacent game-watching concessions as is a very successful wildlife tourist paradigm in South Africa's world's top international African wildlife-watching concessions where you have to have a bed in the lodge and design number of beds limits the tourists allowed vs. helter-skelter drive in or thru as at Yellowstone NP where there are too many cars, too few wildlife to be seen. i.e. tourists have to have a bed reserved to get in, control the bed numbers to not have too many tourists (lodge vehicles) at any time as in southern Africa's best run international African wildlife watching lodges. That's where (IT) had to book in ahead to somewhat limited beds. That's if the solution to winter built summer (IT) ANWR access is not`interested' (OO). Currently (IT) access, enjoyment of ANWR is lost with but a few who are flown into ANWR to land on watercourse gravel bars in STOL (short-takeoff-and-landing aircraft) or helicopters to camp out but on foot they can see very little to be devoured by summer mosquitoes vs. wildlife viewing via air conditioned vehicles on winter-built-gravel roads from over night beds in for (IT) guest lodge facilities.

As to international-wildlife-watching tourism, in South Africa in the top half dozen lodges you have to book ahead up to a year to get in, and pay cash cow bed prices to make it a viable wildlife-watching-destination industry. It works beautifully there. (IT) would fly into like Dead Horse air facility at Prudhoe Bay. All further transport would be provided from the overnight lodges for vehicles (guide driven) that knew the strict ANWR photography rules and all to limit the `in ANWR' wildlife watching vehicle numbers to protect wildlife photograph quality. (OO) or their construction contractors have proven from before the 1970's Prudhoe pipeline facilities construction they can work in frozen dark winter, that caribou could care less about roads, other oil facilities. By chance with my worldwide heavy construction experience I also can claim experience as a wildlife ecosystem aficionado, guru. See my two bleeding heart Internet sites www.savethesan.org a 501 (c) (3) not for profit for the Kalahari Desert Bushman an endangered human species and `green' cause and fragile wildlife ecosystem the Kalahari Desert.

That's "The Gods Must Be Crazy" movie people per my book *BUSH FOR THE BUSHMAN* (1992). Kalahari Bushman are endangered as are their God given wild animals, plus fragile Kalahari ecosystem like Alaska's Inuit and their wildlife and ecosystem. Let the Inuit have their involvement (employment) for letting (IT) shoot Inuits wildlife only with film. There's also www.savemec.org with 501 (c) (3) IRS status, book titled SAVE MOZAMBIQUE'S ELEPHANT COAST, *Recreating Mother Nature's Wildlife Wonderland Africa* (2007) `green' cause to provide the how-to and cost to create a 4000 Sq Mi Mozambique (MZB) wildlife botanical NP via the book's provided published feasibility plan and economics. Its plan is updated, expanded after Government of MZB (GoM) approval of an initial 914 Sq Mi develop-operate-99-year-NP concession lease in 1996. But its American developer who I was key man for on a winning feasibility study failed to perform, then died in 1999. From my key man MZB experience I learned from premier wildlife management, wildlife tourism gurus in South Africa lessons to be applied toward developing ANWR for international wildlife watching ecotourism (IT) as a high-profile-world-wildlife-watching destination be it in ANWR or Africa. South Africa has Africa's largest economy in which Africa's continent is 3.1 times the size of USA with our Alaska in. Our total US lower 48 fits inside only the North African Sahara Desert for comparative size.

In South Africa pre-2005 gold mining was always their top GDP contributor to their largest-in-Africa economies. Now with the international-wildlife-watching craze their number one GDP item post-2005 is now international wildlife-watching tourism as a prime international destination. Per African experience an ANWR-wildlife-tourist destination would be a substantial cash cow-cum- Alaskan GDP enhancer. Per African equatorial and S wildlife tourism evolution and experience an ANWR development per the well established African paradigm would be world class substantial as a North American (IT) industry that has gone bonkers in Africa south of the equator or Alaska's summer only version. With a now booming international -lidlife-watching msrket craze it is sad a Mother Nature's quality of attraction happening each summer in ANWR is not readily (IT) developed and accavailable . My herein proposed approach get (OO), objecting (NOO) talking objectively towards a both pro (IT) and (OO) resolution to give Congress reason to vote for (OO access to ANWR as within USA's needed or desiveable in-country oil (with ISIS and the whole Muslim middle East being progressively worse bad news. If ANWR oil is ever extracted after a time well heads would be removed , former (OO) roads and gravel pads now available, turned over for (IT) use. ANWR is is a world class special region which only needs access to join our world's first ever NP Yellowstone created in 1872   .   2nd   was   South   Africa's   Kruger   NP   for   (IT)   wildlife-watching.

1991 Finland reindeer (Webster calls them `Old World caribou'). Failing to find my Alaska 1970s caribou pics I offer these their European ANWR cousins instead for the migrants that calve on ANWR's Arctic Ocean coast.

1974 on Yukon River to Prudhoe Bay pipeline road. This Alaskan wolf joins BLM inspectors to keep an eye on us wild road builders that we don't disturb fragile summer thawed (winter frozen) inside the Arctic circle tundra.

1974 Alaska grizzly bear keeps an eye on our Yukon River to Prudhoe Bay pipeline road construction. Bears like this broke into our camp refers for watermelons. Helicopters took bears far away, only to soon return.

1975 NOY above ground 48" diameter pipe where ever the terrain is `thaw unstable' and the hot oil has to be above ground on piling or it would melt its permafrost support. About half of 800 miles was so above ground.

That's `a-maybe' by harnessing (OO) help for a frozen-winter-built-summer-access-gravel road for (IT) access (finally) achieved. That's to then esperience an ANWR development touristic industry per the African paradigm would be world class substantial as an (IT) draw as a wildlife-watching-summer destination with no guns, just cameras. With a now-booming-international-wildlife-viewing- craze market it is sad an attraction the quality of what Mother Nature puts on in ANWR each summer is not readily (IT) accessible. This proposed approach could get (OO) , objecting (NOO) talking objectively toward a pro (IT) and (OO) resolution to give Congress reason to vote for ANWR's access by (OO) as within USA's needed or desireable more USA in-country sourced oil. When ANWR oil (if) has been extracted well heads would be removed, former (OO) gravel pads now available , turned over for (IT) in-ANWR use. ANWR is a special region which needs access by joining our world's first ever Yellowstone NP created in 1872 to accommodate growing international wildlife-watching tourist destinations which needs only a frozen winter built access roads to add a wonderful summer-wildlife-watching NP.

That's (maybe) by harnessing (OO) help for frozen winter built summer thaw access roads the belated process could finally let (IT) in, access be achieved. It's possible this simple outside the box avenue could provide an ice breaker to quell the no ANWR oil (NOO) angst to win (NOO) conservationist like objective `tree huggers' et all public opinion to allow (OO) their day. That's plus get across the aisle cooperation toward this achievable win-win solution so Mother Nature's ANWR gift is no longer denied to international wildlife watchers or (IT). Where are the (NOO) folks coming from? ANWR is a God given asset. So is the oil under it to be extracted environmentally. As a wildlife habitat for (IT) to see, enjoy it is now denied (undeveloped) and inaccessible as Mother Nature's `diamond in the rough' tantamount to we are going to lock the gates to Yellowstone, East Africa's Serengeti, South Africa's Kruger, Botswana's Okavango Delta to wildlife watching (IT) also? That's by we American's the first to the moon? Then if ANWR's oil can't be touched what about plan B, or others building tourist access roads in winter so (IT) has summer access? But who but (OO) would help pay for it? Per my MZB experience on creating a CPD-NP concept, what about Alaska having an ANWR feasibility study development plan performed? If it comes out as an undeveloped cash cow from (IT) harvested asset, offer it to entrepreneurs outside of (OO). I've seen it via our winter built 1974 pipeline road in all seasons, in summer, the summer wetlands, caribou calving, waterfowl nesting, 24 hour sun's blooming botany would sell as an (IT) international-wildlolfe-watching destination for summer months as Alaska's well up on Antarctic for their now Emperor penguin migrations as a top wildlife watching tourist draw destination worldwide.

People pay big money for all kinds of garbage as entertainment while this Mother Nature's show goes on annually virtually unattended. (OO) people are a now possible option to break the current no (IT) access to ANWR log jam. If (OO) builds roads in winter it would open things up for others to develop ANWR as a seasonal-international-wildlife-observing destination. But (NOO) people what do they really want? Are they also anti international wildlife watching (IT) tourism? It seems that where they are coming from is negative political anti `green' development dogma. There needs to be ecological development like the 1970s Alaska oil pipeline to let (IT) have access to the natural wonders of ANWR's summer thaw wetland extravaganza. We pipeliners say "Do something even if it is wrong." It's wrong to do nothing with our ANWR asset, not give USA and international tourists ANWR access. To get oil out is a more positive sell if it simultaneously opens ANWR up to (IT) or the internationally booming wildlife watching industry a cash cow GDP augmenter like it has proven in South Africa and the whole S of the equator Africa. Let Alaska test that cash cow international wildlife watching market or industry too. Thanks for your time and attention.

Best Regards

John R Perrott
(savesan@sbcglobal.net)

5

The African Impala Paradigm

This chapter is of Mother Nature's type lessons learned while hunting African wildlife after having grown up in a livestock raising environment finding many African wildlife parallels. Thus via wildlife and domestic livestock Mother Nature has a story to tell us which most people are unaware of. To get straight into it I grew up as part of the 4th generation (we five siblings) on our 1865 family 640 acre Federal Land Grant livestock ranch in Northern California's Redwood Empire. That's on Table Bluff Ranch one learned a lot from our livestock about the `birds and bees' early on a mile E of Loleta, 13 miles S of Eureka on Humboldt Bay. Our ranch was on Pacific view Table Bluff dividing our rainfall drainage runoff between the Eel River's mouth S into the Pacific Ocean or N into Humboldt Bay. Our residence's elevated view growing up was six miles from the Pacific Ocean beach with a W sundown to die for. Our dad ran sheep till I finished grammar school then from high school (1946 thru 50) we ran beef cattle. What our dad called invasive `poverty oat' grass proved to be too rank for sheep. But it could sustain beef cattle or this was his announced reason for changing from sheep to raising beef cattle plus his economics per acre cash flow records and estimates. We kids now had a higher social class, cow boys vs. sheep herders. We could now wear pointed toed boots, big belt buckles, and broad brimmed TX cowboy hats.

As a youngster we fed sheep or cattle , horses, chickens, hnnd milked cows thus came to know a fair amount of animal husbandry. In our current stage of human evolution we generally practice monogamy. That is except Muslim males who are allosed four wives , Mormons whow at least used to practice pologamy. But my fourth generation came to know what we called ewes or later female cattle called cows. Then there were rams and bulls For livestock there was no monogamy. The their male `survivor' partners. Our male-ratio was something one male to breed 30 or so females that was the critical mass or economy of scale number. More males they would be fighting to maybe not produce offspring which was what one sells in the livestock business. Meanwhile too few males could lead to unbred barren none productive females. But this is just background for when the light went on when I first met Mr and Mrs Impala gazelle in Kenya in 1965.. But first I had to spend five years in the Sahara Desert of Tunisia, Algeria and Libya with Bechtel International. Only then did I take a side trip as a contract completion vacation trip to Kenya on a travel home's detour. That's in route out of the world's largest sand trap Sahara Desert back to Bechtel's San Francisco home office for a year's HQ coat-and-tie duty. In late 1964 I went circuitously from the Sahara work place to equatorial Kenya for my then (most probably) once in a lifetime ever African hunt which I'd long dreamed of doing as my Teddy Roosevelt and Ernest Hemingway to-do thing. '

That was with Ker and Downey professional hunters in Nairobi. My prohunter was John Kingsley-Heath (JKH) a Brit. Then I experienced a very exciting introductory African hunt. On this Kenya hunt one bought a general liscence for a laundry list of common game then purchased added on supplementary licenses for the choicer game as lion, leopard, Cape buffalo, elephant, eland, oryx, etc. More common impala, wildebeest, hartebeest, topi, zebra, warthog and such were covered on the general license. A common game animal was the impala found in most everywhere in equatorial Africa on S. It is medium small by African standards about the sie of our costal deer where I grew up in CA or whit tailed deer where I now live in the San Antonio TX region. Impala females are without antlers, slick headed as with CA and TX deer. There is no confusion between male and female impala. Cofnfusion may occur in Africa whith the likes of the bigger oryx where the females can be longer antlered as a trophy so it takes care to bag only the redundant males. Impala males are often bagged early in a hunting block for leopard baits. I learned the 1impala paradigm' or how polygamy works in Mother Nature's African wildlife.

1973 Zambia a statue of two cheetahs pursuing a herd of bachelor (all antlered) impala males, great leapers, high and long used to avoid their carnivore pursuers. Breeding herd has one alpha male only which stands out with 30 slick headed female impala. This leads to my `impala paradigm' where wildlife is polygamist, a majority of all the males are `breedingwise' redundant .

1971 Masal Steppe TNZ two Masai gals wash with baobab tree background. This is a few and far between wildlife water hole where elephant come after dark to bath and drink, from which we track (all day) any big footed bull elephants we find the next morning. The track could be up to 20 miles. A bull will stop 10 AM thru 3 PM, lean against a tree for his rest. We have to track or find him by 3 PM to have a look at tusk size.

1971 Masal Steppe TNZ Wandorobo tracker Ngwira, he lives in a Masal thorn bush manyatta with his Masal wife, Masal cattle at night for protection vs. lion, hyena. He's is a bush hunter for bee trees for their honey, small game bagged with his diminutive bow and arrows. He's an excellent tracker, finds a big bull foot print to track at daylight at water hole to track.

1968 Masal Steppe TNZ, a Masal mother with gourd milks cow, mixes milk with blood drawn from cow, their only diet. She is bare footed, has her baby on her back, lives in a thorn bush enclosure with Masal cattle at night vs. lions, hyena. Masal are tall in stature, men are armed with Cape buffalo hide shield, spear vs. lion cattle attackers. Warriors dress in red robes.

Most often a best trophy impala is with his breeding hered of 30 or so females as the sole antlered alpha male. sd yjr dp;r sn hmale. He stands out for his horns vs. his harem having no antlers. Over a hill a few kilometers away was the bachelor herd of approximately 29 other all antlered males, no females. Wow this was in your face strange to enlightening! The breeding herd had one antlered male and his harem. The separate bachelor herd had 29 or so all antlered males banded together but separate from the breeding herd. So if we were to choose to bag the one male in the breeding herd what would happen? The most alpha male in the bachelor herd would take over as new king-of-the-impala-breeding herd harem. That's over his now 30 none antlered females. Or if some hunter didn't bag him he would eventually pass beyond his prime state. Then the strongest bachelor male would then challenge to take over the breeding herd's male position or the same result. So why not shoot the breeding herd single male to retire him a bit early to get an infusion of new genes or blood line from the next strongest male? Then on this hunt a light went on for me. This was just like my dad except he had a herd of more than 30.
That's in his sheep or beef cow breed herd he religiously had just one ram or bull for each circa 30 breeding herd females the same order of magnitude number as African impalas! I thought about all this `coincidence'. My dad sold off all his year's crop of castrated males he called weathers for sheep, steers for beef. He imported his very small number of needed breeder males. That's one male to about 30 females ratio.

That's to get an expected near 100% production of lambs or calves annually. In our dad's case he had white faced Romney ewes. He chose black faced Suffolk males for cross breeding for heaviest lambs. Also Romney ewes produced more wool. Later with cattle he chose white face Herford breed cows. That's with Black Angus bulls for the cross to produce heaviest calves. He went to bull sales to buy his breeders while in Africa it came from a battle in an impala bachelor herd. Here our basic paradigm is African wildlife impalas. How was it with other African wildlife species? One observed a similar system with large African antelope herbivores as eland a single dominant male in his prime with his eland female harem. That's again with the African sable and roan antelope with one sole alpha male and his harem. It's just that the waiting-in-the-wings-other males with these other species did not seem to be so regimented in a bachelor band together as an obvious observable male bachelor herd as with the impala. The other male bachelors were spread out in singles or in waiting pairs in the region until it came time for them to vie for sole king of the breeding herd. Or other bachelor males were less banded together. If one observed an impala bachelor herds over 15 years only three antlered male impala would graduate to being sole herd sire. Thus the majority of other males (80 to 90%) live lives without `breeding her' duty.

But they consume grass in competition with females and young. There are carnivores as leopard, cheetah, lions, hyena, African wild hunting dogs that figured in the impala et al survival numbers or which would consume some of the females and young or maybe less `survival' females substituting rather `redundant' bachelor males instead especially as they aged or slowed. Let's take elephants. I hunted elephants (males only) mostly in Tanzania's Masai Steppe. It was quintessential dry-thirst-and-thorn country in August thru October dry season. There were no running streams. Any water left over from rainy season was seasonally in depressions (ponded water holes). But there were only in a few of the ponds or natural depressions. Water holes tended to dry up, not all but many in August thru October drier equatorial season. There was an elephant breeding herd of females, young elephants. The males ALL left the breeding herds when they matured only visiting for breeding purposes once like every two years per mature cow elephant. The females all stayed in their breeding herd where several generations of related female elephants made up a breeding herd. There was a female matriarch or dominant older cow that ran the breeding herd. She decided when, where to migrate seasonally for known water holes or better seasonal food. Her experience (good elephant memory) contributed materially to her breeding herd's tough survival.

Then I learned by tracking single bull elephants from their priot night's `big' water hole tracks. I tracked one e elephant via foot size to discover their destructive habits vis-a-vis smaler herd cows. I observed male elephants come up to a 12" tree. This bull put his tusk either side of the tree, ran his trunk up the tree trunk. He then `bulldozed' the tree over, uprooted, killed it. Then he walk around to have access to eat tree top greens. But then he soon moved on to do the same to another tree a few miles on two or more a day. Then he walked away to leave the area in his continuing all night and day circuit. He usually rested from about 10 AM to 3 PM by leaning up against a tree. This let my Wandorobo tracker and I to catch up and have a look at him in what was a 24 hour circuit back to the same or another water hole. Most often the breeding herds and lone bulls drank early after dark (Masai Steppe). Elsewhere they drank in daylight hours if there were no rifle hunters about. Thus bull elephants are destructive to the ecosystem killing trees leading to fires, destruction of NPs for the elephants themselves plus all the other species. Scientist rate the world's mammals as to the most destructive. They are (1) humans, (2) elephants, (3) goats. Female elephants with less body weight or testosterone don't destroy trees like this. They might however finish the greenery on trees the bulls have uprooted and left dead and available. In the 1960s Tsavo NP in Kenya became destroyed or desolate for what was termed `elephant over population'. But most of that Tsavo NP destruction was by over population of male or bulls not female breeding herds.

That's over population of bulls only, or far more than the few bulls needed for breeding or elephant reproductive survival. My dad on our ranch talked of this. He kept the number of rams or bulls down to like one to 30 females or just right for breeding, no excess. Why not cull male elephants in NPs by letting hunters hunt males only, raise revenues for overall wildlife management, ivory poaching control, provide protein (meat) for starving Africans. Elephant meat as herbivores is good red meat, only a bit grainier or with a coarser texture than beef. In my African hunting days I ate elephant meat no problem. Meanwhile in South Africa's Kruger NP with a large elephant population there was the same type of problem. Kruger is with lots of forest as Tsavo NP vs. being more open plains like Tanzania's Serengeti has but few elephants. In Kruger in the late 1970s there was initiated elephant culling for a couple of decades to combat what their wildlife management there termed `elephant over population' or in my experience and view was really too many destructive male elephants. In Kruger there was a quiet culling of some 500 elephants a year for 20 years reportedly to combat the elephant's destruction of habitat on Kruger NP ecosystem. But to me the method of choosing which elephants to cull it was the female breeding herds?

Why was this? It was based on logistics not culpability. Breeding herds could be located in convenient groupings with a whole breeding herd exterminated vs. tracking down lone `guilty' bulls one at a time the real destructive culprits. Then there is what wildlife watching (with cameras) international tourist like to see like big tusked bulls for their take home photos or videos like Kenya's internationally famous Ahmed of Marsabit NP (see photo (pg 61) herein. But in Kruger exterminating female breeding herds didn't solve the NP ecosystem destruction problem. That's letting the problem causing males (the culpable) continue to `kill trees' to cause the NP ecosystem destruction. Nelson Mandela stopped Kruger elephant culling in the mid 90s as being negative to South Africa's growing dependence on international wildlife tourism (with cameras not guns) or wildlife-watching. This was to South African wildlife-watching tourism with gold the country's top GDP earner with wildlife tourism second. But then wildlife tourism became number one in 2005 and forward. A solution being debated in the early 2000s was again to cull (kill) like 5000 elephant to save the Kruger NP's ecosystem. Sadly those elephants nominated for killing were again tragically whole breeding herds vs. bulls because of the convenient logistics of the culling operation involved vs. choosing the more destructive guilty solitary remotely dispersed bulls. Whole breeding herds were chosen with the females and young all killed which only fit the most efficient logistics.

Hunting down destructive bulls one at a time was too hard, slow, and expensive. NPs have operating budgets. This `kill breeding herds' choice was mainly for bureaucratic or logistical reasons despite there was an oversupply of destructive males vis-a-vis those needed for breeding , males being the NP ecosystem destroyers. Female breeding herds were congregated, easily located, all killed fairly efficiently. Why didn't they kill the destructive males, the culprits? In my Bechtel engineering-construction career I developed a saying (like on the Alaska oil pipeline) "degrees and PhDs will get you in trouble." My common sense dad would have understood the source of the problem. He that on our ranch only allowed one ram or bull (male) per thirty females. He'd find out the NP ecosystem destroyers were the bull elephants, then eliminate most of the males. He'd do it right from his livestock husbandry, it being so similar to how Mother Nature operated wildlife. Our common sense dad might come up with a culling plan of: (1) Cull only males. (2) Let international hunters do it (raise money). (3) It's a NP, take hunters out in helicopters to locate bulls. (4) Don't let them shoot bigger tuskers that international tourist want pictures of, are good breeders for future big tuskers. (5) Locate (via helicopter) chosen bulls, drop hunter off with tracker guides vehicles close to-be-culled bulls off remote tourist tracks of NP. (6) With radio contact helicopter to ground have 4x4 vehicles get hunter to near the elephant. (7) Bull elephants I knew slept 10 AM to 3 PM standing up against a tree. (8) The helicopter crew would know where to find `remote' off the tourist track to-cull bulls.

Once cull bulls are eliminated, have crews with refer trucks `butcher' carcasses to save meat for protein starved Africans. (10) Have this operation going more or less year around. (11) Thus reduce the bull elephant population, the destructive culprits, not the breeding herd females. (12) The tourist, public need not know using silenced rifles. (13) This operation would alert guides to where the spared bigger tuskers were (radio contact) so tourist were guided to the take home big tuskers to photograph for a beneficial side effect, a Nelson Mandela like plan. This would be hunting destructive bulls down one at a time (all the time). This was not so logistically complicated, inefficient, or costly. It would stop cows, calves (not destructive bulls) being killed for a useless but costly wildlife travesty like shooting human wives and children of male murders, not those murderers. That's culprit excess bulls not needed for overall elephant species survival. Not killing the innocent cows needed for species survival would be eliminated. That's one or two bulls per breeding herd of 10 to 25 mature cows was all that was needed. If my dad's plan above was adopted, keep statistics, increase or decrease the `helicopter' crew's time needed so that with experience full time (maybe not in the rainy season) the problem is controlled or solved by eliminating only guilty destructive (redundant) bulls. But wildlife management has to know these facts. That's too many males, not females or overall elephant `over population' dogma is a bad bureaucratic term or gross error. My career bag is international engineering-construction. However hunting big game in Africa for several seasons I learned a lot to add to my growing up on a livestock ranch.

Then in 1995 I was the key man in charge of a feasibility study that won a large GoM (UN Centers of Plant Diversity) CPD-NP creating 99-year-lease-develop-operate MZB land concession. It started as a GoM's President Chissano offer of a 63 Sq Mi Indian Ocean peninsula only. Our London Bechtel team (I got my old employers involved) resulted in GoM awarding us a 914 Sq Mi CPD-NP development. In engineering construction they say "plan the work, then work the plan." An international `bankable' feasibility study sells the client on it being a good (best) land use plan, then the details to let them know the cost but cash cow return. Creating a NP fits this approach be it in Botswana, MZB or Alaska's ANWR as herein. In the 1995 MZB situation I was able to interact with top South African wildlife-tourism management PhDs thus learn a lot more about endangered African wildlife and creating NPs to save ecosystems "native and unspoiled for future generations" this book's main message and aim. International tourist like to see big horned (or tusked) males in African NPs like Ahmed that my USA childhood friend Kent and I saw in 1973 in Marsabit NP in N Kenya. Ahmed was slowed of older age. He thus had four afoot armed NP guards surrounding him night and day to ward off poachers after his big 148 lb. per ivory tusk weight. Thus Ahmed in his 50s lived to die of natural causes the next year.

He is now a full body mount in Nairobi in a natural history facility. If you're in Nairobi inquire its location to see him. But the special case of elephant males being ecosystem destroying and because one male will care for more or less 30 females who needs breeding only once in two years that's a sexual encounter for a bull like once a month in meetings with breeding herds at water holes or river drinking locations. Thus most of the males can be culled without effecting the species survival negatively, rather putting a brake on NP's ecological destruction, dead trees, fires. That's culling up to a majority of elephant males has merit (only when needed). Keep the bigger tusked ones (10 to 15 %) to upgrade the elephant herd's gene pool as my dad did on his sheep and beef cattle operations has merit. He learned animal husbandry graduating from now Oregon State University in 1929 along with our Pendleton Oregon `wheat Finn' mother. Our dad sold his entire male crop yearly as feeders for meat in the Safeway store. He bought his few needed of chosen breeder males at annual fall ram or bull sales. In Africa (per the impala paradigm) most male bachelors are species-reproduction-survival redundant. They are not in the game. Male impala are not destructive as male elephants are but male impala can still over graze vegetation. The impala's habitat is thus indirectly threatened via survival of their species where wildlife's turf diminishes. That's where human populations are balooning. That's thus declining land ldedicated to wildlife in Africa is problematic.

Yes both impala males and bull elephants are nice to have as wildlife viewing photographic opportunities. But in bachelor herd of impala as few as 10 % will evolve to be an alpha male needed by a breeding herd for impala species survival. A Kruger NP male elephant culling plan could (should) keep the bigger ivoried males to produce more of the same. In the last century hunters have done just the opposite. They've killed off big ivory so now big tusked elephants are rare, as Kenya's mid 1970s Ahmed. How big were Ahmed's weight matched (often one tusk is larger). That's 148 pounds each tusks. In a wildlife records book thru 1986 the largest African elephant tusk was 226 lb, with its second tusk at 214 lb the longer (lighter weight) at 10' 5" including the part embedded in the skull. These tusks were found on Kenyan slopes of Kilimanjaro where the elephant died of natural causes. There are 28 elephants listed heavier than Ahmed but none of recent dates, which says due to sports hunters shooting larger tuskers we have evolved to no or fewer big tusk genes (DNA) being passed on to current African elephant populations. This is sad. Big tuskers should be breeders. That is my dad's plan. That's cull out most small tusked but destructive NP's elephants living redundant while being major NP ecosystem destroyers bulldozing over trees.

Let foreign hunters pay to bag excess bull elephants for funds for conservation with the meat (protein) for starving Africans. This may be judged controversial or an `outside the box' subject, solution but it is worth considering based on observed impala paradigm facts. NPs like Kruger killing off females rather than destructive tree bulldozing male elephants. I'm essentially pro wildlife or anti poacher. vs. over populated humans causing diminishing wildlife ecosystems vs. `civilization'. Some liberal looney will say "but you're a hunter, you killed African wildlife." Yes but as a trophy hunter, I bagged only redundant males (impala paradigm). I bagged my last African trophy in 1973 (at age 40). All my `shooting' since then was with camera film. This book is about increase wildlife NPs in Africa, give me a break. Teddy Roosevelt hunted in Africa, but he was one of our most environmentalist presidents. Most hunters shoot only males as per the impala paradigm. Redundant wildlife males could be food for carnivores vs. carnivores eating young, females. But lions, leopards, cheetah eat what they can catch. In Africa if you slow down, wildlife become prey before they become like bedridden humans. Impala paradigm male redundancy provides facts that apply in wildlife conservation-management thus efficient use of Mother Nature provided wildlife assets vis-a-vis limited availability of NPs or wildlife sanctuary land there is. In human monogamou society most males produce, provide shelter, their families livilhoods. While we see in nature in many cases a few males only provide the reproductive role with little else to offer. Thus only one male in thirty females (impala paradigm) is needed. Take the African lion there are prides of several females then one male or sometimes two lion brothers. The females do most of the actual hunting.

But the pride male lion shows up at the lionesses' kill to take his share first. Sorry gals that's the way it is. The lion's major role is to insure female reproduction. They do provide some security. Lions are often harassed by large numbers of hyena driving lions off their kill. Male lions often kill some such hyenas to keep things under control. This leads to noisy nights in the African bush. Male lion roaring their claim to their territory with the hyena taunting the lions with their answering, tormenting howls. These are lovely night time serenades that are missed unless you are camped out in tents in the remote African bush which I was for months. But dominant male pride lions get their position by challenging or replacing older lions. Like he'll be challenged in a few months or years. Replaced male pride lions don't survive long on their own. They've been spoiled but now no longer have the pride's females to do their hunting. They are male loners in forced retirement. Now they are often set upon by a large pack of hyenas and killed. A rare difference is man-eating lions are often lions that delay this fate. That's by learning they can't kill faster wildlife. But if they learn slow unarmed humans are another avenue.

The famous man-eaters of Tsavo (two killed in 1898) lived off railroad construction men in Kenya's remote bush thus. They were two too old lions too slow to prey on wildlife. But these two learned to prey on the remote area railroad construction workers. In almost a year they killed, ate over 100 Indian and Kenya natives before a British bridge engineer dispatched them. Would you believe in my first Kenya hunt in 1965 in that very same area my pro hunter and I dispatched a lion that had just killed a native hunter at daylight. My pro hunter published the saga as the cover story of Outdoor Life in Dec 1965. The remote area was called Darajani rail station between the W and E Tsavo NPs. The saga's title was `The Man-Eater of Darajani'. In my recent book HUGUENOT ROOTS-cum-SIX CONTINENT ODYSSEY (2015) it was the tale of Cpt 7. Our 1965 male lion was large framed, but in near starvation condition with a porcupine quill up his L nostril, more in his chest when skinned. My pro John Kingsley Heath radioed Kenya Game Department (he hadn't yet bought my lion license) but they let me keep the man-eater's skin. Kenya Game reported not having had a man-eater incident reported in 40 years in Kenya, for one of my more exciting African hunting experiences. A few days later I learned my impala paradigm facts hunting in another Kenya hunting block where I bagged a record book lion on Kenya's one lion per year kenya allowed livcense.

In the man-eaters of Tsavo (1898), thwse two old lions learned to prey on the remote bush railroad construction workers on Kenya's Mombasa to Uganda (via Nairobi) rail construction in 1898. Every two or three days these two lions would pick off one of the well over 100 such workers they killed and ate in nine months back then. This is getting away from the impala paradigm, and wildlife's polygamy and male redundancy or oversupply. Maybe that touches on eugenics which Webster defines as "a science that deals with the improvement (by control of human mating) of hereditary qualities of a race or creed." Like my dad more or less used in his or our family ranch's livestock operation. Or as dog breeders do with hundreds of `created' breeds (called purebreds) that all came from the first wild mammals domesticated by humans in the 10,000 year ago Agricultural Revolution epoch from wolves, fox, coyotes, jackals. What we now call dogs. Today there are 200 evolved breeds called `dogs' now broadly classed as either evolved from one of four sources as (1) wolf like, or (2) herders (livestock), or (3) hunters, or (4) mastiffs like human protectors or watch dogs with all the goofy poodles (toy dogs) that have since evolved. My dad always had one or more hunting dogs, at least one good stock dog which were very useful for livestock ranching and in shotgun bird hunting which our dad did a lot of. XXX stop Wed

That's like `[urebred' dogs that compete at dog shows (173 breeds) . This is according to National Geographic (Feb 2012) in their article `Mix, Match, Morph'. Then there is none purebreds or the village mutt that has evolved bychance and happenstance. I had an opportunity to hunt in Africa which I enjoyed for the challenge and experience. Like facing two Cape buffalo, after a standoff one chargeed at daylight from too close at only 14 paces which occurred and I was saved by divine intervention with one shot to drop the buffaolo dead seven paces in front of me. That's with an elapsed time of no more than ½ of one second!. How do I credit that to divine intervention? That's as my two white mates had their rifles still pointed skyward with safties still on as I killed the Cape buffalo with a heart shot I couldn't see behind his charging lowered head and horns. My snap shot was under his left eye, thru his skull, to an unseen heart stopper was by pure chance or luck. I had another experience where I wounded a male lion with a first shot in tall grass. The wounded lion then charged, my rifle jammed after my second now second charging shot, but was lucky in finally stopping him, as told in my 2015 book Cpt 12. That was about a day with three lion run-ins and getting charged by an elephant breeding herd. What an African hunt day that was! In African hunting I learned about the impala paradigm, how a lion pride works, their interfaces with hyena clans. Then on long all day tracking walks the tree toppling destructive nature of bull elephants. Thereafter by chance I became involved in helping create more and larger wildlife NPs to protect wildlife "native and unspoiled for future generations", which is this book's title. That's all in 17 Africa years, continuing.

1965 Darajani Kenya the scruffy man-eater lion has an 8" porcupine quill well up his nostril, with more quills in his chest. We learned he'd tried to eat a rail station agent the previous night at sundown.

A Kenya Police officer (afoot) measures the partially eaten victim `for the record'. His body was then buried in too shallow (hyenas) grave, no grave marker, end of his life story a la grim Africa bush.

1965 Pro hunter Kingsley Heath sizes up where ME lion killed hunter his bow and four arrows, pool of blood in road to the rail station where this man-eater lion tried to

1965 the pro hunter's article, the cover story of Outdoor Life's Dec 1965 cover story with many pictures. Kenya's Game Department reported this as the first man-eater lion reported in Kenya in 40 years. This was on only the third day of my 1st Kenya hunt.

Yes I trophy hunted in Africa (my Teddy Roosevelt and Earnest Hemingway from youth thing). Bujt only for MALE species of antelope, elephants, lion, leopard, Cape buffalo et al. That's never bagging any females. Only males most of which via the impala paradigm above are redundant to or are largely outside of their species survival reproduction survival needs. No one ever shoots female impala, cow elephants (except poachers), or female lions or leopards. But only a few wildlife (or livestock) males participate in their species reproductive survival while most wildlife males are life time bachelors outside of the actual reproduction of their species survival basis. When I bagged a male of most any species I was just cutting down on redundant males in wildlife's polygamy, where only a very few males ever actually participated in breeding. That's I was cutting down the survival of the species male over supply. There were more than enough other males out there to insure offspring because of the polygamy plus excess breeding capacity that occurs in most of nature's wildlife (or our dad's livestock ranch in CA). Or that in the case of impalas at any given time there is circa 30 bachelor herd males (African plains game) to only ONE at a time is essential to reproduction foir that species' survival.

To those misguided self-proclaimed `Politically Correct' individuals that still admonish me with anti-hunting dogma for hunting African wildlife (yes, but not since 1973) but who eat their share of Big Macs I thus see as their being illogical or ill-informed and hypocritical. Though I grew up on a cattle ranch I very rarely now eat red meet. I get protein mostly from fish and chicken or turkey as recommended by naturopathic Drs. Why? That's because a no to little red meat diet proves to produce the longest healthy longevity. That's while my detractors may be eating FEMALE red meat? Our dad looked at his breed cows teeth annually each fall to see if he thought each breed cows of eight to 12 year olds could survive another winter and raise a calf. Those he `tooth checked' then culled where did they go? To market as what he called `canners and cutters'. But also he sold off like 88% of his yearly crop of female calves for meat as he only needed like 12% as new breeders with an average eight to 10 year productive life span. That's which female's meat well might be in your hate-game hunter's next Big Mac or bought at Safeway's meat counter

Thus as a now predominantly vegetarian I no longer eat red meat. Rather I eat only a bit of fish or fowl as chicken, turkey or duck for protein. This is all food for thought but a subject I don't want to get any further into than what I call the observed-in-Africa `impala paradigm' vis-à-vis my cattle ranch similar paradigm. Or that most polygamous wildlife males are redundant. That is just the observed comparable mammal facts not where that might lead in our human male dominated society. That's where in the USA we've never had a women President. That's stated without getting into human species or women's lib or polygamy vs. monogamy or eugenics and all religious, moral, or political issues which are far beyond a retired construction stiff like me only trying to get more land dedicated to wildlife vs. humans but for humans with cameras to enjoy. But that's for human enjoyment in creating more wildlife watching destinations. Thus read this chapter as `food for serious objective thought' only.

But back in Africa the carnivores are still king. There in Africa life has a rather simple but brutal scheme here on our earth, or in Africa at least. That's a place I spent 17 years from the Mediterranean Sea south to Cape Town South Africa, from the sands of the Sahara Desert to the wildlife kingdoms of equatorial Africa on S. I've lived in San Francisco, but "I left my heart in Africa." And in our modern day, with all the proven scientific knowledge of that the world is round and that dinosaurs inhabited this earth from 65 million years ago back to 235 million years ago, I believe in `evolution' vs. strict Christian biblical creation. Thus I believe in my being an Americo African o (OOA) or if you like an albino African American that has evolved to `white' well away from the Equatorial sun. Also wildlife dominated Africa from south of the Sahara Desert. It's now little different than before the Agricultural Revolution (10,000 years ago).

Africa is a place that has `evolved' too but maybe only more slowly. In Africa there's more `cattle tribes' like Masai, Watusi, Zulu (used to be), Tswana, Hottentot et al. Having grown up in America, but lived, worked then hunted in Africa, I enjoyed some of those good old days in Africa. America is several generations ahead or beyond African bush tribalism. That's into industrialization, and a much advanced society. Who went to the moon? An American. When will a tribal African be advanced enough to accomplish such? But there are different strokes for different folks. Who visits Africa today. Mostly `advanced' Americans (et al) go to African as a wildlife watching destinations, as a back to nature thing. Like to see Mother Nature's gift which industrialized USA has less or little of any more. How many NPs in America have much wildlife? Most have next to none. Yellowstone is featured as having the m any moreost, but for me comparing it to TNZ's Serengeti-Lake Manyara-Ngorongoro Crater are all about `wildlife' NPs which are stunning, even magical Noah's Arc places. For me in Yellowstone the geysers are interesting, but in the subject of wildlife, there are too many vehicles, too few wildlife photo opportunities.

Africa is still more brutal. People come to see `lion kills' as the Romans did before they became Christians in their colosseum. There is an anonymous mantra of how it all works or in Africa wildlife wise: "Every morning a gazelle or impala wakes up. It knows it must out run the fastest lion, cheetah, wild African hunting dog or it will be killed.

Every morning in Africa a lion, cheetah or wild African hunting dog wakes up. It knows it must run faster than the slowest gazelle or impala or it will starve. It doesn't matter if you're a lion , cheetah, or wild African hunting dog or gazelle, impala or zebra.   But when the sun comes up you'd better be ready to still run fast!" Call it Africa's beautiful but brutal survival of the fittest! But for wildlife watching tourist Africa has the best shows. That's with so many exotic species and their interfaces.   Noah's Arc must have left off their passengers mostly in Africa. Who else has anything like Africa's `big five' of elephant, Cape buffalo, rhino, lion and leopard, and tons more.  But now we need more really big NPs to save endangered African wildlife from advancing land grabbing `civilization' and poachers. That's like two African possibilities and one in Alaska. Like two I know about in especially in Botswana and Mozambique.

The real truth is that Africa's (or world's) wildlife's demise is because of `civilized' human expansion taking up the once wildlife grazing space.  Like the demise of the North American bison.  That adds to the urgency of dedicating often worthless `thorn and thirst' land like the Botswana Kalahari to more hardy wildlife that are physically able enough to thrive there if provided drilled-well-windmill water holes as in arid Etosha NP in Namibia are provided. Then wildlife can make it even as mollycoddled domestic (evolved) beef cattle still can't. Then in Mozambique, creating a wildlife NP is the only way to simultaneously protect "native and unspoiled for future generations" such as the UN mandated Maputaland CPD restocked whit Noah's Arcs African wildlife for a saved "native and unspoiled for future generations " win win. Thus ends this `impala paradigm' tale as food for serious thought and action by such as Peace Parks and pro wildlife and pro-native peoples NGOs, charitable billionaires, et al al toward success with GoB and GoM for worthy NP enlargements to insure more special regions are saved for human enjoyment inwildlife NPs (how else) saved UN mandated "native and unspoiled for future generations.", God willing. Amen.

6
Epilogue

There was an original seed idea developing over many years that sprouted into my third book HUGUENOT ROOTS-cum-SIX CONTINENT ODYSSEY (2015). Then this current fourth book revisits book three's Cpt 32 (enlarged consolidated Botswana Kalahari Desert NP proposal) then Cpt 35 was of resurrecting our 1996 GoM awarded 914 Sq Mi 99 year lease now resurrected to 4000 Sq Mi to develop and operate the Elephant-Coast-UN-CPD-NP expanded N to join the 38,500 Sq Mi three country Grand Limpopo TransFrontier Park (GLTP international wildlife sanctuary). Then there's Cpt 39 Alaska's ANWR toward what it takes to get international wildlife watching tourist's in over thawed summer tundra via frozen winter built roads vs. it being a wetland in summer thaw with no frozen winter built access off our 1974 Yukon River to Arctic Coast pipeline road beyond Prudhoe Bay-cum-Arctic Ocean. Then getting it upgraded from a `wildlife reserve' to a full-fledged NP. I was Bechtel's then at site key man in Alaska to launch building out the road N and pipeline project. My 2015 `tell all' book was to pass on what is known about our Perrott family roots and French Huguenot (French Protestant) ancestry and name. That's who our family is, where we came from. That is the surviving paternal side Perrott family name which belongs to the historically colorful 1500s French Protestant tribe called Huguenots of France then via most certainly then several generations in Catholic Ireland. That's with the largely therein uninvestigated maternal side being most recently in American Finnish, British, Dutch, Scotch, then assumed Irish Protestant (Huguenot) on back in earlier generations to French Huguenots driven out of France in 16th century Christian religious war days.

Then odyssey wise I spent 17 years in Africa, thus with a few visits to Washington DC's Smithsonian Museum of Natural History I have come to comfortably believe in some mix of Creation as the 10 Commandments et al then Evolution as to vastly further back answer as to how we now `others' (OOA) evolved earthly humans came to be originally from Africa our surviving second wave leaving the African continent like 60,000 years ago as per the mantra of the bumper sticker IN THE BEGINNING GOD CREATED EVOLUTION. Over the years I have mused at the classification of African Americans. That's for our more sun tanned US citizens (many Pro athletes) who came from Africa, those who fairly recently emigrated by force on slavery ships. That's rather than by a much longer evolution as the rest of us "we walked out of Africa" earlier types. But this current book (herein) is more about saving especially African wildlife havens "native and unspoiled for future generations." That includes the by our same DNA African world's oldest living relatives the few now surviving Kalahari Bushman. That's who we now whiter faces left behind when we walked out of Africa, left part of our tribal clan in Africa when we left in a second wave some 60 thousand years ago. That's with whom we share the same DNA whether we have evolved to be Aborigines in Australia, or native American Indians, or Europeans, or Chinese, or Inuit, or Tibetans, or Bombay Indians, or Japanese, et al worldwide but OOA.

Per *THE JOURNEY OF MAN, A GENETIC ODYSSEY* (2002) by British DNA scientist Spencer Wells, science via DNA indicates we all (today's human tribe) originally came from Africa! So an optional, corrected nomenclature for such as we whites via evolution, my family is that we are now Americo Africans who originated in Africa too, have migrated to now live in America eons later as by now blue eyed blondish albino or largely evolved Africans. Or that human evolution has continued. That's we are now what we are due to adaptions from an Equatorial African to a now Northern hemisphere residing emigrant from Africa with our evolution still continuing even faster. That is to take our family roots story back further than just a fairly recent in transit stop off as Huguenots in France in the

1500s then Ireland before America In 1823 now approaching 200 years ago. For the other barrel of that 2015 double-barreled book is my Greek Homeric like odyssey via which I shared a few incidences with others besides just family which was a rocking chair experience going back, reliving actual lifetime events, with Wikipedia help on historical facts, background, dates, and details of work experiences of 17 years in Africa, and on all six continents except Antarctica. That's 14 years in Muslim countries as North Africa, Saudi Arabia, and several jaunts in Muslim (but not Arab) Indonesia. But the true Muslims are trying to take over especially in western Europe and America which from my living and working experience with them 14 years is a no way or Bah Humbug.

My career work was the cake, with the frosting being later career `adventure travel' to put frosting on the career cake. Per this current book, if I was to leave any legacy it would be for some advance in creating of more endangered African wildlife NPs protected acreage in Mozambique's Elephant Coast and Botswana's predominantly W Kalahari Desert. I could never write imaginative fiction. To me everything herein is nonfictional events that happened, some in the vein of stranger than fiction. This total `we need more wildlife NPs' message or tale (experiences) borders on being somewhat autobiographical. This was not my original intent. It is rather just how it evolved if this tales autobiographical fiber is found to be self-serving.

The simple message is we need some more special African or Alaskan NPs to protect "native and unspoiled for future generations" a more special Mother Nature's GIFT sites and ecosystems. How else will they still be as such in 1000 years? I feel lucky to have lived a fairly active, somewhat unusual to interesting out of the mainstream life or odyssey. Like not being the postmaster of my small home town of 800 people in Loleta CA. Rather my life played out on a broader international stage. I managed to more than just visit, but to live, work in a bigger international world. I had the opportunity to do some relatively new or unusual things with some elements of Walt Whitman earlier quote "Do not go where the path may lead, go instead where there is not a path and leave a trail." Or in my case it is to leave at least a (this) tale. But this book hopes for a lot more advance in upgrading and protecting three very special regions as NPs then to be guarded native and unspoiled for future generations to thus be enjoyed as such forever (however LONG that is for our –this–earth).

So I'd still like to see these three herein NP proposals happen, or even be involved in finishing such as an Endangered African Wildlife Bushman NP in Botswana's W Kalahari Desert (Cpt 2), or the 4000 Sq Mi resurrected Elephant Coast MZB NP (Cpt 3) saga or sorting out ANWR (Cpt 4) so its ummer Mother's Nature annual dazzling beauty show can be accessed then enjoyed as an international-wildlife-watching destination any or all of these choice ecosystems accessible (existing) and protected "native and unspoiled for future generations."

This book is self-published, available electronically thru Create Space the `printers' or their owners Amazon and Barnes and Noble et al in- print-on-demand mode when someone is interested in a copy. As Walt Whitman advised up front, I often went off the beaten paths, or as a Frank Sinatra's song said, "I did it my way." I leave three huge international wildlife NP projects undone at this writing. That's upgraded to a NP ANWR open to Tourists, the MZB Elephant Coast NP at 4000 Sq MI, and the amalgamated Botswana wildlife-Bushman all of W Botswana's Kalahari Sands NP. If you have gone on this literary journey (mini odyssey) with me THANKS. I hope you enjoyed at least some of it. Like an idea of saving "native and unspoiled for future generations" these three nominated sites, now before it is too late. I won't belabor you with more as I've probably said too much already. So be it. Thanks. Please advise if you have ideas toward any of bringing these NP proposals to fruition. Like knowing a billionaire who might be intrigued into at least some first step international-feasibility-study `kickoff' seed money. There's an old saying, "You can't ever FINISH if you don't START."

Annex
Author's Resume

JOHN R PERROTT Resume

17321 Lookout Rd, Apt 2110 Selma, TX 78154, (210) 487-1524, savesan@sbcglobal.net

Education: BS Civil Engineer, University of California, Berkeley (+1969 night accounting courses) **Military:** Ensign, US Navy flight training, RIF, recallable reserve, Honorable Discharged Lt Jg at 7 years (1964).

Key Career Accomplishments: 40 + yr career, early on, key man or Site or Project Manager on 20+ successful mega development projects (petroleum, mining, ecotourism) on every continent but Antarctica, 17 years in Africa as: (1) Key man, PM pioneered $8 billion Alaska Oil Pipeline-Road-Arctic Camp construction, pipeline kickoff then largest such project by private enterprise, credited with saving project in early kickoff stages. (2) Key man w/Bechtel for Kuwait Gov `new' plan reentry into Kuwait post Desert Storm (1991) to put out 800+ Sadaam Hussein set oil well fires in eight months vs. delayed 18 month master plan, limited Kuwait oil loss to $30 billion vs $90 billion via delayed plan. (3) Mozambique wildlife ecotourism Nat Park, upgraded Gov offered 63 Sq Mi to 914 Sq Mi National Park award to save Center of Plant Diversity (CPD) native-and-unspoiled as mandated per UN Rio 1992 Earth Summit's Int Biodiversity Accord, won 99 year Gov develop-operate-lease concession in 10 months. (4) Green causes Botswana, Mozambique, author-publish two green books as IRS 501-c-3 www.savethesan.org, www.savemec.org, plus (1999-2005) plaintiff CA green cause legal when Aunt's will created Charitable Foundation which then despoiled her gifted 14.3 acre Public Nature Preserve www.humboldtexposed.org.

Project Activity List-1958-88 full time with Bechtel, post-1988, call out freelance with Bechtel et al

TX-Mozambique (2006-16) green cause 501-c-3	Borneo (1982) as PM bC p/l for Gov Indonesia
Cal (1999-2005) plaintiff green cause legal	Iraq (1982) consult Gov IRAQ p/l bid philosophy
USA-MZB (1997-13) to resurrect MZB NP project	Sudan (1982) field engineering p/l Chevron
Bolivia (1997) key man bC SA group for ENRON	Malaysia (1982) bEPC as PM for Gov Malaysia
Chad-Cameroon(1996-7) bECP p/l EXXON	Argentina (1982) recruit welders Bechtel Algeria
Borneo (1996) fsd consult LNG M W Kellog	Algeria (1980-82) PM EPC 24" p/l SONATRACH
Mozambique (1995-6) fs EPC Nat Park develop	Borneo (1980) PM bC gas to LNG Gov Indonesia
Argentina-Chile (1995) key bC trans Andes p/l	Algeria (1977-80) PM EPC 36" p/l SONATRACH
Abu Dhabi (1995-96) bEPC ABB Lummus Crest	Sumatra (1975-7) EPC gas field for LNG Mobil Oil
Algeria (1992) key man bEPC 48" p/l Gov Alg	Alaska (1973-5) PM-p/l-road-camps-Alyeska
Bushman Bk Tour (1992-4) 332 media events	TNZ-Zambia (1972-73) CM Gov TNZ-Zambia p/l
Sumatra-Java (1991-2) fsd p/l (s)Gulf of Canada	Irian Jaya (1971) EPC mines Freeport Indonesia
Kuwait (1990-1) EPC well fires out Gov of Kuwait	Argentina (1970) CM EPC p/l Gov Argentina
Papua New Guinea (1989) fsd EPC p/l Chevron	Libya-UK (1969) negotiate claims p/l Oxy Petrol
Alaska (1989) fsd Valdez-oil-spill for EXXON	Canada (1969) fs Alaska oil via Camada ARCO
Peru (1988) fsd Oxy-Shell p/l over Andes	Tanzania-Zambia (1967-8) CM TanZam p/l
Peru (1987) fs trans Andes p/l (s) for ENRON	Libya (1961-66) EPC p/l (s) ESSO, OASIS, Mobil
Argentina (1986-7) bEPC p/l (s) Gov of Argentina	Tunisia-Algeria (1958-61) EPCM Alg-Tunisia p/l
Arg-Uruguay (1987) bEPC major river crossing	N Cal (1958) highway engineer Cal State
Colombia (1986-7) EPC Trans Andes p/l for OXY	US Navy (1957) flight training Pensacola FL
Saudi Arabia (1983-6) EPCM p/l to refiney ARAMCO	N Cal (1956) highway construction State of Cal

Acronyms: bC (competitive bid lump sum to Construct), bEPC (competitive bid to engineer-procure-construct), C (construct won by bid), CM (Construction Manager) or CM (Construction Managed project w/C bid out), EPCM (EP+CM), fs (feasibility study), fsd (feasibility study+preliminary design), PM (Project Manager, Program Manager), p/l (pipeline). More project details available on request

Languages: Authored four books in English, performed as PM in French, Spanish, earlier days ran crews in Arabic and Swahili in Africa. Computer skills-Solo authored 2007 book www.savemec.org via Microsoft Word, plus Excel.

General Comments:

O> Career Bechtel (et al) predominately on remote-area-beachhead-no-infastructure developments for 17 years in Africa, 14 years in Muslim countries predominantly on grass-roots-turn-key projects (w/roads, airports, ports, buildings, all infrastructure and facilities. Generally built, operated our own construction camps, buy, bring in equipment spread, no Motel 6 or Hertz, all work, no play seven-10-hour (+) days per week, no R&R until post 1973, thus like wartime military w/track record of "another ahead of schedule under budget successful project" via proactive, can do proven common sense approaches, with when needed innovative, outside the box solutions, identify the Critical Path problems then organize, plan to solve them ahead of schedule under budget.

O> Such as Colombia PM (1985-86) 283 MI over the Andes EPC 24" diameter pipeline w/suicide schedule, bonus-penalty fixed lump sum OXY-SHELL contract. Colombian Army call out was required to jobsite vs. night attacks by anti-Gov revolutionaries. A Bechtel top supervisor was taken hostage died in captivity. Despite all odds project completed in 11 months for nominal 18 month schedule for contract bonus vs. penalty via identify problems, solved them forthwith.

O> Learned hands-on-bid-build construction in early Libya five years to be Bechtel key man Libya, for ongoing laundry list of global bid-construct-lump sum-turnkey mega projects. Then EPC, EPCM international competitive bidding, sandwich in feasibility studies, bid other projects, construction claims, etc. Thus post 30 year full time permanent Bechtel years received assignments via international networking calls, like one man feasibility study for Gulf Canada (1992-93) which became the basis for their then international-bid-build 300 MI pipeline system in central Sumatra.

O> Post 30 Bechtel years, semi retired in 1988, continued freelance work w/Bechtel et al with more time to sandwich in adventure travel, as 1988 Kalahari Bushman visit, leading to green cause book *Bush For The Bushman, Need the Gods Must Be Crazy People Die?* (1992) with IRS 501 (c) (3) net site www.savethesan.org plus cause book tour (1992-1994) w/332 radio, TV print media, speaking events US, overseas w/appearance on CNN International Hour (1993). Then ex-1995 project in Mozambique, authored *Save Mozambique's Elephant Coast, Recreating Mother Nature's Wildlife Wonderland Africa* (2007) w/IRS 501 (c) (3), www.savemec.org site. (1999-2005) green cause www.humboldtexposed.org plaintiff w/appeal (two) to SF California Appeals Court, two appeals to California Supreme Court to save paternal aunt's 1972 will gifted Public Nature Preserve from despoilation vs. being safeguarded native-and-unspoiled for future generations as per her will and Trust mandates.

Current Objective: Any activity including such as resurrection of Mozambique 4000 Sq MI Wildlife Natural Park development or current fourth book includes plan to create a west Botswana enlarged NP to protect fragile Kalahari ecosystem with Kalahari Bushman involvemet, or any full time or call out as consultant, to share, put to use vast, unique global experience as key man PM, consultant, planner, estimator, bidder, designer, developer, problem solver, advisor as can-do guy fit, ready now, single. Can, will travel, relocate to global remote or difficult destination on short notice as per proven past career track record to insure another difficult project's successful outcome. Fit, health-food-exercise nut, gym for aerobics, resistance train five days a week. I played football at Oregon State, rugby at Cal Berkeley at 247 lbs to currently weigh in at healty 222 lbs. Don't bother considering me unless you have a big mega, tough project, study, task nobody else will touch or can handle. More details on past projects, activities available on request.

Note: Including an author's work resume in a published book is probably unusual but it may help add cohesion, a date-detail fiber in the case of this author's international construction career and experience. What's this book all about?. Saving "native and unspoiled for future generations" three regions I have some knowledge of in Botswana (Kalahari Desert for wildlife and a near extict Bushman haven), Mozambique (4000 Sq Mi Elephant Coast CPD-NP) and Alaska (Opening ANWR to wildlife watching tourist). I have knowledge of these proposed NPs to be a `key man' in their happening, coming to fruition, or being an advisor to someone with the money's chosen key man. The first step is to get GoB or GoM (in Africa) interested in a best competitive land use (which I belive is a wildlife National Park development) identified and proven by an internationally respected organization like Bechtel (or equal) feasibility study' and an individual or organization interested in funding such towards being involved in the `charitable' development costs. Enclosing my resume let's who ever know of my extensive to unique experience in these three `green causes' and a desire to see them lead to their development to save these unique regions as protected NPs "native and unspoiled for future generations."

BIBLIOGRAPHY

Alyeska Pipeline Service Co, ALYESKA: A 30 YEAR JOURNEY (2007)

Darwin, Charles, ON THE ORIGIN OF SPECIES (1859)

Darwin, Charles, THE DESENT OF MAN (1871)

Erasmus, Udo, FATS THAT HEAL, FATS THAT KILL (1988)

Faloon, William, PHARMOCRACY (2011)

Grzimek, Bernard, SERENGETI SHALL NOT DIE (1959)

Gunther, John INSIDE AFRICA (1955)

Hemingway, Ernest, THE GREEN HILLS OF AFRICA (1935)

Ionides, C J P, MAMBAS AND MAN-EATERS, A Hunter's Story (1966)

Life Extension Foundation, FDA, FAILURE, DECEPTION, ABUSE (2010)

Main, Micheal, KALAHARI, Life's Variety in Dune and Delta (1990)

Marshall, Lorna, THE !KUNG OF NYAE NYAE (1976)

Owens, Mark and Della, CRY OF THE KALAHARII (1986)

Perrott, John, BUSH FOR THE BUSHMAN, Need the God's Must Be Crazy People Die? (1992)

Perrott, John, SAVE MOZAMBIQUE'S ELEPHANT COAST, Recreating Mother Nature's Wildlife Wonderland Africa (2007)

Rowland Ward, ROWLAND WARDS RECORDS OF BIG GAME, sixteenth Edition (Africa) (1975)

Thomas, Elizabeth Marshall, THE HARMLESS PEOPLE (1958)

Van der Post, Laurens, THE LOST WORLD OF THE KALAHARI (1958)

Van der Post, Laurens, THE HEART OF THE HUNTER (1961)

Wells, Spencer, THE JOURNEY OF MAN, A Genetic Odyssey (2002)

Wheeler, Jack, THE ADVENTURE GUIDE (1976)

INDEX